SIT STILL, 1

Tim MacWilliam

Dedicated to Katherine

ABOUT THE AUTHOR

Tim MacWilliam is a fellow of the Royal Society for Public Health and the founder of MacWilliam Associates, a training consultancy he established in 2003. A keen runner, writer and broadcaster. Tim lives in Norfolk with his wife Katherine and has two grown-up daughters.

Tim has lived with the effects of ADHD all his life. However, he wasn't formally diagnosed until he was fifty-eight years old.

Table of Contents

www.timmacwilliam.com

INTRODUCTION

People with ADHD are not stupid.
They may be more gifted than 'normal people'.
It just takes a while to work out what the gift might be.
Especially when diagnosed late in life.

The broadcaster Simon Bates would often begin his daily *Our Tune* feature on BBC Radio, in which he would reveal details of a listener's torrid love affair for the rest of the nation to enjoy with the following words.

'I'm going to change the name for obvious reasons.'

Such is the highly personal nature included in parts of this book it led me to consider, for a long time, whether I should write under a pseudonym.

Some chapters were so emotional and challenging to recount that I almost binned them. At one point, I almost binned the entire book, wondering about the people who thought they knew me and may never see me in the same way again. During the writing, research and editing of *Sit Still Timmy!* I have discovered things about myself that I didn't know or want to admit to, and there is content included that I really didn't want to reveal.

I concluded, however, that a book of this nature had to be written with complete and utter transparency. I have always thought of myself as an all or nothing type of person, so these words will, I hope, prove that to both myself and those who know me.

The writing has, at times, resulted in tears of some nature being freely shed. Tears driven by degrees of light and shade, funny and sad, moving and loving. I've tried to be nothing other than searingly honest throughout.

From suicidal thoughts, self-harm and stealing to dodging bullets on the Isle of Wight. Flirting with addiction, taking numerous risks, crazy car accidents, being regularly fired and doing something that I doubt Simon Bates has ever done, taking a radio station off the air.

I would probably be long dead, if not quite forgotten, by now if it hadn't been for the amazing love and fierce loyalty of Katherine, my wife. ADHD can be a relationship wrecking ball, but our marriage has survived both the real and metaphorical stormy seas that I frequently travelled. *Sit Still, Timmy!* Contains the good, the bad and the sometimes very ugly side of ADHD and how it affected both my life and those close to me.

There are many symptoms and signs of ADHD. They include impulsiveness, disorganisation, poor time management, problems with focusing, restlessness, frustration and the curse of low self-esteem, often caused by enduring a torrent of negativity early in life. Further indications of the condition are still being explored and uncovered. Symptoms may vary from one person to another and be extreme or polar opposites. This can lead to acceptance of the condition being more complex, to the point where some people don't believe that ADHD is a 'real thing.'

Believe me, it is.

All the signs were there from an early age as I regularly charged around our living room full of hyperactivity, waving around whatever object I could find. On one occasion armed with the gas poker, a strange metal tool in the shape of a garden rake that was used to light our coal fire, I proceeded to smash the device straight through our rented black-and-white television set.

I was constantly bored, restless and endlessly showing off, demanding attention and unable, no matter what, ever to be still. My family, driven to distraction, would regularly beg me to

'Be quiet and sit still, Timmy!'

I wonder how different life might have been had I received an earlier diagnosis and whether things would have turned out for the better. While ADHD has its disadvantages, it also has a raft of positives that are highlighted within this memoir.

Although, on the one hand, this is a biography, *Sit Still Timmy!* is also very much a self-help book centred on my experiences to give an insight into late-diagnosed ADHD. Writing it all down has been a form of living therapy, rediscovering and reliving parts of my life that were buried long ago, containing a myriad of incidents and demons that I had previously failed to deal with.

There has also been the challenge of additional memories flashing through my brain. At times it felt like a vast jigsaw puzzle that was just beginning to take shape when new pieces started falling from the sky as further reminiscences were uncovered.

Everyone in life has probably decided not to do something because they are worried about what others might think of them. I now realise my own self-doubts, possibly due to ADHD, have held me back in the past and perhaps from writing this book sooner. However, my long overdue diagnosis has finally helped me to discover myself and put pen to paper. I hope by sharing my experiences they will help others with the condition, their friends and their families.

I have read memoirs in the past that appeared to be sanitised, having had important details removed for personal reasons or made sterile by the editing process.

I promise this book won't be one of them.

Tim MacWilliam

PROCEED WITH CARE

This recollection of a near lifetime of late diagnosed ADHD is not that of a therapist or highly qualified practitioner but straight from 'the horse's mouth' of someone whose only qualification is having lived and continues to live with ADHD. I have no mental health qualifications, and the words in this book are not intended to convey that I ever have. I would reiterate that it is vital to seek medical help and professional advice from a suitably qualified source and to take the proper medication when prescribed.

Secondly, the events in this book are how I remember them, and I have told the tale to the best of my ability. Others may remember certain incidents differently, but that is often the way in life. This is my portrayal of a journey through decades of unknowingly and then knowingly living with ADHD. The effect it had on my life and those closest to me. Where appropriate and when specifically requested, I have left out or changed names so as not to identify those people.

There may be wiser and better-read experts to be found elsewhere who can offer more technical insight, depth and medical information. However, I am confident that anyone who reads this book will have a greater knowledge, empathy, and understanding of what living with ADHD might entail.

I have added further help and advice throughout, with an extended section in the final chapter. This advice is based purely on my personal thoughts and experiences. Where appropriate, I have researched, fact-checked, and credited the individuals concerned to the best of my ability. However, it may be necessary to make further enquiries before proceeding. Please also be aware there are chapters in this book that contain swearing and references to sex addiction, suicide and self-harm that some readers might find upsetting.

How to Read This Book

Are you kidding?

If you have ADHD, you've probably already jumped in and read a couple of the more exciting-sounding chapters. That's fine. I've written this memoir for people with ADHD so they can easily dip in and out. However, those without the condition who prefer the traditional way of reading, from start to finish and all points in between, will have no problem navigating their way through.

PROLOGUE

A Christmas candlelit service is an exciting place for any three-year-old, let alone one with ADHD.

Throughout the festive sing-along, I had constantly squirmed, wriggled, and moved around on a slippery wooden pew next to my family near the back of an 18th-century Anglican church. The smartly dressed lady sitting directly in front of us wore an expensive-looking black fur coat with a fluffy overlapping collar that now displayed a glowing orange tinge with the first signs of a flame about to appear. As soon as I swished the lit candle and saw a piece of the fur turn to ash, I got so much immediate attention that I giggled and swished the flame back and forth ever faster.

My dad quickly snatched the candle out of my hand and then did his best to cool the forthcoming blaze by furiously puffing his cheeks and blowing onto the smouldering coat with as much force as he could muster, his face becoming flushed with the effort. My brother was not amused, but my sister was in fits of laughter while my mother continued to sing from her hymn book, no doubt hoping there wouldn't be too much of a fuss.

Fortunately, the smell of burning fur blended in perfectly with the copious amounts of incense and melted candle wax that continued to swirl around the church while the lady in the fur coat remained, remarkably, none the wiser as my dad had, somehow, brought the coat back from the brink of ignition without attracting too much unwanted attention.

I still wonder to this day who thought it was a good idea to give a hyperactive three-year-old a lit candle in a public place, but it was advertised as a candlelit carol service!

The year was 1965, long before any apparent health and safety was required and long before ADHD was formally recognised as a mental health condition. I was still more than five decades away from receiving a proper diagnosis and belatedly finding the answer to the question that I and many others had regularly asked through the years, all of them unable to hide their disbelief and regular annoyance.

'What the hell is wrong with you?'

Fast forward three decades from the incident in the church to a gift shop at the Castle Museum in Norwich.

As ever, I'm keen to entertain my young children to make up for whatever else I lack as a parent, so I picked up a large bouncy superball from a nearby display. The ball was heavy, with colourful swirls trapped deep inside whilst, to my delight, the ceiling in the shop is a high one. My aim was now to bounce this ball hard enough to reach one of the distant wooden supports.

Ideally, it will spin through the largest gap, and I would catch the ball upon its descent. 'It's OK. I'm a good catch,' I assured those present. Of course, my wife would probably be embarrassed by my unpredictable behaviour, but my two daughters would laugh, and maybe the people in the shop would also be amused by my performance.

Any thought of amusement immediately evaporated as I threw the ball, and with some force, onto the ancient stone floor, where it promptly smashed into countless pieces. It seems the 'superball' was actually a special edition glass paperweight.

The stare of the cashier was as cold as that of the stone floor in response to this apparent act of random vandalism as she processed my payment for the damages, and we hurriedly left the scene before we were asked to.

My youngest daughter appeared somewhat confused by my actions. 'Daddy, why did you do that?'

'I thought it was a superball.' I replied.

'What's a superball?'

My diagnosis took the longest possible route. First, I had to play my part in creating and raising my own daughter, who went through school and university before becoming a specialist in mental health. So, it was she who, one day suggested, and seemingly out of the blue.

'Hey, Dad, have you ever thought you might have ADHD?'

At that moment, life began to make sense for the first time in over half a century.

CHAPTER ONE

Growing Pains

*Children with ADHD tend to receive far more negativity from parents,
teachers, adults and peers than young people without the condition.
This is possibly why so many with ADHD grow up
to have such low self-esteem.*

The Roald Dahl story *Matilda* features a terrifying head teacher called
Miss Trunchbull. I had to deal with a real-life version of this fearsome
woman for much of my early school life.

'Mrs. T' warned any child caught swearing that she would wash out
their mouth with soap and water. The threat was regularly carried out
when the teacher proceeded to hold a squirming child under a soap
dispenser, pinching their nose in the process so the boy had little
option but to open his mouth in order to breathe, whereupon it was
promptly filled with the weird smelling liquid soap that had the
consistency of snot. I'm glad I didn't swear, or at least I wasn't caught.

I once hid inside a portable stage to avoid a lesson, having sneaked
out to escape the tedious morning assembly. Predictably I was caught
and feared the worst, but somewhat fortunately, instead of anything
physical, I received an emotional cow-eyed rant about being 'hurt and
betrayed.' This was not a particularly enjoyable experience, but It was
preferable to be shaken up and down or hit.

At the start of a new school year, Mrs T gave everyone a new pencil
and announced to the class that the pupil who could keep their writing
implement looking the newest for the longest time would win a prize.
Unfortunately, I had long stopped listening and already chewed away
the side of the pencil with my name written in full on the carefully

shaved sliver of wood. I was about to break it in half when she grabbed hold of my arm and repeatedly slapped my wrist.

Fortunately, such was the heightened state of her rage that she missed at least half of her attempted slaps and hit herself instead.

Mrs T's predecessor had me physically dragged out of assembly along with the naughtiest boy in school for mimicking the visiting clergyman. It was thought to have been my first offence, so I was spared physical punishment and told to leave the office while the naughty child, aged just eight years old, was kept behind and hit with a cane.

A teacher like Mrs T, filled with so much anger, was not ideal for a student with ADHD, although the condition would not have been recognised at this time anyway. Therefore I was just labelled as lazy and stupid. Fortunately, for my last two years of primary school, I was in Miss Honey's class, and she protected me from the worst rampages of the head teacher. She, too, would be frustrated by my inability to learn and often softly scold me for seemingly making little or no progress. I think she realised something was genuinely amiss, but there was little she could do to help.

To escape the classroom, I asked if I could take a cassette recorder and interview the public about their shopping habits which, amazingly, Miss Honey agreed to. In addition, I recorded some random comedy shows with another student that was played out for the rest of the class to 'enjoy.'

Although often misunderstood, I always tried to do what I considered the right thing. For example, one boy was so badly bullied he ran out of the school gates in a state of emotional breakdown, so I decided to check if he was all right and spent ten minutes of lesson time searching the local estate for him. I eventually found the boy hiding in the nearby churchyard and accompanied him back to school, where he was sent to calm down with a drink in the head teacher's office. On my return to class, I was fully expecting some level of appreciation, if not a round of applause.

Miss Honey was away on extended leave, and her replacement Mr W produced a rather old and smelly tartan slipper from his desk drawer, beckoned me towards him and said.

'You can't go off school premises in lesson time without being punished, you know.' A weird smile spread across his face. He had a raised eyebrow in the style of Mr Spock, the character from Star Trek.

As I apprehensively made my way to the front of the class to receive 'the necessary punishment,' one of the tougher kids, a frequent receiver of the slipper himself, who had never previously spoken to me, showed some solidarity advising in a low voice.

'Don't say nothing.'

I obediently bent over as ordered by Mr W, to be greeted in return by a sea of faces. Some looked bored, some were aghast, but most were eagerly awaiting for the entertainment to begin. There was a loud 'thwack' and another and another. I tried to count how many times I was hit but couldn't keep up.

The slipper was eventually put away, and I looked up to find my eyes being met by a wide-eyed and contorted grin. Dark greasy black hair stuck to Mr W's head, sealed in place with copious amounts of Brylcreem. Thanks to my classmate's whispered advice, I managed to avoid a defiant 'Didn't hurt' retort to the punishment that would have inevitably led to a second dose.

This, remember, was at primary school. I was barely eight years old.

Prior to a school trip in France, every child was given written instructions for our parents to read on what to wear, what to bring, and definitely what foods not to bring, such as yoghurts or similar desserts that might easily break open and spill into our bags. I'm unsure whether my parents simply didn't read the note or maybe I'd eaten it on the way home from school. Still, either way, a forbidden chocolate mousse split open, covering everything in my duffle bag, including my green cardboard passport that had formed into a kind of chocolate paper-mâché. Even Miss Honey turned on me with an empty threat that the French would be unlikely to let me into their country, and I was promptly removed from a photograph with the ship's captain as a form of punishment for my apparent wickedness.

On the return journey from Dover, a teacher from another school, seemingly tipped over the edge from the day's activities, grabbed hold of my hair as I charged up and down the train with a friend and threatened to kill me.

I wasn't an ideal student and often messed around, but I always avoided conflict and didn't have a single fight until the very last hour of my final day at primary school. Everyone seemed to be enjoying their last playtime of the school year, but I had perhaps got a little too giddy at the thought of leaving this school forever when another child decided he'd had enough of my stupid behaviour. I responded to his mutterings by telling him to 'Get lost!' and things promptly escalated until he angrily challenged me to a fight.

I hadn't expected matters to intensify so rapidly. He was far bigger than me and quite imposing, so the outlook for victory was fairly bleak. Now even more excited than they had been before, the rest of the demob-happy group of kids in the playground gathered around to watch without a single teacher in sight to bail me out. However, It was encouraging that most people were cheering me on. 'Tim! Tim! Tim!'

This gave me a boost, but it annoyed my opponent even more as he let out a loud scream and charged toward me. I shut my eyes and swung some wild punches before opening them again. Much to my surprise, he was on the floor crying, with a bleeding lip. I felt terrible at having caused this boy so much upset, but before I could say anything or he could get up, a loud bell sounded, signalling not only the end of the fight but the end of our final 'playtime' as we were ushered back into class. Mrs T had heard about the altercation, but the school was about to close for the summer, and she knew I would be gone in another hour.

Once we had returned to class, I tried to make it up with the boy, more in hope than expectation and asked if we could forget about our fight and be friends, but he was still raging at being floored by such an apparently weedy kid and growled he was going to 'finish me' after school. So, I returned back to my seat and prepared for the forthcoming pasting, deciding that I wouldn't fight back. I would let him have his revenge and get home with as little damage as possible. So instead of being able to enjoy the good wishes and favourite memories of our teachers, plus a small gift we were given from the school during our final assembly, I was lost in my own world, wondering how I could have been so idiotic, waiting to be beaten up and knowing there would be no one to stop him.

Just as a big cheer went up from the assembled children and the door opened to release us for the final time, the boy, rather bizarrely, grabbed hold of my hand to shake it and smiled. He said we should forget all about our fight, provided I called it a draw. I hastily agreed and breathed a huge sigh of relief. The school probably did the same as it closed for the summer and was now rid of me for good.

News of my fight had spread rapidly, and James, my older brother, laughingly asked for the full details, but the episode had ruined my last day at school and haunted me for weeks afterwards. Of course, I could have walked away without engaging in a fight, but I was young and stupid.

However, you live and learn, don't you? With ADHD, apparently not.

There were two secondary schools to choose from; both were equally appalling. One, referred to locally as 'The Dump', was just two hundred and fifty yards from our home; it also hosted many of my friends there, however, because my brother and sister had both been taught at the slightly less terrible school referred to as 'The Zoo' I was sent there instead and proceeded to waste the next five years of my life.

Like most people with ADHD, undiagnosed or otherwise, I would sit through lessons bored and confused while drifting in and out of the real world. I was regularly told that I was lazy, stupid and occasionally a moron. However, when something interested me or I needed to get a task done urgently, it was like a bottle of fizz had gone off in my brain. I would then complete the work efficiently and usually to a decent standard.

My school report read, 'Tim is a polite member of the class, but his contributions are of little or no value. He could undoubtedly do better if he gave just a little more effort towards his work.' However, there was a glimmer of hope. The report said in English and French, 'Tim's spoken work is good.'

I knew I wasn't stupid and definitely not as stupid as I was made to feel by teachers, my peers and even the occasional relative. But the negativity eventually seeped through my defences. Of course, everyone is good at something—aren't they?

My passion in life was football, both on and off the field. I was a goalkeeper, either making brilliant saves or conceding howlers. My dad pointed out that I seemed to be wondering what to do with the ball before I had it in my hands as yet another goal trickled into the net behind me. Perhaps this was an early clue to my ADHD.

As a twelve-year-old, I was keeping goal for a boys Sunday league team that lost 25-0, but no one who heard the result would have known the detail behind the score that day. Our team was sitting bottom of the league, and only eight of our group had bothered to turn up. Those who did choose to play became quickly disinterested against our top-of-the-league opponents, who spent the entire match in our penalty area, taking shots against me at will. They probably would have scored ninety had I not played so well. At the end of the match, I got a standing ovation but was greeted home in ridicule by those who had not witnessed my 'heroics.'

There was often mob rule at my school where a teacher was usually late or didn't show up at all. At weekends I would travel to football matches where hooliganism was off the scale, and I had learned how to stay away from trouble at these events, so when it kicked off in the classroom, I knew how to position myself so other students got the treatment from the bullies instead of me. However, inevitably, I let my guard down one day and was thrown out of a first-floor window.

I do understand that I was a nightmare of a student, but on the scale of misbehaving, I wasn't even mid-table at this particular school. However, I was occasionally made to stand outside for being too boisterous such as when I climbed on a chair singing jingles from television adverts to the rest of the class.

The clues that I had ADHD were always there, but no one saw them as so little was known about the condition back then. One benefit of this might be that I didn't have to go through school life in the 1970s with the stigma of the condition and who knows what kind of medication with potentially horrible side effects.

I bizarrely ended up in an O-level home economics class. I was the first boy ever to do so. After the first term, the teacher threw me out, and it was agreed I would go to the library and 'study.' But, instead, I just went home. However, karma eventually caught up with me as I walked home one day. I was identified by a group of particularly unpleasant students who were also playing truant. They proceeded to chase me through some woods, eventually following me to my home. I wasn't even safe there as they proceeded to chuck eggs that cracked open against our windows.

I'm not sure what was more challenging for a kid with ADHD, queuing for school dinners or eating them. One lunchtime and while making my best attempts to line up with friends on a short flight of hard squared lino steps that led to the school dining room, we began to light-heartedly re-enact the previous evening's adventures on the East Bank at Aldershot, where fans of nearby rivals Reading FC were made to feel most unwelcome.

We playfully surged forward and promptly scattered all of our fellow pupils who stood in front of us to produce a scene akin to life on a 1970s football terrace.

A stern-looking teacher, reminiscent of Rosa Klebb, the evil spy who starred in The James Bond epic *From Russia with Love*, soon emerged from the staff room to restore order. We'd often joked that she might have a poison-tipped knife in her toe cap that could be deployed at any opportune moment, and this might have been it.

I had never experienced such a contorted and angry face as she lurched forward through the crowd and grabbed hold of my hair, proceeding to drag me through a sea of bemused, amused and slightly horrified faces. My feet flailing helplessly behind me. We travelled down two flights of stairs, accompanied only by the smell of floor wax, plimsoll rubber, and some form of dubious cooked meat from that day's school dinner.

I'm not sure exactly what kind of retribution Rosa had in mind, but it wasn't going to be pretty. She eventually dumped me on the floor next to a dead-end basement. There was no realistic option for me to defend myself or escape, so I considered curling into a ball with the hope she didn't have the poisoned-tipped knife in her shoe that day when the red mist appeared to clear from her mind, her face softened, and she proceeded to walk off without a word. Whether this one incident ended her career or it was the last straw, having experienced one too many misbehaving students, I'm not sure. Still, I don't remember ever seeing her again.

I had problems with some of the other students too. While hyperactively playing five-a-side football one afternoon, I completely took out an opponent with a two-footed tackle. Unfortunately, he just happened to be best buddies with the school's most extreme bully. He spent the next week hunting me down, threatening to give me a kicking.

Fortunately, my ability to find endless hiding places and pretend to be ill so that my mother kept me off school for a couple of days meant I was eventually forgotten, and the bully had moved on to his next victim by the time I had returned from 'sick leave'.

Parents' evening was initially one of dread but, in time, became a source of entertainment to my family at just how awful some of the comments might be.

My dad said the teachers all said much the same thing.

'Tim. Oh dear,' and we all laughed at his comedic descriptions of how terrible I was.

I reasoned that if I was being laughed at, then at least I wasn't being told off. So the next time, I drew cartoons of various teachers, gave them nicknames and acted out some impressions so my parents might giggle when they next met them.

Following the umpteenth attempt to explain an apparently simple rule of mathematics, my exasperated teacher shouted, 'Are you unwell or stupid?' A fairly below-the-belt insult, but there were crueller staff members, including a sizeable Welsh history teacher with wiry red hair and a matching beard who would mumble on about his doppelganger, Henry VIII, while scrawling tiny illegible notes onto the blackboard. His homework was to copy out long passages from a textbook. I refused to do this as it was utterly pointless. He wasn't impressed and gave me a detention, but it seemed optional to attend.

I had warned my dad about this guy who had such disdain for me and openly labelled me as a fool to the class. During the next parents' evening, this teacher told him I was possibly the worst student he had ever encountered and suggested I was incapable of retaining even the simplest of facts. My forewarned dad produced a football history book and told him that I had no trouble learning from that.

The school careers teacher said I should join the police force as I liked sports so much, this sounded like a bizarre suggestion for a kid with, albeit unknown, ADHD, but in retrospect, I would love to have done the training.

By my fifth and final year, my friends who'd previously messed around with me were mostly ordered to avoid 'the naughty kid' by their parents, who now considered me a bad influence. They apparently didn't want me to hinder their chances of passing important exams. But I didn't seem to care.

I've already mentioned that I was often labelled as lazy or stupid, but that isn't the case. On the contrary, if the spark in an ADHD brain could be harnessed academically, it would probably result in that student being at the very top of the class. However, not surprisingly, I was ungraded in all of my O-levels and left school with just a grade 3 CSE in European Studies.

It seemed to my family that I had failed these exams on purpose, through sheer laziness. I obviously had the capability to do well but seemingly couldn't be bothered. My mother wrung her hands in despair, upset that she hadn't sent me to the posh grammar school by the railway station, but wherever I had gone to be educated, I would undoubtedly have underachieved with the same poor results.

I just wasn't compatible with education…Oh yes, and I had undiagnosed ADHD!

Due to a staff shortage near the end of one term, we had a mixed PE class. The male teacher, all blond floppy shoulder-length hair and a matching shock of Chuck Norris chest fluff sticking out from beyond his tracksuit top, reeking of Hai Karate aftershave, would shamelessly flirt with the impressionable fourteen-year-old schoolgirls. He spent the entire lesson leaning against the trampoline under the pretence of 'spotting', thus preventing any of the girls from falling and hurting themselves. In reality, he was blatantly up-skirting, a permanent grin on his face, mock wiping his brow with the effect it was having on him. Other boys took their cue from this pervert to join in with the lark.

Perhaps it was because another school year was coming to an end, and the staff no longer cared. But, later that same day, I was asked to take a written message to our form teacher. I finally located him in the empty dining room, hiding among the stacked tables and chairs.

He had a female colleague partially suspended against the wall with his groin and one hand supporting her lower back. I couldn't see where his other hand was located, but the flushed look on her face probably gave a clue. I was tersely instructed to leave the message on a nearby table by the male teacher, and the breathless woman gave an embarrassed smile and gestured for me to leave as speedily as possible. Maybe the note I delivered read, 'You're fired!' as neither returned for the following term.

I clearly remember both the male teachers involved in these incidents were seen as cool guys, a crush or a good laugh, and therefore they must be good at their job. My classmates thought it strange that I disagreed with their perception. It's thought that ADHD helps you to be a good judge of character, and I could see right through these two charlatans.

With role models this poor on impressionable young minds, I wonder how some of the students turned out with or without ADHD.

When a young French student teacher took over our class for the day, it may have left a lasting impression on those present for life. She had the looks of a model and matched the world's longest legs with the world's shortest skirt.

In her soft French accent, she started a varied classroom discussion on growing pains, puberty and school life in England. She glided around the classroom barefoot from student to student, smiling just enough to encourage interaction. Then perched herself on the edge of a desk to inadvertently reveal her underwear for all to see. Most thirteen and fourteen-year-olds are struggling with raging hormones at that age and are very likely to be distracted by anything that bears even the slightest sexual connotation. The teacher had already provided a decent stream of one-line put-downs to the usually unruly boys in the class, who were all now seemingly owned by this woman.

The classroom was now silent, with all eyes focused on our teacher for the day.

The girls in the class were also becoming increasingly unsettled by the flamboyant and overt behaviour. They may have also felt a little intimidated, undermined or made to feel inadequate by this super-confident French woman. One of the girls who saw the effect the teacher was having on her boyfriend got up and walked out, slamming the door behind her, while another later begged,

'Miss! Please can you stop this now?'

'Stop what?' she replied, genuinely perplexed and not realising that a majority of the boys were now in a state of trance.

It took some time for our regular teacher to get the class back on track when he returned the next day.

Sex education classes were virtually non-existent. The only lesson I can recall on the subject was being made to sit through a rather vivid and unpleasant film about gonorrhoea. That was the absolute sum total of anything remotely close to resembling 'the birds and the bees' at secondary school.

As far as passing exams were concerned, I was seemingly beyond help, so instead, my father spent a significant amount of time, effort and money helping one of the more underprivileged students in my school year so that he would gain the necessary qualifications. He also helped to get him an interview for a position at the factory where he'd worked for over two decades. When the boy wasn't offered the job, my father was apoplectic with rage. However, the following week I was offered an interview for a similar role at the same factory and was immediately successful. I would imagine, purely through the fear of my dad's potential retribution, had I not been offered the job.

Prior to that, when school ended for me that May, hypothetically for revision, I saw it as a holiday and a chance to mess around. I do wonder If the prize of passing my exams had been an apprenticeship at the BBC, Capital Radio, The Football Association, or possibly even *The Bracknell News,* where I had already filed some match day reports and been paid £4 a time for doing so, I would have made more of an effort, but ultimately working in that soulless factory as a commercial apprentice was the stuff of nightmares.

I've no idea what a commercial apprenticeship involved. I should have listened to my friend who joked. 'When you finish being a commercial apprentice, do you become a commercial?'

I can remember being shouted at by those in the finance office of the vast factory and continually told to do one thing at a time. A sergeant major style supervisor destroyed an invoice I had produced from a large archaic printing machine and screamed at me, 'You can't send that to a customer!' proceeding to throw the scrunched-up paper at my head. I was left red-faced and humiliated in front of the entire department.

Waiting for the exam results to drop in August was a time of dread but also provided a spark of excitement about what would happen next, knowing full well that I had failed them. A part of me looked forward to the jeopardy of how people might react as I was hoping for an escape from the factory to something more suitable, although I had no idea what that might be.

After my four ungraded results had been confirmed, I was awarded a job in the factory that was effectively unlocking a cupboard each morning while I was given a chance to re-sit my exams, but the same ungraded results were duly repeated, and my opportunity to complete my commercial apprenticeship ended. Still, I stayed in charge of unlocking the equipment cupboard for three more years until, much to my relief. I was finally made redundant.

This had all seemingly been a complete waste of my final three teenage years. However, even in that dead-end job, my mind would be whirring with ideas for a new venture and I set up a small business selling football memorabilia. Yet, my older and wiser colleagues would assume I had nothing going on between my ears and would love to unkindly tease, 'Look at him, brain in neutral, finger up his bum, wasting another day.' But, of course, they had no idea what I was really thinking or what I was going through.

When management finally let me go, the vacuum of two years unemployment began.

So yes, I was now technically unemployed amid the recession of the early 1980s, but the entrepreneur that many with ADHD seem to have would now come to the fore. My football souvenir business had become somewhat renowned, and I had a kiosk at a football ground that opened on match days. My shop had collectors' items from virtually every club in the country for which people would travel from far and wide to visit, and the mail-order catalogue would attract business from across Europe. Another source of income was made from persuading the general manager of a local football club to let me use the rickety old team bus as part of a Wembley Stadium package with tickets and travel included to attend England internationals. However, this project was short-lived, as we arrived late for one match and left a passenger behind for another.

Eventually, I became disenchanted with running what had essentially become a mail-order business from a bedroom office. It was far removed from the way a twenty-year-old should be living. I began to regret my wasted school years and spoke to a careers advisor who told me I should have studied harder at school, and I was now effectively an old man in their eyes.

Things were not easy. My dad had just had a stroke and needed time and space to recoup, while the spectre of depression was creeping into my soul for the first time, mainly from an undue feeling of failure.

I sold my business as a going concern for £50 so that I could look for a proper job, but no one would employ me.

I felt so lost and alone that, in desperation, I applied and was accepted onto a medical project to be given a dose of flu and become a 'guinea pig' testing the effectiveness of drugs.

Fortunately, before the first dose of flu was given, I was offered a job at Pontins on the south coast for the season.

So, I spent the next couple of summers messing around, working in various holiday camps where there was so much going on that my unknown ADHD behaviour was embraced if not entirely understood.

In the winters that followed, I was in and out of casual bar work, never quite sure which way to turn next.

CHAPTER TWO

Love, Sex And A 'One-Night Stand'

This woman had somehow remained practical
even when 'taken hostage'

———————

Impulsiveness is often a symptom of ADHD that may lead to either a one-night stand or jumping into a relationship without much forethought.

I never intended to have a one-night stand, and to date, I still haven't. But as impulsive and outgoing as I may have seemed, I was inwardly lacking in confidence to an excruciating level, particularly when it came to the matter of finding a girlfriend.

There were probably opportunities for romance at the various live-in seasonal jobs that I remained oblivious to, including the nice girl in the snack bar who bought me food from the grill every night after our bar had closed, as she knew I couldn't stomach the cuisine offered in the staff room. This was so awful that a colleague once threw his meal on the floor, announcing it as '…a waste of a pig's life!' I think the girl in the snack bar may have liked me, but if she did, it sailed right over my head.

Another female colleague decided to leave halfway through the season to become a glamour model. She knocked on my bedroom door and politely asked in her very broad Welsh accent if I would kindly go to her room, take her dress down and kiss her.

I was too stunned to move, but when she insisted further with a full-on pleading smile, 'Come on!' There didn't appear to be much of an option to refuse.

This particular holiday camp held folklore of some women who had apparently planned to sleep with every male staff member during the summer, collecting us like some kind of sex world cup sticker album. So maybe it was my turn, but this girl literally had the looks of a model and was leaving the site in a few hours, and I was absolutely certain she wouldn't want me in her sticker collection.

Upon further investigation and having managed to untangle her Welsh accent a little, it seemed she had merely asked me to retrieve a heavy case down from her dressing table.

There was always plenty of work in bars and hotels, and I was offered five jobs in one day, but I couldn't seem to stay anywhere more than a few weeks, bouncing wildly from one dead-end job to the next.

I had an interview with the owner of an employment agency that I hoped would be a career turning point. But having read through my CV that illustrated how I'd been starting a new job, on average, every six weeks, he ripped me apart in the style of the television show *The Apprentice* when the failing candidates are fired. He virtually ordered me out of his office with the parting shot, 'You have a problem, don't come back until you find out what it is!'

I wonder if I should contact him these decades later and tell him that I have ADHD.

My parents begged me to find some stability, but I didn't know what this apparently essential life ingredient looked like, let alone where to find it. I'm told it takes time to achieve, but I couldn't stay in one place long enough to find the stability I desperately needed. It was a vicious circle. My dad would say that I was lucky to be young, free and single. But, it felt like torture, underachieving on a daily basis with no one to help with my future and no one special to share my time with.

I walked out of a residential job in Beaconsfield before I had worked even a single shift after another employee broke into my room in the middle of the night. Then, feeling completely numb with life, I went back to live with my parents in Bracknell and started yet another dead-end job at a large four-star hotel.

17

Beginning a new job was always highly stressful, yet another lonely first day spent at ground zero. I didn't intend to stay there very long.

My latest employer hired a group of feisty middle-aged women. To them, it was a part-time job, a chance to let their hair down, get away from their offspring and partners for a while and earn some extra cash.

I was meant to be supervising these women, all of them a fair bit older than me, but I would often be groped and jokily propositioned as they tried to break me down with innuendo, bum pinching and the odd grope, perhaps viewing it as a kind of harmless game. Some evenings would descend into a surreal edition of *The Benny Hill Show* as I was virtually chased around the bar. In the present day, this kind of behaviour would have led to their dismissal, and as the only way to defend myself was seemingly to retaliate in kind, I too, would no doubt have been given notice and shown the door.

Maybe these women picked on me as I was fun and seemingly harmless, but I was hardly a catch physically or otherwise. If I had followed through on their raunchy innuendo and suggested we use one of the empty hotel bedrooms, I'm sure they would have run a mile.

One miserable colleague spread rumours that I was having an affair with her. She did this so effectively that many people, including her own husband, believed it. One male workmate simply refused to accept my honest denial of the tryst. But, there was nothing whatsoever going on between us or ever likely to be, but she perhaps enjoyed the fantasy as an escape from her turgid reality. This silly pantomime clearly affected her husband and possibly her young children too. Yet, I continued to ignore her ridiculous fantasy and should have put a stop to the nonsense far sooner than I did.

In July 1985, after a particularly long shift that went on into the small hours, another female employee, ten years my senior, with something of a reputation for bedding men, invited me back to watch the end of *Live Aid* at her flat, but as I waited for her to make the first move, I started to focus on the concert finale, live from Philadelphia, and perhaps didn't give her the expected attention. I was tersely instructed to let myself out when I was ready as she slammed her bedroom door shut. Apparently, she had felt humiliated by my behaviour and resigned soon after. I still have no idea why.

I knew deep down that leaving this job would be the wrong thing to do, but I couldn't help myself. I had already decided to quit, ignore reality, and work for yet another seasonal holiday camp on the coast.

The following day our neighbour frantically knocked on the front door, completely panicked. 'Thank God you are safe! Your hotel is on fire!'

The entire building was smoke damaged, and the conference suite had been completely destroyed. That night delegates arrived for a dinner dance dressed in smart evening wear, angrily demanding that we do something to ensure their event went ahead. Meanwhile, the fire brigade continued to damp down. I wonder how they expected us to magically create another venue from the smouldering ashes.

Things changed from this point. The hotel was closed for the next few weeks while the damage was repaired, and several colleagues, especially underperforming middle management, were let go. However, those who remained discovered a renewed work ethic, pulling together and working extra hours to get the hotel open again. A social life began and colleagues became friends.

When the hotel finally re-opened, the remaining members of the 'Benny Hill Gang' focused their minds, once more, on finding me a girlfriend. There were lots of new female staff to consider as my suitor, but when I was caught sharing a smile across the open plan lounge with the new assistant restaurant manager. I was given a scolding.

'No, Timmy! Not her!'

The social life and camaraderie continued with a fun evening spent with workmates that ended back in the small apartment of the forbidden assistant restaurant manager with whom I had been chatting most of the evening. This hadn't gone unnoticed by others, who soon realised there was a spark in the room that didn't involve them and quickly left the scene, dragging those with them who hadn't yet cottoned on to this unlikely liaison. Giggling as they departed at their perceived impromptu set-up.

The two of us were left sitting on her bed together.

Once on our own, words were quickly replaced with smiles. As I brushed my arm against hers, there was that uncertain, almost surreal, dizzying moment just before you kiss someone for the first time, but there was also a flood of doubt in my mind. I hadn't kissed anyone in ages and had no idea how she would react. So, I wondered whether she even wanted to kiss me or whether I would be pushed away and told to get lost. Or perhaps she was waiting for me to make the first move—the procrastination ADHD brings with it arriving at a typically inopportune moment. To stop any further speculation, I reached forward and kissed her. Thankfully, she didn't hesitate, returned the kiss and didn't stop.

While I was speculating just how far we were going with this, she had, in the style of Wonder Woman, sprung from the bed, returning moments later sporting nothing more than a pair of gold dangly earrings.

Our night of uncontrolled passion was amazing as it was unforgettable but also probably quite reckless. I might have made this woman I hardly knew pregnant, and either of us could have had an STD. The government claimed, incorrectly, that AIDS was only a problem for gay people back then, so at least we didn't have to worry about that just yet or, so we thought, such was the misinformation at the time. Fortunately for us, not one of those problems ever came to pass. It is, of course, essential for everyone and particularly those with ADHD who are often likely to be more impulsive, to practice safe sex, and I was very fortunate to get extremely lucky that night in every way possible.

My lover asked me to stay until morning, but instead, I made excuses and left, something I still regret. I could have woken up next to Wonder Woman instead of my parents' snoring dog.

I also regret my subconscious, uncontrolled and often unacceptable catalogue of bad behaviour that followed for the next few weeks. ADHD can be a wrecking ball to any relationship, particularly a fledgling one. However, I was seemingly oblivious to my appalling conduct.

I completely ignored her for the next two days, even though we worked together in the same building. Perhaps I was embarrassed, waiting for a put-down or to be laughed at by those who thought they'd cleverly set us up. Maybe she would now regret our liaison, thinking it had all been a terrible mistake. I also wondered how the disapproving members of the Benny Hill Gang might react once they found out.

Earlier that year, I had finally been released from a toxic and, at times, abusive relationship with a woman who had the temper of an emotional wasp. She would ridicule and humiliate me on a regular basis. Whenever we met her friends, she insisted I remove my glasses so as not to embarrass her. Perhaps she thought it was OK for her friends to see me but not for me to see them. On the way home, she would continue to reprimand, lecture, and scold me about my apparently unacceptable behaviour correcting me like I was a naughty child. 'You never listen, you don't think, God, you are stupid, what am I doing with someone so stupid!'

If it were known I had ADHD back then, she would probably have dumped her shameful boyfriend without ceremony. Also, to my humiliation, she was openly two-timing me with her long-distance partner. I clearly had no self-worth whatsoever.

I was once woken by her shaking my arms and slapping my face. My crime? I had apparently been talking in my sleep.

I felt continuously embarrassed and self-conscious, with no idea how to protect myself or process what was going on, only that it was nice to have a girlfriend and I should be grateful. I was oblivious that friends, colleagues, and my entire family all felt she was totally wrong for me. My thought at the time was that beggars can't be choosers. This was perhaps a result of the negativity thrown at me from an early age, something that many people with ADHD experience. Some of her comments still affect me today.

Perhaps it was the remnants of that toxic relationship, the undiagnosed ADHD, and the often-excruciating underlying lack of confidence that left me a little confused by that night of passion with the assistant restaurant manager. Being genuinely liked for who I am and by someone so lovely was a new experience for me, but she was not unsurprisingly hurt and angry by my furtive behaviour. She cornered me late one evening while I counted the bar takings, clearly annoyed by my continued avoidance to ask why I was dodging her after the night we had together and what on earth I was playing at. The answer was that I didn't actually know, but no words came to mind, so instead, I offered her my best apologetic smile and shrugged, to which she gave an exasperated sigh and walked away, only to return a minute later with a smile of her own and then enquire.

'Are you coming then?'

The takings with piles of silver coins, five and ten-pound notes loosely spread across the counter were left abandoned like something akin to the late-night bar on *The Marie Celeste*.

Her tiny apartment was located within the hotel building, so we didn't have any distance to travel. No one knew of our relationship, but any secrecy was put paid to by the newly installed super-sensitive fire alarm that rang at the most inopportune moment as we hastily dressed in whatever we could find. Many of our colleagues were working late that night and met us with surprise, followed by knowing smiles, as we belatedly arrived at the fire assembly point wearing various items of each other's clothing.

The next morning, to my horror, all the cash had disappeared from the bar, but my panic was fleeting as, fortunately, the night porter had found the money and put it in the safe. I thought I might be sacked, but there was more interest from management in that day's gossip, and I was asked with a smirk as to why I was listed on the 2 am fire alarm roll call when my shift ended sometime earlier. I didn't care, and I would quite happily have shouted it from the rooftops. As the news spread, two more of the Benny Hill Gang handed in their notice as a clear sign of their disapproval of my choice of date.

I tried to make amends for previously ignoring my new girlfriend by arranging a day out together but overslept, leaving her to believe I had stood her up. Later I bought tickets for a Paul Young concert. Unfortunately, the gig started late as Paul had a few issues with his voice, so the event overran, but I insisted we stayed for the encore, fully aware that we'd now miss our last train home.

We were duly stranded on platform 4b at Reading station, a less-than-perfect place to be in the small hours of the morning. Fortunately, we knew a kindly taxi driver who rescued us in exchange for a packet of cigarettes.

I had recently bought a new wallet, and as I changed all the varying bits and pieces over, including old parking tickets, receipts and out-of-date membership cards. A passport-style photo of the emotional wasp fell out, much to the understandable upset of my new girlfriend. It was a ghastly moment, but I had simply forgotten the photo was there. If I had known, I would have ripped it to pieces. Can I blame ADHD for this? Bizarrely my ex continued to scold me from afar via airmail, perhaps attempting to keep some form of control.

This would be the final straw for most people, but there was still more for this poor woman to endure.

ADHD can sometimes result in significant, unmanageable, and often horrible mood swings. These moods can be mistaken for bipolar but are different as they often come and go in a few hours. I understand that bipolar may be more gradual, deeper, and may last for days and sometimes weeks.

I was still decades from any suggestion of ADHD, let alone a diagnosis, and my mind had descended into a dark place that I couldn't escape from. I hate it when this happens, especially as there was no apparent reason.

Normally, these feelings have gone by morning, and the best place to go is bed and hopefully sleep it away, but I knew that my girlfriend wanted to go out on her rare evening off. My dark moods often begin due to something minor that I've irrationally escalated, thus beginning an unstoppable downward spiral. Sadly, there is little I can do to flush it through my brain. I realise now this is a condition known as rejection sensitive dysphoria, an unwelcome but regular companion to ADHD that is difficult for a partner to endure or understand. There is more about this condition in chapter six.

We arrived at a nearby pub for a meal, primarily to see if it would lighten my mood, but it didn't, and my behaviour became ever more sulky and agitated. Before we had time to order our food, my girlfriend tearfully asked me to take her home, and a part of me died with shame as my mind fell ever deeper into a darkened pit. As we left, I caught sight of myself in the bar mirror and shouted, 'Stupid idiot!' fortunately, those sitting close by chose to ignore me, so the potential 'Are you talking to me, mate?' scenario was thankfully avoided.

We drove in silence back to her apartment. My mind was now troubled and full of almost blinding self-hatred. The negativity bouncing around my brain had become relentless and unforgiving. I couldn't believe that I'd behaved so badly. I had, at last, found someone really kind that, incredibly, seemed to like me too, and I was pushing her away. I didn't think to apologise as I was too involved in my own self-pitying darkness, an ongoing theme of my ADHD.

I couldn't bear to let the evening end like this, but if we had gone back to her apartment, my behaviour might have deteriorated further and would probably have led to the end of our relationship. I wanted her to understand how much I was hurting from upsetting her. I needed to apologise, but I couldn't find the words to articulate it. As we neared the motorway entrance, I was overcome by the feelings that fizzed in my brain like a bottle of shaken cola that has no escape and made a flash and risky decision to swerve erratically onto the westbound carriageway of the M4.

'What are you doing? Where are we going?' asked my passenger, now somewhat alarmed.

'Wales!' I replied

I had decided that a hasty and insane one-hundred-mile trip to the Severn Bridge would actually improve the situation and win her back.

The sudden jolt onto the motorway must have alarmed her, but she managed to calm things down a little, and by the time we approached Swindon, she had successfully talked me into abandoning my intended destination based mostly on the fact that we both had work the next day, we didn't have enough cash to get across the Severn Bridge or to buy petrol to get there, let alone back again as the tank was only a quarter full.

This woman had somehow remained practical even when 'taken hostage.'

I'd hit the self-destruct button, behaved appallingly and upset someone who was only ever kind to me. I had put her life in danger just to demonstrate how my demons were affecting me instead of driving her safely back home as she had requested. I knew my behaviour was erratic and, deep down it wasn't normal. But, whatever my problem, it looks to have spectacularly ended our relationship, as this idiotic performance would be too much for even the most understanding of souls to take.

As we got closer to home, it appeared we might just have enough petrol to get us back, and the darkness slowly began to lift from my mind. I attempted to lighten the mood further by making weak jokes and taking my foot off the accelerator, pretending the fuel had completely run out just to get a reaction.

'Tim, don't!' She fell for my joke every time. Her Essex accent rose through the panic to become more prominent.

We arrived back as the needle on the fuel gauge was in the last of the red zone. The car was now running on fumes. At least we had avoided the ignominy and expense of being towed away from the motorway's hard shoulder, but it didn't exactly save the wreckage of our traumatic evening. On the plus side, I had managed to kick most of the demons from my brain. I'm aware that my lightened mood is entirely due to my passenger, or was she technically now my hostage? Either way, this loving woman had somehow found a way to blow away my toxic cobwebs. It belatedly dawned on me that having someone this calm and understanding was the missing piece in my life.

The stability I craved and needed was right here, right now. All packaged in the form of a beautiful, kind, loving, fun, patient and caring woman. I didn't even have to wait another moment. Instant stability was mine! Or perhaps it was something entirely different. Maybe falling in love gives you all the stability you ever need.

Unless, of course, you behave like a total jerk and drive it away!

I wish I had thought to apologise and take her home rather than enter a spiral of self-pitying road rage. However, ADHD doesn't always give you that option, and a lack of empathy can be a symptom. Sadly, the reality had come too late. Maybe the scars were still raw from my relationship with the emotional wasp, but it's always easy to blame someone else for your troubles rather than look in the mirror, and maybe I was part of the reason why she was so often angry with me. Either way, I'd scored yet another spectacular own goal in my life, and I needed to face facts.

Who on earth would ever want to be with someone so unpredictable, unreliable, difficult and temperamental as me?

This relationship was seemingly about to end, all through my stupidity and ridiculous behaviour. I can't bear the thought of losing her, but perhaps, parting would be the best option for her own safety and quality of life, as, despite my hasty actions, I'd become somewhat protective of this lovely woman, and that undoubtedly meant getting her well away from me. With ADHD, sometimes you don't know what day it is, and other times it feels like you have already seen what has happened and are trying to change things for the better.

I genuinely want her to find someone nicer, safer, calmer and better than me. Someone she deserves who will make her feel happy and secure to give her the normal, carefree life she deserves. Probably someone without ADHD and the baggage that comes with it.

But it seems she doesn't want an easy life, and it was already too late to save her from this timeline's particular fate.

This amazing lady had apparently seen something good in me that I'd never even seen in myself. Her life was drifting too, and she was already emotionally invested with the wildly unpredictable guy who she intends to stick with through hell and high water and see where it takes her.

So, instead of ending the relationship that night, she looked across from the passenger seat and said,

'I'm visiting my mum and dad next week. Do you want to come and meet them?'

I married Katherine exactly two years on from our first night together.

———————

My employer had sent me on a three-day residential training course in Oxfordshire to learn supervisory and management skills. Fifteen delegates from various hotels in the group were present. When we were asked to stand and introduce ourselves to the others in the room, I proudly told them about my forthcoming wedding.

A woman sat directly opposite informed me that she was a part-time palm reader and clairvoyant. She immediately demanded I inform her of our star signs. She then announced to the room that a marriage between an Aquarian and a Scorpio was doomed to failure. She insisted we immediately call off the wedding as it would avoid the cost of our certain divorce.

I eventually managed to break the stunned silence by replying, 'I've decided not to invite you.'

My planned stag night was cancelled at the very last minute by a nightclub in Windsor upon discovering we were an all-male group. As an emergency alternative, we ended up in the local Indian restaurant in Bracknell before descending, late into the night, to the hotel where I was employed. We found the keys to the swimming pool, jacuzzi, and sauna, where we were joined by various semi-naked members of female staff as they finished their shift for an impromptu party. It was a very sackable offence for everyone involved and multiple times over. Fortunately for us, the night porter chose not to report anything untoward happening that evening, and a rather large blind eye was turned, although my car never quite recovered from the chefs covering it in eggs and flour.

Once married, we were still living in the staff quarters of our workplace hotel and were now looking for our first house together, but there was little chance of finding an affordable property in the South East, so we took a chance and bought a bungalow in Norfolk, where we already had friends and knew the area quite well.

However, I had no job and little prospect of getting one, and to compound things, Katherine was now expecting our first child.

We both really wanted to start a family but thought it might take years to conceive, and we were prepared to have loads of fun trying for as long as it took. However, we hit the jackpot in the first couple of months and were absolutely delighted. We knew we were going to be the best parents ever! That was the plan anyway.

My in-laws were not impressed, and with hindsight, I can see why they were concerned. 'Golly' and 'Didn't you take precautions?' were the collective responses as her mum disappeared off to make tea and Katherine's dad endlessly re-measured the size of their living room carpet while they came to terms with our unexpected announcement.

It was quite deflating for our exciting news to be received this way, but you always got it straight from Katherine's parents, and they probably, rather naively, thought their youngest daughter was still a virgin on her wedding day. However, a positive response is important when you are given life-changing information, even if it is through gritted teeth. We were both really happy, I was going to be a dad, and it was something I was really proud of. They soon got used to the idea, became pleased for us and looked forward to welcoming their latest grandchild.

My mum, on the other hand, was jumping for joy. She probably had the same concerns but never showed it, although she did bizarrely let slip, 'Are you sure about this darling? My dad said that it was too early to know if Katherine was 'properly pregnant' yet.

Another relative simply couldn't believe it and treated our news as a joke. I can't remember if I threw the phone down on them. They did try to lighten the mood at our next family gathering by giving me a copy of the *Sunday Sport* newspaper with the headline 'Baby born with two heads' complete with a mocked-up graphic, thinking it would make me laugh. But for some reason, It didn't.

Not for the first time, it was thank goodness for my sister, who was genuinely thrilled for us.

Of course, we might have delayed for a while longer and perhaps we should have, but if you wait too long, then opportunities can be lost. We had friends who had struggled to conceive and suffered the agony of miscarriage, so we were concerned this might happen to us. Anyway, things always work out for the best, don't they? But if having a baby was a risk, uprooting from Berkshire to Norfolk with no job or prospect of getting one was enough to leave some relatives open-mouthed and buying extra popcorn to watch how their prediction of epic failure would unfold. They were almost proved right.

Katherine was eight months pregnant and had already moved to our new house, It was meant to be easy for me to get a job and follow her, but it just wasn't happening. I was stuck working in Bracknell, awaiting the outcome of multiple job interviews in the Norwich area, and things were getting somewhat desperate with a new house and a pregnant wife living on her own 150 miles away. There seemed little prospect of finding a job paying anywhere near enough to cover a mortgage with a very high-interest rate.

Katherine could tell our risky adventure, driven by my unknown ADHD and '…things always turn out for the best' mantra, was now wearing thin. When yet another job application was rejected, I put my head on her shoulder and wept. She had never seen me cry before and started to fear for our immediate future and wondered how her family might react to the predicament.

Fortunately, soon after, I was given a provisional job offer at a hotel complex in the Norfolk countryside. Then, quite out of the blue, I was offered a cancellation appointment at a hospital in Norwich for some long-awaited routine surgery. However, as the availability was in just three days time, I would have to quit my job immediately, but my contract required a month's notice to be given.

I decided to refuse the offer of surgery out of loyalty to my boss in Bracknell, as I couldn't leave him in the lurch.

I was rapidly talked around by Katherine and my colleagues, who ordered me to put myself first. A fellow employee told me, 'You don't owe this huge organisation anything!' I took their advice and left just 24 hours later to prep for my operation, but with a feeling that I had badly let down my former employer.

I soon discovered they couldn't care less about me. The general manager had hired my replacement some time ago, and he was just waiting for me to leave. So much for loyalty! I learned that day that in business, to always put yourself first and that you can never fully trust anyone.

Happily, the surgery was successful, and I was formally offered the new job just a short drive from our new home, all in time for the safe arrival of our baby daughter.

CHAPTER THREE

Risky Business - Going It Alone

In business, trust no one.
I seemed to have forgotten my own advice already.

———————

I had left for work, as usual, one morning, only to return home an hour later. Katherine saw the look on my face and braced herself for the bad news that she knew was coming.

'I've just been sacked.'

Two children under five, a new mortgage and now without an income, all amidst the deepening recession of the early 1990s. It was difficult to find a positive.

My built-in ADHD self-destruct button meant that I would sometimes almost dare an employer to fire me when I got bored or frustrated with a job. But I was still a bit shaken by the abruptness of this decision.

The recession had started to bite, and I knew cutbacks were about to be made. I thought I'd been proactive by creating a self-funding role to protect my position within the organisation and my young family. I proposed that I be paid a reduced salary, thus saving them money. However, in addition, I would be given twenty per cent of all the income generated from providing a training service to other hotels throughout the UK. If the scheme hadn't made a profit for the company in two years, which it surely would, I boldly declared.

'You can make me redundant, and I'll walk away.'

However, the new management regime wouldn't take the risk, and I was told somewhat coldly that the decision had already been taken and I was being made redundant with immediate effect.

I had only been there for five years, so the redundancy cheque wouldn't keep the wolves at bay for long.

I had no choice but to take my rejected business plan and go it alone. This gave me sleepless nights and more stress and anxiety than I have ever known. It was an almighty risk. If the plan had failed, the bank would surely repossess our house. Happily, crisis bought out some of the more positive aspects of ADHD, and I found hyperfocus and determination in spades. To quote Albert Einstein, who was also thought to have ADHD, 'Adversity introduces a man to himself.'

'At least you can't fire yourself,' said Katherine helpfully.

If it weren't for ADHD, we might still be sitting in the dark, and no one would have a telephone. Thomas Edison simply refused to give up on his light bulb moment, and Alexander Graham Bell found a way of making a machine to chat with someone in another room.

Both were thought to have ADHD and benefited from enormous willpower and the ability to think outside the box. I read a few chapters of a book written by Richard Branson on how he would have an idea for a new business while taking his morning bath and have it up and running that evening. That is exactly how I liked to think, too. Why faff around with a business plan? Just do it! It wasn't much of a surprise to find Branson is thought to have ADHD too.

I found myself acting on a piece of advice that the Virgin boss had written.

'If someone offers you a fantastic opportunity and you are not sure, say yes, then learn.'

My business had initially started as a management and training skills organisation, but during the recession of the early 1990s, there were cutbacks in this kind of development, so I needed to find additional strings to my bow. I would phone hoteliers to offer my team building courses or NVQs only for them to enquire about the basic food hygiene certificate they were now required to provide following the introduction of The Food Safety Act in 1990.

'Did I offer that training course?'

'No, I'm afraid I don't… er, yes I will be very soon!'

The opportunity to increase income and steer my fledgling business through that recession was the fleeting opportunity that Branson had suggested. I just needed the foresight to grab it.

I set about gaining the necessary qualifications and became registered with the lead food safety organisation in a super quick time, powered by ADHD hyperfocus and the not-inconsequential thought of having our house repossessed. So, my business took the first of many new directions into what was mandatory for a client rather than a nice-to-have facility. I soon added further health and safety qualifications and, in time, became a Fellow of the Royal Society for Public Health.

Whatever a client required, I would, within reason, find a way to deliver it. I'd endlessly phone and doorstep businesses until they either gave me some business or, as one hotel owner did tell me, to '… go and jump in the lake!' The survival of the fledgling business was very much touch and go for the first year, but thanks to the new supply and demand of statutory training, we got through.

On a snowy Sunday afternoon, I set off on a long journey to North Yorkshire to present a training course on food hygiene, but just as I drove away, the client phoned my office to cancel. These were the days before mobile phones, so Katherine called the local radio stations all along my route to ask if they would give the message on air requesting me to return home. Unfortunately, I was listening to some football commentary on national radio for the entire journey.

Nowadays, we take our mobile phones for granted, and I wonder how many relationships Google Maps has saved, although I do miss Katherine turning the old-fashioned paper map in the direction we were travelling as it made sense to her.

On the occasions we drove abroad, she also knew that when she instructed me to turn left, I would turn right—I have ADHD.

The following year, Katherine was painting our living room ceiling, but when I returned home from a day on the road, she had made very little progress.

'Every time I climb up the ladder, our phone rings.' She said before presenting me with a list of potential new clients and dates for training courses. It was a seminal moment, and we both laughed out loud, mostly from relief. Our business would not only survive, but it might even flourish.

I got so busy that when my daughter was five, she hid my car keys so I couldn't go to work. My family were all I really cared about, and I changed the way my business operated so I could be home more often. However, I was never completely off duty as the phone might ring at any moment, day or night, but it did allow plenty of quality family time. Being self-employed is like having lots of spinning plates constantly on the go, desperately trying to stop them from smashing on the floor, and that includes the most important plate—family life.

Having my proposal rejected by my former employer really was the best thing that could have happened, and they were happy to become my first retained client, remaining so until many years later when the newly installed managing director, who wasn't exactly my biggest fan, phoned me early one morning.

'Tim, we've known each other long enough to be honest with each other, haven't we?'

'Er, yes,' I replied, intrigued but already alarmed at where this conversation might be heading.

'Have you, or have you not, been spreading malicious gossip about my working relationship with the new general manager?' His tone was quickly escalating. It was fairly well known they couldn't stand each other, and I had been enjoying some gossipy chat the previous day with some department managers I had known for years. I couldn't wriggle out of it, so my association with that hotel group ended rather abruptly.

This wasn't the first or last time my loose tongue and candour cost me rather dearly. One of the upsides (and also the downsides) of ADHD is quick thinking, but it can be a bit too quick at times, and I often find myself saying the wrong thing. As a result, I've almost been beaten up, lost work, been sacked, and alienated loved ones through my filter-free gob.

One potential new client began our meeting by refusing to acknowledge my presence, let alone look me in the eye or shake hands. He then continued in a rather aggressive manner that he resented paying money for people like me.

I never knew when another client or pay cheque would come along, so I would do whatever it took to get a contract over the line. But on this occasion, I was so annoyed that I just got up and walked out, only to have him chase after me, offer me a drink and declare, 'I think we may have started on the wrong foot, old boy.'

Whenever the phone rings or an email pings on my computer, my heart skips a beat. I've never got entirely used to the stress of being self-employed. Usually, when I receive a message, it's nothing untoward, but occasionally, it would be something significant.

My youngest daughter, Vicky, had just started a new job, but unfortunately, her car had a flat tyre on her very first day, so I immediately travelled to the stricken vehicle to help.

I was struggling to remove the damaged wheel in the pouring rain. So, I was cold, wet, and dirty when the phone in my pocket rang. It was Piers, the managing director of one of my biggest clients. He rarely talked with me directly, so it would surely be bad news. Either there had been a major incident, or they were firing me. It's the latter, and I couldn't be in a more compromised position or sound any less professional with a poor phone signal next to a busy road, my nose now streaming from the cold, wet weather. 'I'm afraid we need to have a difficult conversation,' Piers informed me in a falsely compassionate way.

They had been so faux-friendly, telling me that I was part of their team and how they wanted to grow with me having recently taken on several new properties, but it now seemed they had already completed a deal with a competitor behind my back. So after ten years, I was kicked into touch without a backward glance.

I know it's part and parcel of being self-employed, but any time I lose a client, it hurts. It really hurts. It's embarrassing and damaging to our welfare. At first, there is shock followed quickly by denial, anger, self-loathing, and fear. The thought of letting Katherine down with a significant drop in our income makes me feel physically sick.

In business, trust no one. I seemed to have forgotten my own advice already.

We can get by, but it was a massive blow to my confidence, and, not for the first time, imposter syndrome set in. My hair began to fall out, and I developed an infected rash on my face. I felt so dizzy, sick, and unwell that I was given a brain scan. I almost hoped they would find something so I could opt out of life for a while. However, the tests were all negative. It was apparently a psychological reaction, although the accompanying physical pain felt very real. Katherine told me business would pick up again and as ever she was right.

It seems none of us are exempt from the axe man, and soon after, Piers received a phone call of his own telling him his services were no longer required.

Within a small business, you may not have colleagues or a human resources support team, and you can't expect your clients to be up to speed or sympathise with your personal life. However, one of my clients was being threatened with prosecution while my mother had become terminally ill. Still, neither my client nor my prosecutor cared about my life-changing situation or the enormous emotional stress that was bearing down on me.

During a food hygiene inspection the previous year, this client had an unacceptably dirty kitchen and was given a verbal warning by the authorities. Now, twelve months later, they had failed to act upon even one action point that either the inspector or I had previously made. The hotel cannot keep a chef in place for more than a few weeks. I would meet with each new incumbent who told me of their urgent plan to clean the area to the necessary standards, so I would then smile and nod, knowing full well that they would have moved on long before I returned next, so the problem wouldn't be resolved. Meanwhile, the manager would shrug his shoulders and tell me he was far too busy with customers.

The inspecting officer had, by now, decided to prosecute the hotel, and as a result, I would be going to court too. The paperwork and procedures were in place, but they weren't being followed. Surely any half-decent organisation should be capable of employing a qualified chef to keep their kitchen from becoming a pigsty.

I felt it was unnecessary for the visiting officer to prosecute, but this person had a reputation for going in hard and, for some reason, didn't like me at all. Although her boss advised there wasn't enough evidence to mount a successful prosecution, she insisted on continuing her vendetta.

My terminally ill mother was now in her final days, and I couldn't see her as often as I would like. I tried to explain my plight to the prosecuting inspector and begged them to reconsider, but her unforgiving mind was set.

I worked around the clock to get the hotel in the clear. The additional paperwork and planning were well received, plus the latest chef finally cleaned the kitchen. Meanwhile, there was a significant incident elsewhere in the county that put this relatively minor misdemeanour into context. As a result, the case was downgraded to an official warning so we could all breathe a sigh of relief.

I received the welcome news while at a meeting in the Midlands. After driving home, I got out of my car and collapsed with the mental and emotional exhaustion of this incident and my mother's imminent death. I promised I would search for a new career, maybe something outdoors like cleaning windows. It's another promise I failed to keep.

Bizarrely the general manager had somehow kept the whole episode from the owner of the hotel, who had a tinderbox temperament and an unhinged dislike for the authorities. Unsurprisingly he found out about the pending official warning that would stay on record for five years and phoned me just as we were leaving for my mother's funeral in Berkshire. He proceeded to give me a highly unpleasant fifteen-minute verbal kicking and refused to accept the down-graded warning that I and others had worked so hard to acquire, insisting he would battle the authorities through the courts as he hated civil servants. Fortunately, this ridiculous man was eventually talked around and belatedly took the warning.

You can argue that the inspecting officer was just doing their job, but they had seemingly caused a similar rumpus at a number of other properties and left their role soon afterwards. I have never loathed anyone as much as this person for causing me so much unnecessary distress and misery and for making the lowest point in my life even more unbearable.

The damage was done as the time lost with my mother could never be replaced. Sometime later, I realised my mental health had been affected for years by these events, which caused further emotional distress to my family as my inability to cope grew.

Three years later, I recounted this episode to my producer when I was just about to go on air for my weekly radio show. I was still blurting out fantasies of unhinged retribution for this inspector whose actions stopped me from being with my mother on her deathbed.

I was in full flow, ranting that I wouldn't cross the street to piss on them when my producer grabbed my arms and shook me.

'Stop it now! You are better than this. Come on! We have a radio show to do!'

Amazingly that did the trick. She is one of the most relentlessly positive people I have ever met and reminded me of what I was once like or perhaps pictured myself to be.

'Time for a new career?' I laughed while getting my senses back.

'Yes, definitely,' she replied, red-faced and shocked by witnessing a side of me few people get to see. At least I remembered to keep the microphone closed during my rant.

My dream of a new job or career never materialised, and I'm not sure what else I was qualified to do. Working outside would be lovely, but I'm not much of a gardener, and my ADHD meant that windows would be highly unlikely to be cleaned to the necessary gleaming standards. My dream was always to work in radio, but there are countless broadcasters far more talented than I could ever hope to be, all now looking for work. Sadly, many established local radio stations have disappeared from the airwaves resulting in very few opportunities. Those that remain are often poorly paid with short-term contracts of just a few months.

Of all the occupations for an adult with ADHD to have, being a health and safety consultant probably wouldn't feature very high on the list.

At various points in my life, I have touched a live electric fire bar to see if it was working, and I've stuck a metal knife in a toaster attempting to release some fresh bread, which gave me such a strong electric shock that I fell backwards over a table. Of course, I wasn't expecting much sympathy from my random act of stupidity, and the emotional wasp didn't disappoint. 'You complete fucking idiot!'

More recently, I tested with my hand to check whether a strimmer blade was still rotating. Fortunately, metal blades have been replaced with nylon cords these days. I like to think I'm road-testing hazards and risks so my clients don't have to—I have ADHD.

However, ADHD may also help me to find potential workplace hazards for my clients and view issues and solutions in more than one dimension. I like to think I am good at my job, if I hadn't been, I doubt I would be approaching my fourth decade in business.

The interpretation of legislation is often in shades of grey rather than black and white. This can make things tricky for a consultant when you don't know how the guidance might be interpreted from one inspecting officer to another.

A visiting fire officer described my risk assessment as the best he had seen. He asked if he could use my document to train his cadets in the correct way to format an assessment, as it ticked every box from the new guidance. Yet, when he retired, his replacement visited the same hotel and described the document as non-compliant and not fit for purpose. Legislation shouldn't allow for such polarised views.

Incidents are thankfully rare, but they can happen, and when they do, blame is often pointed back at the guy who wrote a document rather than the person who decided to behave in an unsafe manner. This can allow a visiting official to have their 'pound of flesh' and a potential day in court.

Is it really my fault when someone decides to empty boiling chip fat into a plastic bucket that predictably melts, causing a serious incident, a person gets their toe cut off by a petrol mower as they have decided to wear flip flops instead of steel-toe-capped shoes, a drunken mother-in-law knocks herself out by tripping over the red carpet laid out for the bride and groom at a wedding reception or a plumber decides to jump off a high water tank in an attic, falling through rotten floorboards and down three flights of stairs?

No wonder I'm constantly stressed!

As a safety consultant, people probably think I'm some kind of a bore. However, they have no idea of the constant turmoil and fizz that goes on within an ADHD brain. This can make me feel so trapped that I'll leave the room during a training session to see how far I can run while they are watching an information video. I even dared myself to paddle in the sea at a coastal hotel during a film on manual handling.

One client has an unusual transparent glass lift. I rode to the top floor while in a plank position. I later found it was a one-way mirror, and people had gathered to watch. I was doing press-ups in a walk-in fridge when the door opened without warning, and the manager stood somewhat surprised to see my prone body. I immediately dropped to my knees to crawl under the bottom shelf, informing him that I was checking for evidence of mould.

'I know I can always trust you to be thorough,' he smiled.

However, ADHD has probably caused me to lose clients by being too opinionated and making the occasional error of judgement.

I travelled early one morning to Hampshire for a potentially significant new contract, but after visiting the gents and washing my hands, I was too impatient to wait for the old and ineffectual hand drier. As I left the toilet, the company managing director strode forward to shake my hand, and I had no choice but to offer my cold and soggy hand in return. 'Ugh!' he said, jumping sharply back, and it would appear deeply offended. He continued to stare at his hand in disbelief while I mumbled like an errant schoolboy about having just been to the toilet.

The meeting was uncommonly brief. 'We will let you know' was all he said as I departed the building, but he'd disappeared before I could even say goodbye, let alone shake his hand again. After a seemingly never-ending journey home, I was greeted by Katherine.

'Did you get the contract?' She asked hopefully

'I think it's doubtful.' I replied.

42

Most training sessions are well attended by delegates who will at least make some effort to engage. I'm usually pleased by the results, as are my clients, but it is not always plain sailing. One example is harassed young mothers who would bring their babies or young children with them as they had no other option if they wanted to keep their job as their manager had told them attending was compulsory. The babies would proceed to cry throughout, or a young child would be traumatised by the accident graphically re-enacted in my training film.

On one occasion, while awaiting delegates to arrive at a client in the East Midlands, a young woman who was a part-time employee entered the room with a face like thunder. She had a badge with a name on it: Charlotte.

'How long is this crap going to take?' enquired Charlotte.

'About an hour,' I replied, in my most patient and smiley way.

'I ain't sitting here for an hour!'

'Don't then.'

'I 'ave to.'

'Sit down then!' I replied in a sharper tone. She tutted, then complied before sitting in the back row and staring at the wall.

Management will sometimes introduce me by unhelpfully announcing, '…I know safety training is boring, but it's important.' However, I always do my best to make training relevant and as interesting as possible. To my mind, there might be boring people, but there are no boring subjects, and it is in everyone's interest to engage with health and safety.

I have been where they are working long hours then dragged into training, often without pay and under threat of being fired for failing to attend, so it's not surprising there is an occasional hostile audience.

The final part of this training session involved a short film on fire safety that demonstrates how a small flame on a hotel bedroom chair can soon become a huge exploding fireball.

I asked the group how long they thought this would take. Charlotte is looking away, her arms folded with a poisonous and sulky look on her face. I'm not a teacher of an underperforming school, so I usually ignore these people and ask those engaged in order to get the session finished and get away. But not today.

'How many minutes do you think this will take, Charlotte?'

'Dunno.'

'Two minutes?' I suggest. She shrugged her shoulders.

'Three, four, ten? Have a guess!' I wasn't going to back down.

We stared at each other for some time before I eventually prevailed, and she mumbled, 'Five.'

Triumphantly I turned back to the rest of the group.

'Let's see if Charlotte is right.' I clicked a button on the DVD player, which promptly spat out the disc and switched off.

'Fuck it!' I said rather too loudly. Everyone laughed, and the session ended with me on my backside. Charlotte gave a smirk akin to a middle finger as she walked past and out of the room.

After the session, I asked the deputy manager who also attended if they bothered with interviews or just collected people off the street. I dread to think how much business I have flushed away with my random ADHD fuelled comments.

The next day the hotel manager telephoned me to apologise and told me they had fired Charlotte. Of course, this was not what I wanted or expected, but I couldn't help thinking about the rather threatening looks she had given me and double-checked that our doors were locked at night for a week or two after.

The young and perhaps not so young people who attend my training probably don't want to be a waiter, barman or a cleaner. They want to be a DJ, actor or pop star and believe it's only a matter of time until they are. I guess that included me not so long ago. However, there does seem to be some added pride and importance evident in those attending in more recent years, but perhaps that is due, in part, to those who attend. I don't think I have ever encountered a problem with an employee whose first language wasn't English.

When a session goes well, I often receive excellent feedback and thought-provoking questions from those gathered. It is always a good feeling to know the training has raised the level of awareness and made the work environment safer. However, the questions I receive aren't always the ones expected.

During a level two food hygiene course, while I was doing my best to explain the transition of pathogenic bacteria and food-borne disease, a delegate raised his hand in front of twenty others to ask,

'What about oral sex, would it be safe?'

There were stifled giggles followed by a few moments of silence from the other delegates before I finally replied. 'But I hardly know you!'

Among a group of forty or so people attending my short presentation on health and safety, there was a very mouthy middle-aged waiter seemingly out of his comfort zone, probably due to being in a classroom environment for the first time in many years. He had been making sarcastic and unhelpful comments throughout. When I decided to counter his ridiculous words, he retorted, 'Do you even have a life, mate?' The comment stunned me like an uppercut through a poor boxing guard, and I started to rock backwards and forwards, fearing I was about to boil over, but I'd just bought a new car and couldn't afford to give the reaction this buffoon deserved. It wasn't easy, but I smiled and swallowed down the insult.

I used to be where he is, laying tables then serving food and drink morning, noon, and night until my ankles were swollen and my legs grew varicose veins. I know what it is like to work in junior hotel management too, dealing with every problem imaginable from slow service, undercooked steaks, corked wine, petty crime, and on more than one occasion, attempting to unblock a bedroom toilet complete with accompanying 'floaters' armed with only a bin bag and a metal coat hanger as plumbing tools. All the while as the guest who had recently produced the aforementioned floaters vented their anger, having been embarrassed by the inadequate flushing system. I believe this was the moment when I realised I no longer wanted to be employed in the role of duty manager.

Now, many years later, I'd worked even harder to build up my own business and should perhaps thank the resilience ADHD gave me to set it up and fight through the challenges. I had probably earned more that morning than this man would earn in a week. Furthermore, it was only 11 am, and I had now finished my appointments for the day. So I drove home in my new car and took my wife out for lunch at a restaurant overlooking the sea.

Yes, 'mate' - I definitely have a life!

CHAPTER FOUR

Diagnosis and Denial

'I know he doesn't really think that everything is cool, and he knows that I know he doesn't really think that either.'

———————

Everyone remembers where they were on 'Super Saturday' during the 2012 London Olympics.

I was on a train and missed the whole thing.

The Rumble in the Jungle, epic Ashes victories, regular England penalty shoot-out agonies, the Lionesses finally ending fifty-six years of hurt at Wembley, or a five-set Wimbledon classic. These and other great sporting moments will stay with us always.

But I associate the day when things in my life changed and finally began to make sense with a football match that probably passed most people by.

Norwich City 0 Stoke City 1 (Klose 35, own goal) - 6th October 2018

I had commentated on the football match between Norwich City and Stoke City for the blind and partially sighted fans at Carrow Road, the home of Norwich City Football Club. It's a service known as Soccer Sight. The fans tune in through an induction loop that transmits the commentary around the entire stadium. It's one thing that keeps me focused and concentrated that I can do at a passable level, with occasional compliments hidden among the complaints. Radio and football were two passions in my life, but both had now gone stale.

My task was to make this terrible match sound exciting for my listeners, but it was easier said than done. Stoke City had just been relegated from the Premier League and were perhaps expecting to quickly bounce back to the big time. However, in their bid for a goalless draw, Stoke parked a 'defensive bus' along their goal line before benefitting from a freak own goal, prompting them to park two defensive buses in front of their goal line until the final whistle.

My brain was in some form of a toxic neutral zone, but I made it through my commentary duties, and there were no negative comments from my listeners this week, as they were mostly angry with the result of the match and had gone straight home. I knew the guys in charge of Soccer Sight were getting tired of my moody behaviour and unreliability, but, as ever, they gave me the benefit of the doubt.

'That's fine, Buddy! everything is cool.' The supervisor was always genial and friendly but obviously hiding his true feelings.

I know he doesn't really think that everything is cool, and he knows that I know he doesn't really think that either.

Such was my behaviour during this time; one of my fellow commentators won't even speak to me now, so I hope this book will explain something to him and some others involved who I may have alienated.

They would have had no idea what I was going through or that a week later, I would be standing on a Norfolk beach, waist-high in freezing cold water, searching for the courage to swim out to sea and make my sack of shit brain close down for good.

I walked like a zombie from the stadium back to Vicky's flat on the outskirts of the city. We discussed the awful match before I asked her about taking medication for depression. My brain was constantly misfiring, whirring and unable to focus, like an engine in neutral unable to travel anywhere. I felt like I was wading through mud, misunderstood, disliked, paranoid, and full of self-loathing. I began to question whether my life was worth living anymore.

The symptoms of ADHD were there throughout my life. No one saw them, not me, not my parents, teachers, doctors, therapists, or anyone else. It took so long that I had to play a part in conceiving, then waiting for my youngest daughter to be born, go to school and university, get a degree, then study and work professionally in mental health for several years to ask the question that finally made the past fifty-eight years of my life make some sense of order.

'Dad, have you ever thought you might have ADHD?'

Frantic internet searches were immediately made with reputable online tests completed. I purchased every book available, and so finally, I think I know what may be 'wrong' with me.

I phoned my sister and told her about my discovery. She ran to find a picture book from her shelf called *All Dogs Have ADHD*, reading each page aloud before exclaiming,

'How did we all miss this?'

The more I looked into it, the more obvious it became. The school work, the jobs, inattention, and constant underperforming against all expectations.

Not everyone agreed or supported me, though. Some laughed or scoffed or made stupid comments.

'Timmy! Just like the kid from *South Park* Ha! Ha!'

Some confuse it with autism, and another tells me they don't believe ADHD 'is a thing.'

My life had become ever more fraught, and I realised the diagnosis couldn't wait any longer. However, there was a three-year waiting list for an NHS diagnosis, so Katherine agreed to cash in our Premium Bonds, and for almost the cost of a foreign holiday, I found the most reputable ADHD private consultant available. I know I was lucky to have the resources to jump the queue, but I justified it in my mind that in doing so, I was helping the National Health Service, although this later proved to be untrue.

The private consultant is based in Harley Street, and I'm told this is the gold standard diagnosis. I had two sessions that were spread over two days with a psychologist and then a psychiatrist. They also required input from someone who knew me as a child, so a questionnaire was duly sent to my sister.

There are endless questions to answer but little opportunity to discuss them. So it's either 'Yes' or 'No.' At the end of the consultation, I have a 9/9 score for inattentive ADHD and 8/9 for the hyperactivity side of the condition. My diagnosis is conclusive.

During the follow-up session, my results are discussed, and I am prescribed Concerta, a long-acting methylphenidate. However, the consultant ended the session early, but I still had many more questions to ask, and by my calculation, there were two minutes left at £7 a minute. I wanted to get every second of value for money, but the prescribing psychiatrist wouldn't budge.

'We've run out of time, and I have another person waiting. Just take the pills and not just for a day, you will feel better!' At this point, she ended the session rather abruptly.

When the prescription finally arrived at the pharmacy, I almost sprinted the mile there. After a tetchy exchange over the exorbitant price of a private prescription, during which the pharmacist ultimately threatened to destroy them. I backed down and paid. Taking the first dose before I left the pharmacy. By the time I got home, I could feel the drug's effect spreading through my body towards my brain like a mixture of caffeine and steroids. It was a new and not unpleasant sensation.

On my first day of taking Concerta, I was running down the street like George Bailey in the Christmas movie. *It's A Wonderful Life*, greeting everyone with a big silly grin on my face. Hooray! I'm cured, and my life is going to be brilliant from now on!

But of course, I wasn't cured and soon received a plethora of unwanted side effects, so within a couple of weeks, they were thrown into the bottom drawer.

Disappointed and disenchanted, I wondered if it was all a big commercial venture taking advantage of the growing number of late-life ADHD diagnoses.

There are also large fees to talk with their team at regular periods. In addition, there would be recurring hefty bills for prescriptions and compulsory private consultancy fees that I hadn't expected. I had assumed it would be a shared agreement with the NHS to avoid the high costs. However, my doctor told me this treatment wasn't covered by the NHS and advised me to stop taking the drugs immediately due to my ongoing issues with high blood pressure.

Regarding the costs, I was advised by my doctor to contact the local MP, which I did and to his credit, he took the necessary steps to ensure a shared agreement of this kind would be far more straightforward to obtain in the future.

There is more information about my ongoing battle with ADHD medication in chapter eight, with a potentially happy ending in my quest to find a suitable remedy.

I had researched several top private ADHD clinics throughout England and chose one of the most respected specialists based in Harley Street. But I had become rather sceptical of them and what appeared to be a rather flimsy diagnosis procedure. I wondered whether I had been ripped off for hundreds of pounds or misdiagnosed, as my diagnosis was so overwhelmingly conclusive.

Apparently, I was in the next stage of the process: denial.

Denial.

I had expected to be relieved and happy to have finally been given my ADHD diagnosis after decades of waiting, but instead I was shocked, slightly annoyed, and a little embarrassed by it, and I continued to believe my results were probably a mistake. I could have appeared purposely a bit jittery, over-talkative, constantly moved around, and then answered the hundreds of questions falsely to ensure I got a positive diagnosis. Instead, I'd just made the whole thing up for attention. So no, I don't have ADHD, not me!

Of course, I don't have ADHD. I'm not at all impulsive. Other than when I tried to mortgage the house for a surefire bet, that lost and would have left my family homeless.

I can't have ADHD. I've never had risky sex. Other than the one-night stand of passionate unprotected sex. That doesn't count because it turned into a relationship that is now well into its fourth decade.

I can't have ADHD. I've always been a safe driver. Other than for the time I drove on the wrong side of the road, had several speeding fines, and wrote off three cars in a pile-up on a humpback bridge.

I can't have ADHD. I'm never angry or moody except for kicking in a few doors, smashing four mobile phones on the floor, and throwing another into the Norfolk Broads. In addition, I now have to live with the shame and long-lasting effect that my mood swings have had on some of those close to me.

I can't have ADHD. I have never thought about ending my life. Other than the time I planned to swim out to sea and when I visualised myself hanging from a rope in our garage. I've never tried to self-harm other than when I poured boiling water over my hand, cut my arms with a kitchen knife, and bit myself
so hard that blood ran down my shoulder. Self-harm and suicidal thoughts are public health concerns that disproportionately affect those with symptoms of ADHD, and that definitely isn't me…Is it?

I admit I don't or perhaps can't always listen; I zone out, get a bit stressed, and leave everything I do half finished. I left school with no qualifications, I'm overly sensitive, battled back from the brink of addiction, got fired from so many jobs I had to employ myself, and hadn't before read an entire work of fiction. And my mind often bounces around like the ping pong balls in a bingo machine.

OK! I admit it I have ADHD!

After three more years of waiting, I was given a thorough ADHD assessment from the NHS that confirmed the private diagnosis and there was no more room for denial.

Following the second diagnosis I had regular catch-ups with my ADHD specialist. It's rare to find someone that I am entirely at ease with and who will laugh, understand and then make an attempt to correct my behaviour without being judgemental. Since then, I have met a number of excellent ADHD consultants. For anyone looking to get a diagnosis, the worst part may be the wait, but once you are through the queue, the treatment on offer from the National Health Service, in my experience, is exceptional.

The day after the soulless one-nil home defeat to Stoke City, following which Vicky first suggested I might have ADHD, I bumped into Timm Klose, scorer of the unfortunate own goal. He had somehow managed to park his giant Mercedes into the tiniest of spaces next to me in a cramped car park on a hill. He then marched into Norwich city centre disguised only by a pair of Clarke Kent-style glasses in the hope he wouldn't be recognised. Life would get considerably worse for me before it got any better, but for Timm Klose and his team, things improved significantly from that day on as the Canaries barely lost another match all season and won the league at a canter.

When diagnosed with ADHD …
Own it, live it and love it - It's part of who you are.

———————

If you have ADHD, it is also likely that someone else in your family has the condition too, usually a sibling. If this is so, I'm quite sure it is not my brother who appears to bound through life, grabbing every opportunity to seize the day. I've often wished I could be more like him.

My sister completed a master's degree and had decades in a job with a huge amount of responsibility. However, she can't find her way out of a car park, will burst into loud song while in a library, and rush excitedly into the sea, having brought no change of clothing or a towel. Whenever we are in a queue together, we will both jump up and down, unable to bear the slowness of those serving, eventually deciding to go somewhere else even though we both know this will take longer. I believe that my sister is even worse at queuing than I am (see chapter 14). If Alex does have ADHD, she makes it seem like a breeze compared to my endless battles, and nothing ever seems to derail her. She has been one of the biggest influences in my life.

However, symptoms in women and girls may present differently, and this can lead to diagnosis being missed. For example, whilst boys may be tearing around full of hyperactivity, girls may be more likely to show signs of inattention and disorganisation.

Since my diagnosis, I've occasionally noticed symptoms in others. One of my clients would keep the most disorganised office, leave multiple tasks incomplete and attempt to hold several conversations at once. Although a successful businesswoman, she admitted to being rather 'scatty' and struggled to get things done but didn't know why. It was still quite a risky thing to suggest she might have ADHD. But, of course, I did. 'How would you know?' was her rather forceful reply.

I then took the additional risk of telling her of my condition. This seemed to resonate and led her to seek a diagnosis of her own. There were also people who rather unkindly laughed out loud when I first told them I had ADHD. However, when I study their own behaviour more closely, I'm tempted to suggest they might take a diagnosis test themselves.

As I tell more people about my condition, a growing number wonder if they, too, might have ADHD, as some of the symptoms sound rather familiar. Of course, I suggest they get a professional diagnosis, but I also enquire about their DIY habits as these might offer a clue.

When painting a wall or a garden fence, I wonder whether they complete each panel methodically and evenly, checking to see if the first coat is dry before continuing, then ensure they have enough paint to complete a second coat, or do they start at one end, paint a bit at the other end, then go to the middle, stop midway through to cut the grass, returning to complete the job before running out of paint and deciding one coat will do.

Similarly, when they receive a piece of flat pack furniture, do they read the instructions before starting and lay all the various tools out as detailed, or do they instead empty everything onto the floor and open all the screw and nail bags, ignore the guidelines and make a complete mess of the assembly before searching through the rubbish bin to find the instructions that were it seems, rather necessary after all.

Of course, this is in no way meant to be a scientific diagnosis, but perhaps it might offer a few tiny clues.

CHAPTER FIVE

Suicide, Grief, and Self Harm

Recent research shows that adults with ADHD are five times more likely than those without the condition to have attempted suicide

——————

I was nine years old when I confided to my big sister that I was feeling 'semi-suicidal.'

We were close to a large dirty lake on some scrubland in Berkshire where hundreds of new houses would soon be built. The water was deep, dangerous, and filled with weeds, bricks, and other debris. My sister Alex proposed that she would push me into the mucky water. If she added, I then tried to get back to the safety of dry land, I would have my answer as to whether I wanted to carry on living. I declined the offer and we walked home.

Fast forward several decades later, to November 2018, when I planned to test this particular theory once again. I had driven to a small seaside resort a few miles up the coast from Great Yarmouth, where there is a little car park next to a block of toilets and an ice cream van. I was smiling and greeting everyone I passed in a slightly vacant and falsely jovial manner. It occurred to me these might be the last people I would ever see. Ironically, I'd left the keys under the car wheel, so for once, they wouldn't get lost in the sea, as they had so many times before.

I planned to swim out as far as I could, then take in my final moments before the cold numbed my body, and I slipped below the surface. If I changed my mind, I could, perhaps, scramble back to shore, but only if I had enough energy left before the cold entirely took over and halted any movement.

My misfiring brain has invented the ultimate game of 'Dare'.

If I had Pebbles, my beautiful golden Labrador and constant companion for the past fifteen years with me, she would have known what was happening and do something about it. Maybe she would have run back to the car, so I'd have to chase after her and insist we go home or, perhaps, swim out to sea herself, so I would have to save her like the scene in *It's A Wonderful Life* when James Stewart's character, George Bailey, jumped into the freezing water to save his guardian angel rather than going ahead with his own planned suicide. But my canine guardian angel isn't there anymore, and it's her death that I still can't get over more than a year later that's led to my crippling depression and confusion.

Due to injury, I was now unable to feel the release that exercise brings, and a lifetime of failure and bewilderment from undiagnosed ADHD has led me towards this empty and hopeless end. It had been two weeks since it was first suggested that I might have ADHD. But, unfortunately, the initial bounce from the potential diagnosis hadn't dulled my downward spiral that was yet to be halted, and it would still be years before I would seek any professional help.

It's weird the thoughts that go through your mind when you are on the brink. Before I swim out to my potential demise, I'd like to know whether Norwich City are winning. I still had my iPhone with me and clicked on the live scores page. I had carefully left my keys under the wheel and my wallet in the car so they wouldn't be lost forever in the sea, but three things to leave behind was apparently one too many for my brain to 'forget,' so my iPhone would now join the collection of my many other items that had been lost in Davy Jones' locker—once I'd checked the football scores, of course!

Norwich were indeed winning two-nil away to Swansea City, and I wondered if they would hang on. It didn't occur to me that I would never discover the answer. I also, quite literally, had no idea what I would do next. It felt as if I was watching myself on a screen as my brain proceeded to have the mother of all arguments with itself.

'You know full well you're not going to do this.'

'Are you daring me? Do you think I won't?'

'Just go home, idiot!'

'Maybe I'll just plough into the waves and see what happens next.'

'Don't be stupid. Just go home now!'

'No, come on, let's do this. It will make the pain stop, and the people you've hurt will have a better life without you.'

And with that, the more agitated side of my brain took hold.

The tide was going out as I took a few small steps over the wet sand towards the grey foamy water. The waves were not huge but swept over my trainers before the water splashed higher, covering my knees and soaking into my shorts and the bottom of my shirt. I gasped as the shock of the freezing water hit me, and the part of my brain that needed to take control seized back power as I realised with shame and embarrassment that I was just a useless coward acting out a toxic charade. There was never any serious intention of being brave enough to go through with my pathetic game of Dare.

The suffering must be unimaginable for those who decide they can no longer bear to live.

I stood there almost waist-deep in the icy water, and I screamed, and I screamed, and I screamed towards the windy ocean. I swore and screamed again. Finally, when I had no voice left, and tears were burning my cheeks, I turned to see a young family with their small dog making a hasty retreat away from the noisy, crazy guy who was wading fully clothed into the freezing sea.

I departed the beach and trudged slowly back to my car, the icy water sloshing in my now ruined trainers that I had paid £90 for in the futile hope they might have the magic cure to help me run without pain.

Fortunately, the car was still there with the keys undiscovered behind the front wheel, and I travelled back still dazed, confused, helpless, empty, and ashamed. Keeping my brain focused on the ever-passionate local radio football commentary helped to get me back home in one piece.

As I walked through the front door, I quickly hid my wet shoes inside the porch before my wife noticed them. I painted on my 'everything is fine' face, but Katherine knew it was a lie, although she didn't know quite how bad things were and wasn't exactly sure where I had been either.

'Did you have a nice time?' she asked doubtfully.

'Yeah, Norwich won 4-1.'

I wanted to unload all my problems, but there was too much anger, shame, hurt, and embarrassment for me to do so.

A mental health professional told me that If I had gone through with my swim to oblivion that day, it would probably have been recorded as death by misadventure rather than suicide.

Whatever the coroner's verdict, I realised that I hadn't left any goodbye notes and began the grim and emotional task of doing so. I knew the dark clouds might descend back into my brain, and there may soon be another time when I would stand back on the precipice.

I left details of passwords and legal documents, a copy of my will, and my life insurance, although I doubt it covered suicide, so I would need to make it look like an accident.

One in four women with ADHD are thought to have attempted suicide, although statistically, more men than women die from taking their own life as a man will often use a more violent method and, therefore, be more likely to complete the act before anyone can intervene. I know I am more in danger of an 'Oh fuck it!' moment where I may become overwhelmed by a situation rather than making a detailed plan for my demise.

Vicky went through some very challenging times when she was young, so to protect her, we entered into a bizarre suicide pact that, if one of us decided to go, we had the knowledge we were taking the other one with us, so this is a tricky one. I remind her that she has two young cats to look after, so she had to forfeit the deal and stick around to keep them safe. I ask others to remember the good times, to know they were always loved, and I promise them things will improve one day and to keep believing in themselves.

Although, I truly wondered if people would even care or notice if I was no longer around.

I was writing the farewell notes on my computer while other family members were in the same room, all watching *Saturday Night Takeaway* on the television. Involuntary tears pricked my eyes as I rewrote the notes again and again.

I thanked Alex for being the most amazing sister and attempted to write a caring and loving note to my brother, laced with some poor humour that I knew we both shared that would perhaps still make him smile after I had gone.

But, the more I wrote, the more I realised that it wrongly lay guilt at other people's door when in reality, it was my own failings and mental health problems that needed to be recognised and treated.

As I began my letter to Katherine, I only had Smokey, our elderly cat, for company with his ever-present grumpy face staring back at me from across the room. But I was unable to write a single word. It's one heart that I could never break, and I felt paralysed. So I hid away, curled up in a ball and cried, unable to stop. Hoping and praying to whoever was listening that there was some kind of help, if not for my sake but for the others in my life.

Writing goodbyes to those I love and am closest to proved cathartic and demonstrated the unimaginable hurt and grief I would have caused. I began to realise what I would be leaving behind and started to fight back against the toxic rot invading my brain and the part my

60

undiagnosed ADHD may be causing. Of course, people would care if I died! Wouldn't they? It was probably the lowest point of my life, but it was also a turning point.

* Samaritans 116 123

Grief

My mind and body were numb as I marched along a quiet South Norfolk bridleway. I had never felt such desperation as I continued to frantically search for my missing dog. I was travelling so fast that I was almost running. The warm autumn sunshine had brought out the smell of stale dog urine in the dirty old blanket I had clutched tightly to my chest. A woman passing the other way gave me an understanding smile and opened her mouth to say something but then thought better of it and walked on.

I hadn't seen my dog for days, but a small part of me knew the desperate search for her was completely futile.

So, it was with some relief and not a little surprise when I spotted a lady in her sixties striding ahead of me with my dog on a long pink lead.

I'd had Pebbles by my side for the past fifteen years since she was just a few weeks old. A beautiful golden Labrador with soft brown eyes and a faded pink nose that changed to black during the winter. A one-of-a-kind friend and never judgemental. A canine guardian angel, she had, as my symptoms worsened, kept me safe and away from the cliff edge, seeming to realise I needed protecting, most of all from myself. Her happy, joyous face and thick wagging tail with its light tuft of fur were unmistakable, and I had fully convinced myself that the woman just ahead of me had stolen her.

Dog thieves are an evil stain on society. I hate them. The punishment needs to be far more appropriate for the pain and suffering they cause to the animal and owner than the current law provides.

I was overjoyed to have found Pebbles but unsure how to proceed. Nothing too hasty, I decided to follow the woman while she continued ahead in the same direction. She had short grey hair, wore a green top, dark trousers and brown boots. I was getting a description in my mind for the police. The dog thief was now just twenty metres in front of me, and her footsteps crunched on the loose stones and dry twigs. The tension rose as she picked up the pace, now fully aware of my presence, nervously looking behind at the fast-approaching angry looking, dishevelled guy staring back at her. I was rather surprised that Pebbles hadn't noticed me yet. What the hell was this woman doing with my dog and holding a long pink lead that I had never seen before? My plan was to snatch Pebbles and get away quickly, or perhaps I'd attempt to keep the woman there until the police arrived.

My brain was tired through lack of sleep but also spinning with crazy thoughts. Part of me knew the thoughts were crazy and irrational, but not enough of my brain wanted to believe or accept the truth. The incessant noisy chatter inside me had become almost disabling.

At this point, I'd advanced to just a few paces behind the dog thief and was about to grab Pebbles away from this lady and run when the tiny remaining scrap of reason left inside my dishevelled mind took back control and silently screamed at me to stop.

A surge of uncontrollable grief overtook the anger, hatred, and injustice as I narrowly swerved the absurd confrontation. I knew it couldn't be my dog, as she died in my arms three days ago.

The naturalist and television presenter Chris Packham first realised he had autism when he struggled to get over the death of his dog. I can't either. So am I autistic? Is that the problem? ADHD and autism are known to share some of the same traits. My ADHD diagnosis was still years away, but I knew something was going on that wasn't normal, which had been there for much of my life, but I had no idea what. However, I continued to scoff at the suggestion from my wife that I had depression or any other mental health issues.

I couldn't let the grief go for days, months, or years. However, time does eventually heal the pain, although it may also leave a permanent scar.

I've cried and grieved more at the passing of a pet with open raw emotion, and I didn't care who saw me. It was later suggested that I had unresolved issues regarding my parents' death that magnified when Pebbles died. The dark clouds only truly started to lift when I had the ADHD diagnosis and finally accepted treatment.

When our much-loved elderly cat died just before Christmas one year, I knew more than anyone how much it was hurting others, yet I couldn't find the right words to help with their pain and instead seemingly made things worse.

You have to travel down the road of grief at your own pace. It wasn't possible to get another dog, but it helped that we got a couple of kittens a few months later. Another pet doesn't replace the one that has passed on, but it is a new relationship that allows the healing to begin.

Shortly after Pebbles died, the Blue Cross, a wonderful charity that offer help and support with pet bereavement, were the most welcome guests on my radio show. Later, I bought a tiny fir tree with scruffy branches that reminded me of Pebble's tufts of ruffled fur and put her ashes in the pot. The tree is now over six feet tall and grows new shoots every year.

Self-Harm

My mother-in-law passed away just before her 96th Birthday. A truly remarkable and inspirational woman, part of the greatest generation. She was sixteen when the Second World War broke out and was asked to work in Lincolnshire. Upon arrival, there was no one to greet her and nowhere for her to stay, so she went to the local police station and spent the night sleeping in the cells as this was the only accommodation to be had.

Sadly, just like a classic car, she had come to the end of her time. Dementia was lurking around the corner, so it was, perhaps, a relief that the end came when it did. Katherine had her own health problems, so she couldn't be involved as fully as she would have liked to be with the funeral arrangements, but as the youngest of six, I was glad that she swerved some of the potential disagreements.

In the week prior to the funeral, I'd arranged a family afternoon tea. I hoped we would enjoy some time out of the house and clear our minds a little, but even before we reached our destination, some intense feelings overflowed, and we had little choice but to head back home again. There had been undercurrents of emotion and other difficulties in our household for a while that weren't helping when matters unnecessarily boiled over.

My spirits were now at breaking point, but there was no longer a dog to greet me as I arrived home that would come to the rescue by requesting a long calming walk. So many difficulties and potential confrontations had been avoided over the years thanks to an hour in the fresh air walking with Pebbles in the countryside. Although, more recently, I have realised that my weakness of avoiding rather than facing such disagreements and confrontations had been a failing, perhaps causing more problems than it solved.

I entered the kitchen and closed the door for some privacy while I made tea. I wanted to cry and scream, kick in a door, throw a cupboard full of glass on the floor or slam drawers shut. But those options weren't available to me. Still, I needed to get rid of the intense feeling of injustice, grief, self-loathing, and annoyance, however extreme the remedy might be.

I was told by someone who suffered acute mental health problems that they self-harmed because it numbed the other kind of pain they were feeling, and it actually made them feel better for a short while, even though the injuries they sustained required an urgent trip to the hospital.

I deliberated how it would feel to pour boiling water over my hand and then to stop myself from wondering any further. I decided to find out.

I picked up the glass kettle with the blue LED lights still flashing at the base and splashed the boiling water liberally over my left hand and wrist, then waited for the split second to pass and allow the pain to reach my brain. A sensation of scorching blades and stinging nettles coursed through my arm, but the pain was also weirdly comforting as it temporarily wiped away the intense and desperate feelings. I immediately stuck my bright red hand in cold water then added some random frozen veg from the freezer in an attempt to halt any blistering.

However, it wasn't enough, and the surge of emotion quickly returned. I apparently required more pain and further punishment. So I located a sharp black-handled kitchen knife from the magnetic block and dragged the pointed blade down, then across my bare arm again and again, leaving a badly scratched noughts and crosses board. I hadn't realised I had gone in quite so deeply until the blood flooded through my skin and ran down my arm. Next up was a plastic carrier bag which I stuck tightly over my head, breathing in manically as I did so and wondered how long it would take for me to keel over. Too fucking long! I ripped the bag from my head and continued to make the tea.

I tried to hide the damage by pulling the shirt sleeves over my arms with a makeshift kitchen towel bandage placed underneath as I belatedly took the tea tray into the living room as if nothing had happened.

In moments of need, ADHD minds can focus well, and I was determined to do my absolute loving best for Katherine at this time of sadness and grief. She knows I will always be there for her with a shoulder to cry on or a cuddle, we can talk all night, or I will just sit and listen. But I was completely ashamed of the self-harming and didn't want her to see the damage, so I kept my arms hidden, but I couldn't stop the blood from seeping through my sleeves.

'What have you done to your arms Timmy!' Katherine asked, somewhat alarmed.

'Er... It was the cat. I was brushing a knot out of his fur and he scratched me.' I tried my best to make the words sound convincing.

The grief Katherine was going through made her oblivious to the reality, and although our cat had once given me sepsis from a bite while I held him so the vet could inject a microchip into his neck. He was rather elderly now and probably not capable of causing that amount of damage, especially in the style of a manic noughts and crosses board. When I recounted this to my then-therapist, I laughed at the absurdity of the words leaving my mouth. I was a little embarrassed that she failed to see the funny side.

Self-harm can occur when there is nowhere else to go. When life occasionally became toxic, I continued to self-harm, mostly with a kitchen knife. Once you have started something, it's often easier the next time. On another occasion, when life had become particularly tough, Vicky asked me how I was. Instead of replying, I just lifted my sleeves to show her the damage.

'Oh, Dad,' she said with an exasperated smile, but never judgemental. Her support through some of the darkest times was probably lifesaving.

Whenever I sent the sharp blade down my forearm, I felt a release followed by an almost instantaneous surge of regret, especially on the occasion when there was a family event the following day in London, and I needed to hide the evidence. I arrived at the gathering with multi-coloured kinesiology tape (used by athletes to support and heal sporting injuries) strapped down my arm, that did an excellent job of soaking up any remnants of blood and hiding the scars, but it still looked faintly ridiculous. I was ready with a long-winded story about a torn muscle and tendon, but I needn't have bothered as no one noticed or pretended not to anyway. A couple of days later, the tape fell off while swimming with Vicky, who asked the obvious question about the cuts on my arm. Again, I didn't bother to lie.

Some years later, while out for afternoon tea with Katherine and Vicky, I was sporting some dramatically healing wounds from scratches that ran the entire length of my arms. They both took a little convincing of the truth that I had been the victim of multiple attacks from our rose bush while trying to paint the garden fence, having forgone any protective wear. The fallout from a history of self-harm is that when you get injured 'naturally,' there are always a set of eyes on you, assuming something else more sinister is afoot. Although, of course, they are just looking out for you.

To think I once laughed at the thought I had mental health issues and, to my shame, felt wary of those who had them.

There may be an event, argument, or difficult situation that leads to self-harm, but it is not the fault of those events or another person. It is ultimately a result of a mental health problem or a choice. There are options and help available to at least try and overcome some of these intense feelings, although I fully understand this can be very challenging.

The mental health charity Mind has some excellent information on their website to help with the issues of self-harm.

The other technique to get me through difficult times was to daydream that I was someone else, somewhere else, or perhaps the same person but younger, happier, and successful, living in a different time.

These daydreams would get ever more life-like with characters that might have been invented for a film or novel, so when the real world got too much to bear, I went into another kinder, friendlier place. I have since learned this is known as maladaptive daydreaming, a form of intense daydreaming that is little known at present, but I fully expect it to be a huge area for therapy in the future.

I have included a section about this condition in the following chapter.

CHAPTER SIX

Toxic Outriders

ADHD seldom travels alone

There are several conditions that may co-exist with ADHD, and this is a significant reason why the disorder can be such a challenge to diagnose correctly. These conditions may adversely affect an individual every bit as much as ADHD, and that is why I refer to them as toxic outriders

I have decided to only include conditions in this chapter that have affected me personally. I haven't necessarily been strictly diagnosed with every one of them, but they have all, at some point in my life, taken a toll on my mental health. These are my personal thoughts and experiences.

- Depression
- Rejection Sensitive Disorder (RSD)
- Maladaptive Daydreaming
- Obsessive Compulsive Disorder (OCD)
- Epilepsy
- Anxiety

Depression

People who are depressed don't pretend to be ill;
on the contrary, they often pretend to be well, and depression
is a common bedfellow with ADHD.

Statistically, those with ADHD are more likely to suffer from depression, and the two conditions are commonly found together. Furthermore, ADHD can be misdiagnosed as depression, and the medication offered to treat the issue may cause inconsistent changes and potentially aggravate the symptoms.

'What have you got to be depressed about, for goodness sake?'

Many depressed people have heard these words that are as unhelpful as they are ignorant.

I've always been prone to low moods, and this is, in part, likely due to the lack of an earlier ADHD diagnosis.

'There are always people worse off than yourself.'

Being reminded of this is seldom a helpful comment, as no one really knows what you are going through. However, a school friend with wisdom beyond his years once told me that 'Happiness is a state of mind, not a state of circumstance.' Until recently, I would have agreed.

A few months before my initial ADHD diagnosis, I booked a week in Menorca with Katherine, but even on holiday, I am not immune to moods that descend into a dark place.

Although it's another perfect sunny morning, and I have the woman I love lying next to me, I had, for no apparent reason, woken up in a low mood. Later in the day, we agreed that a change of scene might help, so we left our idyllic resort for a one-hour drive to what looked in the photos to be a beautiful sandy beach, but when we arrived, it was hot, smelly, and crowded with a film of scum on the water.

Katherine had been unwell and couldn't walk for long distances, so we had the use of a wheelchair but no accompanying blue badge. This meant we couldn't use the disabled spaces that were closer to the beach without fear of fine or retribution, so instead, we navigated a tricky route pushing the wheelchair to the beach via a very steep and heavily potholed road.

We lasted for just twenty minutes at the hot and polluted resort before travelling back up the steep hill to the air-conditioned car. I was upset and annoyed that I'd subjected Katherine to this, as we should have stayed by the pool at our lovely hotel. That same day news broke of a broadcasting colleague who had sadly passed away.

She was a woman with an amazing spirit who had remained on the air for as long as possible, knowing that, without a doubt, her time on the planet was short, desperately wishing she could live longer for the sake of her young family.

It isn't fair that someone so full of life and talent is taken so early.

On our return, I jumped into the Menorcan hotel pool for a bit of underwater screaming, promising to appreciate my life more and live better for the sake of those who have no choice. Another promise that I regularly struggle to keep.

It sometimes feels like I am standing on the edge of a deep dark pit. I become so tired of who I am and think of others who are terminally ill and deserve to live far more than I do. If I could make a deal to gift them my life, I would because I just don't seem to be able to use mine properly. In the past, I've told Katherine I want to walk into a hospital and give away my organs to those who need them so that at least others may be happy again.

'I hate it when you say that kind of thing' is her naturally upset and exasperated reply.

These instances are thankfully quite rare, but when my dark moods occasionally descend, I would upset Katherine through my stupid behaviour and then wish myself dead for doing so rather than looking to find a way to control my demons. I considered myself normal and assumed there was no remedy for my personality flaw.

If only someone had handed me the ADHD label back then, things may have transpired differently.

My doctor had previously suggested that medication such as Selective Serotonin Reuptake Inhibitors (SSRIs) would only be 50-50 effective at my age. We agreed that exercise, diet, and therapy were a better route.

However, there was no thought or suggestion of anything else going on, such as ADHD.

Post-holiday blues would be an extreme feeling of being unable to cope. I would almost rather the plane crash as a better alternative to returning to work. In 2001 I went to a doctor, telling him I felt depressed, and he suggested a holiday. When I replied that I had just returned from Florida, he gave me a look bordering on contempt, and I was shown the door.

I was told, 'Tim, you are not depressed.' and that was it.

Six months after our holiday in Menorca, I hit the rocks again, so I contacted my doctor requesting anti-depressant medication. I was given Sertraline but told that it would take many weeks to work if it did at all, and there would likely be some side effects for me to endure.

During my appointment, I told the doctor that I'd had some suicidal thoughts, but he made no comment.

Sometime later, I was duly sent a 'How are you doing?' questionnaire in the post to complete. Unfortunately, I was in a particularly bad state when I filled in the form, highlighting the turmoil I was going through. So every alarm bell should have sounded at the answers I gave. My score from the questionnaire was almost off the scale.

However, I'd forgotten entirely about the questionnaire when I received a phone call some weeks later from my doctor while I was stuck in traffic and running late for a meeting. This meant I was far too preoccupied to talk properly with him, so I decided the best route was to pretend everything was fine.

It's not that difficult for a person, even on the brink, to act like everything is OK, so I gave my best happy and upbeat voice to cover my embarrassment and tried to sound as nonchalant as possible.

'Oh, that form, yeah, just a bad day. I didn't mean what I said. Everything is fine, no worries.'

'That's what I thought...' answered the doctor... 'but it was flagged up by the system to call you. If things get worse, let me know. Bye.'

I don't criticise my doctor or, indeed, the health service for this at all. The NHS is overstretched and underfunded, plus they have a thousand and one more important things to deal with each day. So if I tell my doctor that I'm fine and sound OK, but I'm telling him a pack of lies. What is he supposed to do?

When I was finally diagnosed with ADHD, it was a relief to know why I had these feelings throughout my life, although it is frustrating and difficult not to grieve for the lost and wasted years or what might have been. An ADHD therapist advised me to be positive about the loss and drew a huge graph on a flip chart of the 21,170 days I had lived so far, then dramatically ripped the page from the stand.

'There is nothing you can do about this lost time, so look forward, not back.'

This is good advice, but easier said than done.

More recently, I booked a holiday for Katherine, Vicky and myself in Cornwall, but Katherine had been further affected by M.E. Her condition takes more of a grip as each year passes. She wasn't well enough for the eight-hour road trip but insisted we go without her, even though I would be away for our wedding anniversary. I didn't want to leave her, but Katherine insisted once more, as she didn't want Vicky to be let down, and told me that I needed the break too.

I thought back to how unstoppable Katherine was, always active and making plans. There was no problem she couldn't solve.

The morning we left, I made the mistake of looking through some old photos from when we first met, looking young and carefree, running along the same Cornish beaches we were due to revisit. Two people in love, fit and healthy, splashing in and out of the waves laughing together.

I'd taken Katherine some tea to drink in bed, but she was still fast asleep and looking frail. The bitter injustice and sadness engulfed me like a tidal wave. I sat on the stairs and completely broke down with tears and snot running down my face. Dolly, one of our cats, heard my loud sobs and climbed up the steps to see if I was OK. She sat with me as a comfort until I managed to stop.

Katherine was right, as always. I did need a break and enjoyed the time in Cornwall, but there were times when it felt like there was a stone in my heart.

The following month to make up for missing the holiday, I had arranged a visit to see my sister and her partner, Mary, on the local Suffolk coast, staying over at a hotel for the night. It's *déjà vu*. Katherine was too unwell, and I was on my own once again, curled up on the hotel bedroom floor in another flood of tears. But there was no Dolly around to offer any comfort this time.

I think back to my school friend's claim that happiness is a state of mind, not a state of circumstance. I seriously doubt the validity of this statement.

I realised that I needed help and went to the bottom drawer where I had kept a stash of various prescribed mental health medications that I had taken for a short amount of time and then rejected. I found some atomoxetine, which I took for a few days. The side effects hit immediately, they are horrible, and my brain is seriously annoyed, so the pills are thrown back into the bottom drawer. It is like I am giving out a final warning to myself.

'Look brain, if you don't get your act together, you will have to take this medication, so behave or else!'

My brain was pleased to be rid of the intruder, and it reset back to a better place for the time being.

I should, of course, point out that this behaviour is mine. It isn't wise or in any way a recommendation. Most people who are prescribed medication get through the side effects and are much better for it.

There is more on this subject to be found in chapter eight.

I found that I detested autumn. It signalled the end of summer, the nights grew dark, and perhaps worst of all, it meant a return to the torture of school. A place where few kids with ADHD, diagnosed or not, are likely to be happy.

When I was ten years old, I went into the kitchen and told my mum, who was struggling with her own depressive demons, that I hated this time of year and was feeling sad and fed up. She suggested everything she could to help, but once the clocks were put back, there was little going on for a young boy with an attention disorder, particularly in the early 1970s when power cuts were the norm.

It took another fifteen years until I could finally make peace with the changing seasons. This was entirely due to my new girlfriend, who told me how much she loved this time of year and would jump in and out of the fallen leaves, pick them up, throw them in the air, and then throw them at me before running away laughing, something that, many years later she encouraged our two young daughters to join in with.

Taking up new hobbies, quickly getting bored or frustrated with them, buying tickets for an event, and then making excuses not to go became another familiar symptom of whatever was 'wrong' with me.

I had purchased tickets for a big England international match at Wembley. Katherine had always wanted to see David Beckham play. (I think she had a secret crush on him!) Of course, I wanted to go too, but I had stupidly booked a work meeting that involved a long journey and a very early start the following day, so I took it as an excuse to back out and give the tickets away. However, there were no takers, and the tickets were thrown in the bin. It is something that I still regret.

As Katherine's health has dipped in recent years, every missed opportunity to have done better and make her happier cuts deeper into my soul.

Shortly before Katherine became unwell, we were walking together on the sandy beach at Sea Palling. She turned to me and said, 'Timmy, we should move out to the coast soon. Why wait? Let's enjoy our lives now while we are still young enough. We don't know what might be around the corner.'

It turned out to be quite prophetic.

Carpe diem - Memento mori

Rejection Sensitive Dysphoria (RSD)

Rejection Sensitive Dysphoria is an intense vulnerability to the perception but not necessarily the reality of being rejected, teased, or criticised by other people in your life.

Dysphoria is Greek for 'difficult to bear,' and it may cause a disproportionate amount of emotional pain that can also be triggered by a sense of failure or self-imposed unreasonable expectations. This may lead to flashes of annoyance or anger or a deep and sullen mood that may last all day and potentially affect or even end a relationship.

People with ADHD are known to be more sensitive to teasing, criticism and rejection. When this is noticed or pointed out, there is often a further wave of disappointment in ourselves. This has become so common that some specialists believe that rejection sensitive dysphoria should be added to the list of ADHD symptoms.

Even small, fairly insignificant events are stuck like tiny thorns in my mind, causing pain as they are randomly recalled.

Eleanor Roosevelt was thought to have said, 'No one can make you feel inferior without your own consent.'

There is some conjecture over what was actually said, but it seems the former American first lady may have been asked to comment on a snub that was delivered to a member of Roosevelt's administration.

'A snub…' defined the first lady, '…is the effort of a person who feels superior to make someone else feel inferior. To do so, he has to find someone who can be made to feel inferior.'

Those with ADHD are likely to receive a disproportionate number of negative messages, particularly in their early life. Therefore, if you are constantly branded as thick, stupid and lazy or regularly told to shut up, sit down or sit still throughout childhood, it isn't surprising that you arrive on the other side of puberty with little or no self-confidence. This can lead to rejection sensitive dysphoria.

I detest the term 'low self-esteem', but it is another frequent symptom of ADHD and something that has followed me throughout my life. It feels like I am being continually judged with every comment I make dissected to find a connotation of disapproval.

People with rejection sensitive dysphoria can go from having a feeling of contentment to suicidal idealisation very quickly, and I have personally experienced this. For example, Katherine may ask me how I am feeling after a difficult turn of events and then has to deal with 'I just want to die' as my extreme reply.

People with ADHD often love wearing bright colours, which can attract the wrong attention. After various unkind comments regarding my super comfortable soft pink t-shirt, such as

'Wow, Tim! It takes a real man to wear pink.'

I know it shouldn't bother me, it's just 'banter' albeit, I would suggest, a little homophobic, but it does. Then the inevitable second wave of discontent arrives at my apparent weakness of letting myself down and being unable or strong enough to be true to myself. So I just gave the shirt away and searched for a plain white top to wear instead.

People may laugh, get annoyed or be frustrated by my perceived stupidity, physical and verbal hyperactivity. Even close relatives would sometimes be embarrassed by my silly behaviour. This results in a constant effort to stay quiet while my mind fizzes over.

Rejection sensitive dysphoria can lead to a social phobia due to the fear that you might publicly humiliate or embarrass yourself, as I often found out.

At our regular post-Christmas family gathering, the rules of a card game were being explained in detail by a relative. I was probably keeping up with things as well as anyone in the room. With my confidence newly buoyed by the realisation I have ADHD, I made a light-hearted attempt at self-deprecation and said, 'This is way too much information for my brain to take.'

I almost announced the news of my diagnosis to the entire room but decided instead to keep my secret for a little while longer because, as of yet, I had only told the few people closest to me, so most of those present at the gathering are still unaware of my disorder.

I have regularly tried the route of self-deprecation, but all too often, it backfires as my comments are taken literally, and it becomes another opportunity for others, all be it in apparent jest, to rejoice in labelling me as an idiot. So I often found the best way to deal with such jibes was to laugh along at my apparent foolishness, although a part of me would be simultaneously burning with the humiliation and secretly dying inside.

The opportunity was predictably seized upon as it has been so often before to poke fun and enter into seemingly harmless teasing as I struggled to follow the rules, although I'm obviously not alone.

It seems others can't understand the explanation of the card game either and, as Mrs Roosevelt suggested they might, are deflecting their own apparent shortcomings onto me.

So the teasing begins with a familiar mocking voice.

'To Tim, It sounds like you've just said blah, blah, blah, blah, blah, he hasn't understood a word, don't worry, he is a bit thick, so keep going.'

I know it's a joke, they were just teasing and probably didn't mean any ill will, and the comment might even be viewed as a strange form of endearment. Perhaps, to a 'normal person,' they are just a few humorous words easily swatted away with a witty retort. It's meant to be funny, a joke, a bit of banter, or just a throw-away comment that's laughed at and quickly forgotten. The reaction of those who laugh at my expense only deepened my intense feelings of discomfort while the words bounced around my brain on an endless loop like a wrecking ball eroding my self-worth.

Those with ADHD endure a torrent of negativity from a young age, and inevitably, it takes its toll as the drip, drip, drip of niggling comments slowly erodes my defences. I find these comments ever more difficult to swallow. On this occasion, it has caused a disproportionate feeling of shame, nausea, and frustration resulting in a surge of anger coursing up towards my brain that fizzes like a shaken bottle of cola with the lid screwed on.

I'm not sure how I will react, and for a moment, I fear for my sister's newly decorated living room.

There had been a noisy police raid at one of the nearby homes across the road from our house the previous night, to which I had given my best and probably unnecessarily talkSPORT style commentary. Unfortunately, the event left Katherine with little sleep and a migraine the next morning, so she couldn't face travelling.

Fortunately, Vicky is on hand. She knows I'm hurt, grabs my arm, and does her best to distract me by finding the latest football results on her phone. It gives me a few seconds to collect myself while I manage a few deep breaths and a tired smile.

On the rare occasions I have bitten back at those who regularly throw barbed comments in my direction, I'm accused of having no sense of humour, being easy to wind up or having a bad temper. Surely even the friendliest dog will retaliate eventually?

Events such as this are a 'double whammy' as my inability to take such episodes on the chin leads to further inner turmoil, so the damage to my self-worth is increased, and should I decide ever to retaliate in kind, the emotional impact only intensifies.

When I examined these feelings later, I realised that it was my own reaction to the comments rather than the behaviour or words of others that caused me the most harm.

Rejection Sensitive Dysphoria and Intimacy

Symptoms of ADHD are so wide-ranging they can be extremes of the same thing. Hypersexual (high sex drive) or Hyposexual (low sex drive). So It is no surprise that issues with intimacy often affect those with the condition.

Adults with ADHD may be promiscuous, have risky sex, and have one-night stands. There is also the issue of heightened sensitivity to touch and smell. ADHD has the potential to disrupt and even ruin a close relationship. A person with the condition may blurt out something inappropriate about shopping or a work appointment, be put off by a smell, or appear to lose interest mid-way through lovemaking. Moods can change suddenly with the slightest perceived negative comment or action, potentially switching off the passion in a moment, leaving a frustrated partner to enquire.

'What's wrong? Why did you stop?'

'Oh nothing, goodnight.' might be the sulky reply

Even a well-meaning casual compliment can lead to a surge of self-doubt. I can remember Katherine telling me.

'You are so much better than you used to be.'

Negative thoughts and doubts immediately surged through my brain...

'Was I rubbish before? Did you just pretend in order to get it over with? Why didn't you say something?'

Dealing with such a sensitive partner must be like walking a long emotional tightrope.

It is important to be completely honest with your partner about what your ADHD symptoms are. As with many things in life, communication and honesty are key, and reassurance is a two-way street. Some ADHD medications can either boost or lead to a loss of sexual desire.

There is plenty of good information available online in regard to helping those with ADHD and their partners to get the best out of their love life. There are also options for talking therapy available. I have written more on this subject in chapter twenty.

Rejection Sensitive Dysphoria and People Pleasing

'Tell me what you want, and I will try my best, but please don't get annoyed with me if I get it wrong.'

Those with ADHD and rejection sensitive dysphoria are likely to be constantly seeking assurance and may even seem needy. So, they often become people pleasers, hoping that friends and family will like and approve of them.

People pleasing may also be seen as a form of high-functioning anxiety.

I dislike conflict or upset of any kind partly as I know the RSD has the potential to unhinge me, so it's difficult to stand up for myself until I get pushed too far, and then the red mist will likely descend with varying degrees of ugliness. Either way, it will usually end in humiliation.

There have been times when I don't care about my own feelings as long as everyone else is happy. I have tried to please everyone, but the result is that I please no one and succeed only in losing my identity. You would think this might win a degree of approval and respect, but if anything, the opposite is true.

I watched the owner of a springer spaniel training their pet on the beach. The dog's only goal was to please its owner, but the dog looked sad because it had failed to do so. That, I realised, was my own behaviour in a nutshell.

I have, at times, become so focused on pleasing individuals I have lost sight of my own feelings and real opinion because I'm so busy nodding at someone who is loudly spewing out their one-sided viewpoint. As a result, I've fallen into the trap of agreeing with something to be better regarded or gone to the extreme of absurdly making a point that I think is wrong just to fit in with their warped viewpoint, only to be slapped down and told I'm talking nonsense! I am then literally arguing against myself with every scrap of remaining self-respect lying in the gutter.

Those who are happy in their own skin seem to live the best life, and perhaps the key to being less angry is simply to be true to yourself. I was advised to remember that you choose your behaviour, and only you can control it. I wish it were always that easy with ADHD.

I read a book entitled *Stop People Pleasing* by Patrick King. It suggests that people pleasers are, to a degree, actually selfish as they try to please everyone for their own gratification and to feel needed or wanted. So the way forward is apparently to be assertive, more self-focused and even a little more selfish.

Over the years, I may have overdone family present buying for Christmas and birthdays. Maybe it is part of the people-pleasing thing, although overspending meant the January credit card bill seldom pleased Katherine.

As a child, I remember the unbridled displays of joy as each family member carefully opened one present at a time. Katherine's family ripped their gifts open together like a piranha feeding frenzy.

One Christmas, I bought a carefully selected allergy-free teddy for a newborn relative. When the parents unwrapped the gift, there was an uneasy silence as they exchanged horrified glances.

The reaction was as though we had just given their precious baby a packet of cigarettes. Other gifts were later described as landfill.

On occasions, my ADHD has led me to buy presents for a birthday or anniversary and then get so excited at the prospect of their happy reaction that I can't wait and hand them the gift prematurely, often to their embarrassment and sometimes annoyance. I then have to quickly search for another gift to buy them for the actual day of the celebration.

There are drugs available that may help with rejection sensitive dysphoria, but with so little known about the disorder and some not even recognising the condition at this time, it is still unknown how effective they are. Therapy and mindfulness may help by identifying and then reducing some negative thoughts that potentially cause feelings of rejection.

Remember that your feelings are your own perception and not necessarily the truth or reality, so always be kind to yourself.

Maladaptive Daydreaming

'I try to halt the strangers in my daydream that are demanding access to my mind by visualising a brick wall around my brain, attempting to refuse them entry. If I can starve these thoughts of the oxygen they need to survive, maybe they will cease. But, as I inevitably submit to the pressure, the wall is torn down, and I am forced into a fantasy world that I both love and detest with equal measure' - Tim MacWilliam.

Maladaptive daydreaming can become so intense and penetrating the thoughts interfere with daily life. These daydreams become distracting to the point where the person will stop engaging with the task in front of them and begin actively looking for time and space to enjoy their fantasy world. A sound, a word in a conversation, a song, or a television show may trigger the condition. Maladaptive daydreaming was first defined in 2002 but, as far as I am aware, is yet to be recognised as a specific mental disorder.

Essentially maladaptive daydreaming is a coping strategy, perhaps for an abusive or difficult life or to counteract a trauma. For me, it was an escape from the endless stress of life and, now looking back, perhaps trauma too. A place where I'm a better, nicer, more successful version of myself. It is a place I would go to when things were particularly difficult.

I spoke to a serious gamer who became so involved in the surroundings of his fun online battles that technology now provides, with the special effects ever more realistic. That when they were fully engaged in their game, it was as if they were another person in another world, and perhaps this is a partial insight into what maladaptive daydreaming can feel like.

The lack of knowledge about maladaptive daydreaming is particularly frustrating. No therapist I have spoken to, and I've spoken to many, seem aware of the condition or can offer any practical help.

I thought I had done a reasonable job in describing the issues I was having to a therapist, whom I had been making some progress with until she suggested, 'I was in my own little world.'

The brain may employ maladaptive daydreaming to stop a depressive spiral and give a degree of protection, offering somewhere to escape when times are troubling, but if it takes over your life, there is clearly a problem. I expect this condition to become a big issue in the coming years as soon as it's splashed across a Sunday supplement magazine after a celebrity decides to out themselves with the issue.

My daydreams became deeper with characters and storylines so intense it became a play that I could enter at any time and change and renew or relive my favourite parts. I became so fully immersed in this world, where there are conversations and imaginary conflicts going on, that words occasionally escaped my mouth and into the real world.

Katherine would stare at me, sometimes laugh, and ask who I was talking to. I would then be annoyed at being found out although I always tried to laugh it off.

I learned the key to keeping this issue at bay was to keep busy. Either physically or mentally. If I am more active or feel happy, the intrusion is hardly ever there, but when I am anxious, stressed, or there is nothing going on, then the intense daydreaming will quickly seep back in. My ADHD and daydreaming are always worse when I am stressed or unhappy.

One therapist told me that we all need to escape somewhere, and if we can't do so physically, then it is important to be able to do so mentally. Again, potentially good advice but perhaps without the full understanding of what maladaptive daydreaming entails and the negative effect it can have.

Further Help and Guidance -

Keep your mind and body as busy and active as possible.

Initially, you could set a time where you might allow yourself to daydream but keep it strictly to this time only. Use this as a starting point to ween yourself away from the problem.

Think of real-life thoughts as beautiful flowers and daydreams as horrible bindweed trying to suffocate your mind. Weeds won't thrive where flowers grow.

I read a quote: 'Stop dreaming about the person you want to be and start to become that person' - If you can beat maladaptive daydreaming, this may become a reality.

I found that some drugs for depression and ADHD quietened the unwelcome noise of maladaptive daydreaming and improved the quality of my life in this respect.

There is further information to be found on maladaptive daydreaming at the sleep foundation website.

Obsessive Compulsive Disorder (OCD)

OCD is a common mental health condition where a person has obsessive thoughts and compulsive behaviours. OCD can affect men, women, and children. I have never been professionally diagnosed with OCD, but the clues suggest it is likely. ADHD and OCD share some overlapping symptoms and can have similar effects on how people function.

Most of us have heard someone say, often as a cheap joke, 'I'm a little bit OCD' accompanied by a giggle, but there is no such thing. OCD is more than just wanting things a certain way. It's a disorder characterised by feelings of anxiety and discomfort.

Compared with many others, my OCD symptoms are usually mild, and sometimes they go altogether… and then they come back again.

Is it OCD or 'just' a coincidence?

I went through a nightly routine to check and shut every cupboard and drawer in the house to ensure nothing potentially awful would happen. Finally, I concluded this was ridiculous behaviour and stopped. Within a few days, I lost two large work contracts.

Surely, it's just a coincidence, though. Isn't it?

I went through a routine each and every time I left Vicky's flat to keep her home safe. Again, I decided this was ridiculous behaviour and stopped.

The following week her cat died.

Surely, It's just a coincidence, though. Isn't it?

I touched all four car doors to ensure a safe journey before I left. Again, I decided this was ridiculous behaviour and stopped. My car promptly broke down on a busy slip road with a subsequent repair bill of £500.

Surely, it's just a coincidence, though. isn't it? … Isn't it!?

Of course, all of these events are pure coincidence, but for someone with OCD, it doesn't feel that way.

On the way home from school, aged eleven, I often felt the compulsion to go through a routine whenever certain thoughts came into my mind. An older boy watched me do this a couple of times and shouted insults from across the street. It was rather difficult to offer any pretence or try and style it out.

As a child, prior to a family holiday, I would go through endless routines and then insist on sitting in the front middle seat of my dad's big white Land Rover. When I was ordered to sit in the back but angrily refused, I felt the full wrath of my family for this apparent idiocy, along with the accompanying shouted empty threat, 'If you keep behaving like this, we won't go on holiday!'

How on earth could I ever explain to them?

I would carry out tasks in a specific order, hoping it would stop my mother from having an epileptic fit. But, unfortunately, she would inevitably have a seizure on the days I forgot to go through my routine.

It is purely coincidence. But that is how OCD strengthens its grip on you.

As a child, I would find the largest and sharpest knife in the kitchen and see how many times I could flip it over and catch it without getting hurt. Quite a lot as it happened, so when this got too easy, I would flip the knife with my eyes closed until I could do at least ten in a row.

The damage to the kitchen floor from my failed attempts was there for all to see.

I can still recall my mother's exasperated cry, 'For goodness sake, Timmy, stop it!'

In more recent times, I might touch the front and back of my car before a journey, but I would quite often be rewarded with a painful and crackling static shock, so I took that as a sign that my car was telling me to stop doing it.

OCD can increase in times of stress. I'll still occasionally go through a routine when leaving the house, but if anyone notices, I will feel embarrassed, as though a pathetic secret about my life has been exposed.

My OCD doesn't affect my daily life as it once perhaps did, and I have no idea how I got this mostly under control, and I can go through periods when it disappears altogether. However, there are times when it still finds a way back into my life, and I can't even choose a mug out of the cupboard as they look set in a particular pattern. I will go on a daily exercise streak for months that I struggle to break despite the resulting overuse injuries. Having a fitness watch that gives a mini fireworks display on a small screen whenever you reach a target isn't ideal for an OCD brain.

A relative had warned me not to run a marathon as I would '…piss blood.'

This vision stuck in my mind for some time, although thankfully not forever, as I finally got the London Marathon 'You're in!' magazine through the post.

Like most runners, I enjoy logging every bit of training, including my average pace per mile, heart rate, steps per minute, and the various running kit. However, while looking through the records from my Garmin watch, I noticed that I had completed every distance between one and twenty miles during the months of training, except for seventeen miles. My running buddies said it would be madness to attempt such a long run just fourteen days before the big event as I would surely mess up my chances of a decent marathon experience. Still, I countered that I had just run a particularly good twenty-miler, followed by an unexpected personal best in a 10k race, so my confidence was high. The gap on my list of distances aggravated my OCD senses to the point that I decided to set forth, reasoning that I would never get another chance to do so.

After just a few miles, it became obvious this was a huge mistake, but I refused to stop. It was an ill-advised and horrible run where my Achilles, knees, and stomach protested throughout.

As my friends predicted, my body hadn't recovered sufficiently in time for the marathon. So the 26.2-mile race became a slow and painful plod which took nearly an hour longer than the time I had trained for. I did eventually make it over the finishing line but felt sick, dizzy and shaking with cold, whereupon I burst into tears and was promptly wheeled away to a medical tent. To make matters worse, Katherine had been given some misinformation that led her to believe I hadn't finished the event but had instead been taken to the hospital. Not exactly the scenario I had hoped for.

Can I blame my OCD tendencies for this?

The mental health charity Mind has an excellent OCD resource and help section.

Epilepsy

ADHD occurs more frequently in people with epilepsy than in the general population. The risk of ADHD is also thought to be increased in children whose mothers have the condition. According to the Epilepsy Foundation, ADHD is the most common co-occurring disorder in children with epilepsy. It is also possible that medications taken for the condition during pregnancy can lead to a higher risk of ADHD in their children.

I haven't developed this condition to date, but my mother had regular severe fits throughout my childhood.

How my mum coped with the condition and subsequent side effects from the drugs she took to reduce the number of seizures whilst bringing up three children, including one with undiagnosed ADHD, is a substantial feat. She was the most loving, kind, generous, and stoic person imaginable. Her aim in life was always to make others happy, and with hindsight, I can see she may have fallen into the same trap of people-pleasing as I have.

A full-blown epileptic fit can be a scary thing for a young child to witness, and the house felt continuously on edge. Her seizures were occasionally the cause of some quite traumatic events.

She fell off a boat into the Thames. My dad jumped in to rescue her. She fell onto an electric fire, went head-first through a toughened glass window and smashed her teeth on a stone floor, so she wore dentures that were swallowed during a subsequent episode. It must have been tough for my dad, who had little idea how to cope. He would shove a leather driving glove into her mouth so she wouldn't swallow her teeth or tongue during a fit, but she would sometimes turn blue. The seizures would start at a moment's notice, and our family developed an almost sixth sense of when they would happen a split second before they hit.

I understand that waking up from an epileptic fit is like a toxic cocktail of the worst possible migraine combined with vertigo and a mind of blanks that slowly fill again.

When I was six years old, I begged my father to go with him on his journey into town as there might be a chance of dragging him into the local toy shop. Unfortunately, this led to us being late, and we arrived home to find my mum on the floor in the throes of a seizure for which I was subsequently held responsible. My dad reasoned it probably wouldn't have happened if we had returned home on time. Someone usually had to be blamed whenever things went wrong in our house.

Sadly there continues to be a stigma linked with the condition, although this seems to have improved somewhat compared to fifty years ago when a visit to the cinema ended abruptly as the flashing images from the screen caused my mum to have a seizure.

My grandmother, who had accompanied her, was seemingly so traumatised by the upset and embarrassment she required more help from the medics than my poor mother.

'I'll never go to the pictures with her again!' she yelled like a spoilt brat.

As a teenager, when visiting relatives in Scotland, my mother's violent epileptic fit caused such angst that she was banished from their house and forced to walk around a golf course feeling cold and confused until her shamed father arrived to take her back home. It seems the pregnant wife of the relative feared her unborn child might, somehow, catch the disease. My grandfather was a doctor. I'm not sure if he used his position to help or whether it was just hidden away from the public as an embarrassment.

Such was the stigma, I wasn't even aware the condition was epilepsy. Instead, I was told, 'Mummy's fainting.' When a friend came over after school and witnessed my mother foaming at the mouth, uncontrollably shaking, incontinent, and with blood seeping from her mouth, he said that when his mum fainted, that most certainly didn't happen.

It was annoying not to be given facts or trusted with information. For example, I was ten years old when I was told that 'Granny isn't well.' I thought she had a cold or had a sore throat when in fact, she had suffered a massive stroke and died the next day.

'Why didn't you tell me?' I protested, somewhat shocked.

'We thought you wouldn't understand and just be a nuisance' was the absurd and hurtful reply.

Working late one night at a large four-star hotel, a member of staff found a gentleman who had seemingly walked in from the street. He was assumed to be fast asleep and snoring loudly on one of the large sofas in the reception lounge.

The duty manager considered throwing water over this man before ejecting him back into the cold night. I was amazed that I was the only person who could identify this as an epileptic fit, something that was apparently not covered in the company's in-house first aid training course. I very much hope the understanding of this condition continues to improve.

Epilepsy Action report that eighty-seven people are diagnosed with epilepsy in the UK every day.

Further information about this still seriously misunderstood condition can be obtained from Epilepsy Foundation and Epilepsy Action.

Anxiety

It seems the heaviest burdens are often the thoughts we carry in our heads.

Anxiety and anxiety disorder has a very broad spectrum, and these are my experiences and my perception of the issue.

I find that anxiety feeds my ADHD, and in turn, ADHD feeds my anxiety, so in every scenario, my mind will leap to the worst possible outcome. Half of all adults with ADHD are also thought to have a form of anxiety disorder. Having low self-esteem is also common with ADHD and this may also lead to anxiety.

At times, the stress I receive from my anxiety can feel like my head is about to burst open. For example, every time the telephone rings, my heart beats faster, and my blood pressure spikes, with my thoughts racing as to what the caller might want.

It is possible the stress from my early home life caused some of these issues, or it could be something in my DNA. There appears to be an anxiety condition historically on one side of my family, and it's possible I have inherited this trait.

However, as the previous generation found such talk 'weak and shameful,' I doubt I'll ever find out.

The more I prepared for a day at work, the more anxiety would build. I would go to bed early as I had to be up at 6 am for my journey to a faraway client, but I would continually wake through the night, sometimes sweating with the stress of the coming day ahead. First, I worried that I might oversleep or be late due to travel problems or the weather might cause a delay. Then I feared that I would mess up my work and lose business. If I lost business, we might end up in debt and lose the house—and so it went on.

I did my best to employ a 'What is the worst that can happen?' mantra, as the fear of the imagination is very seldom the reality. However, this mindful tactic was rarely successful.

During my formative years, we had occasional nearby events that were thought of in terms of excitement rather than something to be anxious about and rightly so.

Our house in Bracknell was close enough to hear the loud and distinctive two-tone siren from Broadmoor, a psychiatric hospital. This warned everyone in the vicinity that an inmate had escaped from the building known back in the 1970s as a hospital for the criminally insane.

As children, we always had one ear cocked for the eerie siren that would occasionally fill the streets for miles around, an ever-present cause of excitement mixed with a tinge of fear.

Alarmingly, while the sirens warned everyone to stay indoors, we were let out to play in the twilight and discuss with our friends who might have escaped this time. Possibly the 'Mad Axeman' was making his way to Bracknell, with the ideal place to hide in the woods just behind our house.

The truth was, more often, a terrified patient had not escaped but climbed onto the roof of the hospital in fear and desperation of their situation.

I occasionally played in a local boys team on the pitches directly outside the Broadmoor hospital, where one of the players parents would continuously walk in front of the high perimeter wall carrying a rather large 'Fred Flintstone' style club in which to protect the players, should an escape occur during the match. There was probably more danger from Jimmy Savile, who bizarrely seemed to have his own set of keys to the place.

Phobias and Anxiety

A phobia is, in itself, a type of anxiety disorder. A person may not experience any symptoms until they have come into contact with the source of their phobia. But in some cases, even thinking about it can make a person feel anxious or panic irrationally. This is known as anticipatory anxiety.

Suppose you don't know you are staying in a haunted house. You will, therefore, probably sleep well and just assume those bangs and noises were from the wind outside, wildlife mating in nearby woods or the ancient floorboards creaking above you and not the fictitious headless horseman about to murder you in your bed the moment your eyes are closed.

In the mid-1990s, my young family had a glorious week in Cornwall, camping among sand dunes and marram grass. There was direct access to a perfect Cornish beach with the most beautiful blue sea, large waves crashing over the golden sand and the weather almost Mediterranean. It was as perfect as it could be. Even my daughter's digital pet, Tamagotchi, had survived five whole days before the ghost emoji appeared on the tiny black-and-white screen.

On the final day of our idyllic stay, I walked barefoot and blissfully happy along a sandy pathway close to our tent when I spied a long piece of ribbon blowing along the ground. I almost trod on the mottled cord but pulled my foot back at the last moment, as I realised, with horror, it was a rather large adder!

I've had an irrational fear of snakes since being trapped, as a toddler, in a very large hole with a boa constrictor. I think it was a boa constrictor, my mother always insisted it was a slow worm, but she wasn't there in a deep hole as it slithered around my legs, menacingly poking out its forked tongue as it tried to curl around me. Boa constrictor, adder, or slowworm, this is a phobia I have never shaken off—Google a photo of a slow worm, they might technically be harmless legless lizards, but they look just like a snake, especially to a small toddler with no escape.

My dad once told me during a holiday under canvas that snakes were inquisitive creatures, and a tent would make a nice warm hiding place for them. But, of course, this really didn't help!

I didn't mind if there were adders all over that Cornish campsite. They could be having a snake disco for all I cared, provided I didn't see them or know they were gadding around a few metres from where we slept. But now I do, and I am paranoid for the last night of our holiday, with shivers running up my spine at the thought of serpents bedding down in my sleeping bag. There were probably lots of snakes living in the woods directly behind the house where I grew up and maybe even in our garden. I think I only ever saw one that had slithered its way onto the road that my father threw back into a gorse bush.

More recently, I took Pebbles for a long walk along the sand dunes towards Winterton on the Norfolk coast. When we arrived at the far end of the car park and tea room, that has long since been lost to coastal erosion, I turned to see Pebbles dashing through some marram grass to catch up with me, only to be greeted by a sign as we exited in big red letters stating 'Beware Adders on the Dunes!' and 'Keep Dogs on Leads.'

Everyone should have a happy place and mine is the beach. I will often paddle for miles between coastal towns and resorts just listening to the waves, taking in the view and resetting my mind. It is a place where even I can relax a little. However, rather annoyingly, I had recently been given some unwelcome information, and now my happy place had become one of partial anxiety.

In October, the weather is often warm, and so, comparatively, is the North Sea. On this particular day, I was paddling between knee and waist-deep at Gorleston beach when a well-meaning angler approached me to check that I was not planning to do a 'Reggie Perrin' referring to a long-running 1970s television comedy series where a man leaves his clothes on the beach and fakes his death by swimming out to sea—if only he knew! As we chatted further, he informed me that he had caught two weever fish that day, and they were likely to be lurking around my feet where I was currently paddling.

It seems that weever fish hide in the shallows with their poisonous spines sticking up through the sand as protection. The toxin and resulting pain from the spines can only be destroyed by applying extremely hot water to the wound. My informant described how he had seen grown men reduced to tears from the pain, with one subsequently collapsing and taken to hospital.

In five decades of happy paddling around the coast, I had never once stood on or been stung by a weever fish. I barely knew about the hazard until that day. It seemed I had been playing a constant game of weever fish 'battle ships' every time I took a step into the sea. Finally, the fisherman pointed out to the horizon and gave a further warning.

'There are far worse things out there that you really don't want to know about...'

Anxiety is a difficult beast to control. Armed with this new but unwanted information, I've retrospectively worried about the occasions I took my two young daughters to the beach, where they would jump over and dive into the shallows. But, of course, they were never stung by a weever fish, so why am I still anxious about something that did not, therefore, cannot happen?

It is a difficult question to answer.

If I can't paddle, then a walk on the golden sands of a Norfolk beach is always welcome. However, I still haven't learned my lesson (I have ADHD) and rather unwisely got involved in a deep and disturbing conversation with a local man who had been fishing in the area for more than fifty years. He advised me to 'Beware of the quicksand at Winterton,' a comment that awakened yet another irrational fear.

A phobia can be anything, including the fear of spiders, snakes, flying or perhaps a certain number, mushrooms, cats, or a colour. It cannot be easily rationalised, and it's all too easy for the uninitiated to advise someone to simply '…get over it!

Worrying doesn't change the outcome.

There will always be danger in the world, and being prepared for the eventuality may help reduce at least some anxiety. This was the case when a barrister of Asian descent received racial abuse while travelling on a bus from a female passenger who then proceeded to physically attack her.

The barrister shared this story on social media but refused further publicity to discuss the incident or to take the case forward as she concluded it would take too long and may not ultimately be successful in court. The racially abused lady described herself as a martial artist and managed to restrain the attacker before leaving the bus physically unhurt and continued on her way to work. The barrister said she had been training and preparing for moments like this all her life. No doubt, this training helped to reduce her anxiety.

The first step may be to accept there is an issue in your life that is directly causing anxiety. You should then be in a position to research and find the correct help successfully.

There is some excellent information online, including a section on the NHS website about understanding and controlling this condition.

When a person is lonely, bored, overcoming trauma or has problems in addition to ADHD, then life can be even more of a challenge.

Thankfully, there is more help available now than ever before for mental health issues. For further assistance, it is essential to contact a qualified practitioner or talk with your doctor about the help available.

There are, of course, further co-existing conditions that I have no experience of and have therefore not included them in this chapter.

CHAPTER SEVEN

Anger Management

*'Just because you have ADHD it doesn't give you
the right to act like a jerk.'*

Although anger is not listed as a symptom of ADHD, many adults with the disorder are prone to impulsive, angry outbursts. Frustration, impatience and the ever-troublesome, low self-esteem are often the cause.

'Tim, that isn't frustration. That is rage!'

My latest therapist had called me out mid-sentence as I was recounting a time when I kicked a hole in the front door as '…just a bit of frustration.'

Home life had boiled over once more with accusing fingers unfairly pointing my way, and it felt like the only pressure valve left open to me.

Although, I do realise that it's never an excuse.

Any outburst of anger or misplaced emotion is instantly replaced by regret, remorse, guilt and shame that builds into self-loathing that, in turn, is left open to being misinterpreted as self-pity.

There have been times throughout my life when I have been teased, provoked, and baited until I've verbally snapped back, only to be told I have an anger issue or no control. I've never physically hurt anyone or ever would, but yes, I did kick in the front door and previously put a hole in a wall. Also, I once broke my toe kicking an empty watering can that wasn't, in fact, empty, and I still have the misshapen toe as a daily reminder of my stupidity.

However, sometimes, not even kicking a hole in a wall will help relieve my pent-up anger.

Following a wider family problem, I had become overwhelmed by the situation and was now lost in an emotional dark cloud. I considered all available options, however drastic or life-changing they might be.

Katherine was constantly phoning me, but I refused to answer her calls as I feared that in my current vulnerable state, I would be quickly overwhelmed by a swift piece of her mental jujitsu, and I wasn't yet ready to be talked around.

My brain was numb as I left the house, driving on autopilot in no particular direction, finally stopping at a local nature reserve that hosts one of the Norfolk Broads, where I found a quiet bench overlooking the water.

Now distraught, I was desperate to show the world just how much I was hurting and considered diving headfirst through the reeds, although it was hardly likely to put my life in much danger, let alone bring it to an end. It was August, so the water was warm, and I'd swum across this particular lake countless times before. There was probably more danger to my health from the current blue-green algae, and my random act would merely have served as entertainment for the people queuing for ice creams on the far side had I decided to splash across the water whilst being accosted by swans who would no doubt have been annoyed by my unwelcome intrusion.

Katherine was sending endless texts that were tying me in knots. Finally, when I responded more abruptly to her messages, she became emotional to the point where I decided to bring our conversation to an abrupt end by flinging my iPhone high up and over my head, where I heard it catch on a low-hanging branch before plopping into the water.

There was no plan or build up or a single thought that, if this conversation goes on any longer, I'm going to chuck my phone, that will cost several hundred pounds to replace and contains bank details, every work contact, photos, maps, music, subscriptions, medical information, shopping, notes and all of my passwords, into the water. Instead, it was just an 'Oh fuck it!' moment, followed by the familiar, almost instantaneous feeling of regret. A regular pattern whenever I get upset or angry

The anger I feel is always inward towards myself, usually due to the frustration that I can't solve a problem or be understood. But, as a therapist once told me.

'Just because you have ADHD, it doesn't give you the right to act like a jerk.'

There are relationships in my life that are far removed from what they should be, and I'll often lay awake at night wondering where they went wrong. Of course, there are two sides to any disagreement, but if I had handled my own emotions better, those relationships, perhaps, may not have failed. This is yet another reason to regret such a late-in-life diagnosis of ADHD.

The following day Katherine discovered that I'd chucked my iPhone away in a *fit of pique* and insisted we at least try and locate it.

'Whereabouts were you when you threw the phone? I'm sure we can find it if we search the area properly. At least we should try.'

'We can try, but you will need a snorkel and flippers,' I replied, with the first glimmer of a smile I'd had in days,

'Oh...' she said, barely missing a beat, '...shall we buy some on the way?'

The way Katherine copes with life in general, with me and with others in the house who are, at times, even more difficult than I am, is probably best summed up by a quote from Bruce Lee, who said.

'Notice that the stiffest tree is most easily cracked, while the bamboo or willow survives by bending with the wind.'

Whatever the pressures involved, she simply refuses to break.

In the first year of our relationship, Katherine jumped out at me from behind a wall and shrieked right into my face thinking it would lighten my mood. It didn't, and the shock made me instinctively push her away. Still laughing, she fell against the wall, but the smile disappeared from her face when I petulantly walked past her, clearly irritated by the prank.

Maybe it was the last straw from a build-up of my ongoing behaviour or just the disbelief that I would physically push her away from me. I've since learned that I'm in trouble when Katherine's born Essex accent rises to the surface, as I heard her exclaim for the first time.

'I've just about had just about had enough of this!'

A few seconds later, it felt like I had been attacked from behind by a large wild cat as she jumped onto my shoulders while simultaneously sliding her hands inside my shirt and proceeded to rip her long sharp fingernails deep into and down the entire length of my back leaving eight streaks of torn flesh.

After staring at me for two or three very long seconds, Katherine instructed in a slow, calm, but nonetheless still quite menacing voice.

'Don't ever push me again.'

I stared back at her in shocked disbelief before quietly replying.

'Oh, OK then' although I really should have apologised for the push.

Within a few moments, the scary cat-like ninja had thankfully morphed back into my sweet and gentle girlfriend as she tentatively enquired about the state of my back.

As the blood-stained shirt was carefully removed, Katherine surveyed the *Enter the Dragon* style lacerations splayed on either side of my spine, gasping with horror as the damage was slowly uncovered. The wounds were still numb, and I couldn't see or feel them as the full extent of the pain was yet to reach my brain.

'Oh, my God! I'm so sorry. I didn't mean to do that. I would never dream of hurting you. Oh no!' Her eyes were now wide open with shock, hands covering her mouth. She was completely mortified by her actions, and I didn't know what to do or say. I tried to find some reassuring words but could only laugh at her reaction.

Katherine disappeared at speed from the room, returning two minutes later armed with antiseptic and cotton wool.

'This is going to hurt…'

I'm warned with an accompanying sympathetic smile.

'…but you deserve it.' Her eyes piercing through me once more as I nodded meekly in agreement.

When the wounds had been attended to, Katherine suggested that I keep them covered for the foreseeable future to avoid any potential infection.

That weekend we were team members at an inter-hotel sports day in Basingstoke. Without thinking, I volunteered for the water fight that involved the removal of shirts. A dramatic rainbow of colours from the healing wounds was now fully exposed for all to see. The shock and banter from my teammates came thick and fast.

'Did Katherine do that? That must have been one hell of a row!'

'Do you like it rough, Tim?'

'Wow! Never get on the wrong side of Katherine. Ha-Ha'

'You must have one big cat at home, Tim!'

'Did Katherine really do that? No way!'

I eventually found the voice to reply in my best carefree tone.

'Oh yeah, Katherine did it, but she didn't actually, er, um…mean to.'

However, no one could quite believe this small and gentle woman could inflict the amount of damage currently on display, and the inquisition persisted as they were clearly not buying my explanation.

'Seriously, Tim, what really happened?' asked one colleague for the third time.

Whilst the inquisition continued, Katherine was rooted to the spot, red-faced and embarrassed, her eyes wide and pleading with me to rescue her.

A bonus of an ADHD mind is they can be creative and spontaneous. I managed to invent a tale about falling into some particularly sharp and nasty brambles at Caesar's Camp, a well-known woodland on the outskirts of Bracknell. I described tripping and falling over a tree root and plunging down a hidden bank, landing on my back in a mass of thorns, brambles, and particularly sharp stones.

'Oh, sounds nasty. I knew it couldn't have been Katherine,' said the same colleague, now fully satisfied with my explanation.

Decades later, I recounted this episode to a therapist. She was appalled at the level of apparent violence and wondered if I might be vulnerable to another vicious cat-like assault from my wife. Did I really think it was acceptable to be physically attacked like this, and did I feel safe?

I laughed and assured her that Katherine morphing into an angry cat-like ninja had, to date, been a one-off that happened over thirty years ago and, as far as I could remember, was fully deserved. I then tried to lighten the mood by suggesting that I quite liked the idea of Katherine transforming into Catwoman from time to time. The therapist just stared at me. They never seem to know whether I'm joking.

'I don't believe you told your therapist that!' Katherine scolded later, 'was it really that bad?'

'Well,' I replied, 'if you look closely on a sunny day, I think the scars might still be evident.'

Those with ADHD can be sensitive, and the most damaging reaction to sensitivity is frequently anger, often with oneself. So, perhaps the key to being happy and less snappy, annoyed, irritated, upset, or down on yourself is to find a way to be happy and content in your own skin.

For me, this is still a work in progress.

'One who smiles rather than rages is always stronger'
Japanese Proverb.

Further Help and Guidance -

If you are often upset, try to be honest with yourself to identify why and who you are angry with—possibly yourself. Always try to avoid or walk away from a difficult situation and consider how your behaviour affects others.

If you can apologise, the problem may quickly be alleviated. In addition, you will often feel less angry if you choose to forgive the person who upset you.

As the line from the famous prose poem *Desiderata* by Max Ehrmann states, 'If you compare yourself with others, you may become vain and bitter, for always there will be greater and lesser persons than yourself.' So try to accept yourself as you are and surround yourself with people who will do the same.

I found *Beyond Anger* by Thomas J. Harbin had some interesting thoughts on the issue. The book included a long questionnaire to discover an individual's level of internal anger and frustration. The book suggested that anger isn't just about being angry, as there are many other reasons why we feel these emotions.

Medication for ADHD, counselling and therapies such as Cognitive Behavioural Therapy (CBT) may also help.

CHAPTER EIGHT

Pills, Potions, and Therapy

'It's not your fault! No one asks to be born!'

After another fraught episode and long before any thought that ADHD was on my radar of problems, I'd been told in no uncertain terms by a close family member to 'Get some fucking therapy!'

Up until this point, the only therapy I had ever considered was physiotherapy on my aching limbs from sporting injuries. I honestly didn't think I needed anything else.

However, finding the right therapist or counsellor isn't easy, especially for the first time, as you may not understand what help you require, let alone where to find it.

My sister advised getting as far away as possible, so I wouldn't bump into them at the local shops or running club. The increase in video calling has led us to become accustomed to these meetings via our computer screens, which means, provided you are comfortable with the technology, there is access to virtually every therapist in the world. However, I've found that not every therapist is completely *au fait* with the technology, which can be problematic.

I have lost count of the counsellors and therapists I have worked with. Some have lasted just one or two sessions, perhaps due to my impatience and impulsivity. On other occasions, there is a more obvious reason why they are ditched, such as the time I was informed 'You're not depressed. So what makes you think you are depressed?' based on just sixty seconds of screen time.

I would spend time studying their body language, wondering how sincere the different therapists were. I thought one looked bored, even stifling a yawn, and another was anxiously glancing at the clock as they realised their next appointment was looming. I wondered if others cared or were just in it for the money.

Each new therapist would open with the same question.

'How can I help you?'

I'd describe the issues I was struggling with and then tell them I have ADHD. This has, on occasions, been met with a vaguely patronising smirk or a thinly disguised disbelieving eye roll.

'Who told you that, Dr Google?' Scoffed one therapist.

'No,' I replied, 'a Harley Street psychiatrist.'

'Oh really? Well, don't worry, that's quite OK. It means you are just like Chris Packham,' smiled the therapist, failing to understand that I didn't need any further patronising reassurance.

'No, he doesn't have ADHD, he has autism.' I corrected them.

I had another forty-five minutes left and spent most of my mental energy trying not to end the session prematurely.

Autism and ADHD are related in some ways and share a number of symptoms, but ADHD is not the same as autism, and any therapist or counsellor should know this. Although, having one of these conditions can increase the likelihood of being diagnosed with the other.

Before deciding on therapy, being clear and honest about what you hope to achieve is essential. There have been sessions, after which I feel great, some when I don't, and sometimes I feel awful, but the benefits will arrive in a day or two when there has been a chance to process what has been said.

I have told therapists about suicidal thoughts, self-harm, taking risks, early life trauma, Katherine lacerating my back with her fingernails, and various other incidents throughout my life. I'll often burst out laughing at the absurdity of the words I am saying out loud.

I hope they find it funny too, but I'm often met with a stern or disturbed face. Some sit opened mouthed with a look of horror on their face.

I've always found it easier talking with women, and those closest to me are all women, so I initially only considered female therapists.

For whatever contradictions there may be in this book, I have always thought of myself as a feminist and hope the women in my life would agree.

Some therapists believe they can help with no end of issues, and perhaps they can, but it is also possible they have set up their business as a 'jack of all trades' so if a therapist can't help you, they should always be honest about this.

I would also beware of those who think they can cure a physical condition such as M.E., often disturbingly seen as a psychological issue. M.E. has been formally classified as a neurological disorder by the World Health Organisation since 1969, so for a talking therapist to claim they can help is just as absurd as if they are claiming they could cure Parkinson's disease or multiple sclerosis. The NICE guidelines also state that M.E. is not a psychological illness.

When I first began speaking with therapists, I had yet to receive my initial ADHD diagnosis, so it was a little tricky to get the right help. I often flitted from one person to the next without giving them a chance to make any headway with me.

My first therapist was an excellent listener and helped positively with some early life issues I had unnecessarily clung to, but once I was asked to complete some long-winded CBT forms, I decided to go elsewhere. The second was a slightly scary woman, I surmised possibly ex-army, who chose to stare me out through the entire session. She insisted I pay before I left and kept the door locked until payment was cleared on her banking app. I felt like a virtual hostage and was quite grateful to be finally released. Unsurprisingly I didn't return.

The problem with chopping and changing counsellors and therapists does, of course, mean repeating the same, sometimes upsetting, information multiple times.

Most are easy to deal with and are happy to book one session ahead. But, should you decide to step back, they put no pressure on you and appreciate that you have personal issues. They clearly want what is best for you. I have only been hounded once by a therapist who had sat too far away from her screen and didn't have the correct software, then proceeded to lecture me on using a microphone properly. When I didn't make further contact, they virtually doorstepped me like a needy insurance salesman.

If you don't feel comfortable with a therapist, cannot express yourself or feel unable to be honest about why you are looking for help, then you are probably with the wrong person.

There has only been one person in this field who made me feel uncomfortable to the point of being intimidated.

In theory, this therapist looked perfect. He was experienced with a whole alphabet of qualifications after his name. However, it is important that a therapist or counsellor cares about you or at least appears to be, but this guy could barely disguise his apparent boredom and disdain for the person on the screen in front of him. There was no wish to engage with his client, and he virtually told me to shut up and listen.

The session was via a Zoom signal that continually dropped out despite his claim that he had paid for the pro package. 'The internet is always dodgy this time of day because of kids coming home from school.' he said. I wondered what his excuse was for the last time we spoke when it was mid-morning.

I hadn't realised how debilitating low self-esteem had been until writing this book. However, it is a phrase I've always loathed, but I decided to use it with this therapist and seek his help on the matter.

He replied that it doesn't exist and suggested it is purely down to the weakness of an individual. In other words that, I should just get over it.

This therapist is possibly in the wrong job. I kept telling myself to hang up and go for a run, but I'd already paid £75 upfront via his not-so-personal payment system and decided to tough it out.

I have an addictive personality, and my mind is often at civil war. It's part of the ongoing problems I have. Social media can be a toxic time stealer if you let it, such as getting into crazy disagreements that I refuse to walk away from. So I asked the therapist for help. He looked incredulous and said, 'Just delete your account and then you won't see it!'

I wanted to reply, 'Eureka! I would never have thought of that, all my problems are solved. Please wait a minute and let me write down that unique nugget of genius information.'

But of course, I didn't. I just nodded and looked to the corner of my screen at how long was left of my time with this bullying oaf. Too long! He suggested I consider moving out of the house and stop watching BBC News as it is '…biased, negative and spreads fear and nonsense.'

I still have a BBC security pass from a series of shows I presented on Radio Norfolk in the late noughties. I was tempted to locate the pass and wave it in his face, perhaps telling him I had recorded our session and would be reporting him to the relevant authorities, or maybe I could gently blackmail him into refunding me. But, again, I didn't. Once again, I avoided the conflict and rather weakly thanked him. Unfortunately, I didn't get a chance to say goodbye as he had his finger hovering over the end session button for the last few minutes and hung up his dodgy internet link a nano-second after our allotted time.

I know I should have checked first, but I later found some mixed reviews where he had bitterly and aggressively argued back to criticism from his former clients. It was quite vitriolic, considering those who sought his help were potentially vulnerable. Nevertheless, I imagine he must have had some satisfied customers, or his business wouldn't exist.

A therapist may need to challenge or call you out when necessary, but they shouldn't be aggressive or antagonistic, nor a sycophant that cosily agrees with everything you say.

This particular session did have a positive effect, though, as I went for a run straight afterwards to get rid of the awful feelings I had felt for the last hour and laughed out loud as I replayed it in my mind. I also took the advice and deleted social media apps from my phone, and guess what? It helped. Well, for a few days at least.

I have gained something from every therapy session I've had, even if it was something negative that has changed my outlook and behavioural viewpoint.

An ADHD specialist doctor told me during a rather short phone call that therapy didn't work for ADHD and neither did CBT. However, there is evidence to suggest this is untrue. A condition with such wide-ranging symptoms will likely have numerous techniques that work for many people differently.

As discussed in the previous chapter, ADHD doesn't often travel alone, and therapies may help with secondary problems too, and this can alleviate some of the issues associated with ADHD. However, with so much advice and information available, it can easily become confusing and, at times, exasperating.

After my diagnosis, I had a session with a commercial ADHD organisation. However, the therapist also had ADHD, and we started to duel as to who had the worst symptoms. I think she won. I saw her manically waving at people in nearby offices before telling me about her own life in some detail. I wondered who else might be listening in. She told me that she had tried many different drugs but decided to beat it 'all by herself.' I'm not sure if you actually beat ADHD or learn to accept it.

It was, however, interesting to get the viewpoint of a therapist with ADHD. She told me to own my behaviour and accept that I have the condition, then further advised that I should do something about it myself rather than for other people to change their behaviour around me. She also told me I should try and wake up grateful for each new day.

A therapist experienced in Eye Movement Desensitization and Reprocessing Therapy (EMDR) can be helpful for people who have had a particularly stressful time or suffered abuse. It was an interesting therapy to experience but probably not suitable for my needs as each time I wanted to discuss a particular problem, I was instructed to '…try butterfly wings on my heart,' or I was ushered to an imaginary sandy beach with my favourite people and my dog that died long ago so that I may feel safe. I'm sure this therapy has its place, but we were getting nowhere, and I know I am not the easiest client. After a few weeks, her jolly demeanour was reduced to undiluted irritation. Her parting shot was to tell me with an increasingly reddening face.

'It's not your fault! No one asks to be born!'

However, I was left thinking that everything was my fault.

I did try to use her advice once when I was at the hospital for a procedure that involved lying on a bed where a nurse pinned my arms and shoulders down to stop me from moving whilst the specialist simultaneously inserted a long tube down my throat that made me violently gag.

The procedure caused one of the most uncomfortable experiences I've ever had, so I searched for the happy beach my therapist had recommended in stressful times, but it couldn't be found, and my panic began to rise.

My own coping mechanism was to create even more discomfort in my mind than was currently happening in and around me to deflect away from my growing distress.

I closed my eyes and re-lived as vividly as possible the heat, exhaustion, pain, and discomfort of the twenty-third mile of my first London Marathon on a hot day when everything hurt, and each step sent a shock of pain through my spine. I was amazed at how vividly I could recall the memory.

A minute or so later, I heard a voice saying, 'All finished, well done, Timothy.' So, perhaps entering a world of pain is a more distracting emotion than any amount pleasure.

I have tried Cognitive Behavioural Therapy (CBT) and Emotion Focused Therapy (EFT). The latter is where you tap on various parts of your body and repeat a positive mantra. It sounds silly, and I felt silly, but it did have some good passing effects. We talked, and that helped, too, but as ever, there was an unsolvable impasse, so we parted.

The key to finding the right therapist is to be completely honest about why you need therapy and what you want to achieve from it. This involves trusting the therapist enough to be candid and tell them everything. It took me two years to realise the real issues were those that led to my battle with addiction (discussed in chapter twenty).

After the first session, in which I told him things that I barely even admitted to myself, I felt a bit dirty and annoyed that my information was no longer exclusively mine. Following this, we discussed much broader issues, including those that no other therapist could help with. Later, we managed to overcome the impasse that had ended my time with so many others. It isn't necessarily the most qualified therapist but the one you feel comfortable with.

A person who will listen, empathise and give honest feedback, including things you might not want to hear. However, you may need to travel down a few dead ends to discover your hoped-for destination.

ADHD Medication

These are my thoughts and personal experiences of searching for an unlikely magic bullet to help with my ADHD. I have spent considerable time researching the subject, but I have no specific medical qualification, and you should always seek fully qualified and professional help. Medications and treatments will likely suit people differently, and most of us are holding out, hoping to find one that might work.

There are five drugs licensed in the UK for ADHD in various doses (Source NHS)

- Methylphenidate (Ritalin)
- Lisdexamfetamine (Elvanse)
- Dexamfetamine (Dexedrine)
- Atomoxetine (Strattera)
- Guanfacine (Intuniv)

Another medication, Adderall, is commonly prescribed in the USA. However, in the United Kingdom, it is not licensed for ADHD. Further reliable information can be found about these drugs from the NHS or your medical practitioner.

Of course, medication benefits countless people with ADHD, and as I write this memoir, that includes me, although I know full well that come tomorrow, I might feel differently, such is the complex relationship I have with drugs of all kinds and particularly those designed to help with this mental disorder.

There have been numerous attempts to find a drug that might work for me. One specialist told me that he had changed his mind three times during our consultation about which medication would best suit my symptoms.

'I bet you get this a lot,' I half-joked.'

'No, Tim, I don't, not to this extreme,' was his deadpan reply.

In typical ADHD fashion, I had tried and rejected many of the drugs available to me. In fact, I have completed a full circle, eventually settling back on the medication I was first advised to take. Finally, getting to the point where I felt comfortable with a drug has proved to be a long and often bumpy road.

I had previously been misdiagnosed with depression, or perhaps it had attached like a limpet to my undiagnosed ADHD, leading doctors to hand out various anti-depressants like sweets. So it was no surprise they didn't work, although I doubt I gave them much of a chance to do so.

Initially, I was prescribed Sertraline, and on the first day, I felt great. At last, I was doing something that would help improve my mood and life. 'I'm going to be cured, hooray!' I had one of the best days in many months, I was almost euphoric. But, of course, it was a one-day placebo pill, and I reasoned if I could make myself happy like this, then why did I need pills? The cure was surely in the power of my own mind.

However, I decided to continue to take the medication for a while longer, but the next day I felt awful, and the day after that, I felt weird, so I put the pills in the bottom drawer. Anti-depressants such as SSRIs have, in some cases, make ADHD symptoms worse, although some people do take them successfully for a co-existing condition.

Stimulant drugs for ADHD often get to work immediately, something an impatient mind would necessitate, unlike an SSRI, which may take weeks or months to work and may be of little benefit to someone with ADHD.

A mental health professional explained to me in simple terms how drugs help an ADHD brain. For most people, the road on which we travel life's journey is relatively smooth, but for those with ADHD, there are constant bumps and dips to navigate. The drugs will smooth this road out so regular travel can commence. I wondered what would happen if someone without ADHD took these drugs, and apparently, it is likely to put bumps into their previously smooth road.

The first ADHD drug I took was Concerta, a long-acting methylphenidate prescribed by the private clinic after my initial assessment.

Once again, for the first day on this medication, I was ridiculously happy, walking around with a big silly grin and a spring in my step, saying hello to everyone I met. However, by early evening, there was a crash. I woke at 4 am with my head feeling the size and weight of a granite boulder.

Over the next few days, I felt more confident and a little braver with some of the difficulties in my life, and this was a welcome plus point.

However, some stimulant drugs, including Concerta, can spike blood pressure. Mine is already high due to a family history that had accounted for the death of my father and his own father before him, but I wanted to give the drug a fair chance to see if there might be a positive effect on my ADHD.

My doctor had said he considered it potentially dangerous for me to take this drug without the regular blood pressure and blood tests, which would all need to be done and paid for privately. After recording my high level results, he advised me to stop taking the medication immediately. It was a very deflating moment. I had tried so hard to make progress but now seemingly hit another brick wall.

Still, I was prepared to take the risk and see how my ADHD progressed. Unfortunately, as each day passed, the drug's effect appeared less favourable, and the side effects more prominent. I had a constant headache and a weird fuzz in my brain; I also felt hot and clammy. After the GP's initial concerns, I purchased a home blood pressure kit and found my readings were almost off the scale. Nevertheless, I had reached the tenth day of taking Concerta and was determined to reach my goal of two weeks, thus road-testing the drug properly.

The following day Katherine initiated a morning of passion. Within a few minutes, I was in a pool of my own sweat, my heart beating faster than I had ever known, and my brain felt as if it were about to burst. I'd lost every bit of strength, and nothing was happening, the room spinning all around me. Eventually, I was forced to announce to my wife in a raspy voice.

'I think I'm going to faint…'

Katherine surveyed the wreckage of her husband and rolled me onto my back before suggesting,

'I don't think you should take any more of those pills, Timmy.'

I readily agreed, and they were dropped into the bottom drawer. I really should have heeded the warning from my doctor.

It seems rather irresponsible of the private practice to give these drugs out so readily without a single physical health check, although I guess I must have ticked a box on the health forms at some point during the process. Either way, I was back to square one.

Later that year, I had my second ADHD assessment, this time with the National Health Service, which confirmed my diagnosis. However, they advised that my blood pressure was still too high to risk taking any of the stimulants available to me.

I had never taken pills for a long-term condition; surely that's for other people, not me, I'm fit and I've run marathons!

So now, I was expected to take a blood pressure pill that would enable me to take ADHD medication. I rejected this notion out of hand. In reality, I should thank the specialists and scientists involved for balancing my needs. But, it took some considerable time for me to accept this and a lecture from my big sister, who also suffers from the problem despite being super fit and healthy because apparently

'…you can't fight your genes.'

'Take the blood pressure medication, Tim, anything is better than ending up like Dad!' she continued. This added to Katherine's pleading emotional blackmail. 'I couldn't bear to lose you, Timmy, take them for me' I finally succumbed, although it took four different types of blood pressure medication before finding one that worked and didn't give me side effects, including the one that no man wants! These were angiotensin receptor blockers.

Taking the blood pressure medication finally allowed me to search for a suitable ADHD drug.

I tried various medications, including lisdexamfetamine, after which Katherine told me I was being weird but also said she quite liked me that way. I'd be singing and recounting possibly inappropriate tales of the past, and I cooked lettuce thinking it was cabbage. That night my dreams were in 3D.

I then had a very rushed and abrupt phone call with a private ADHD specialist. He recommended atomoxetine, a non-stimulant, as he advised it was less harsh than more traditional medication and suggested that it wouldn't spike my blood pressure. He concluded that I would soon feel like the other 96 per cent of people on the planet.

However, whether I imagined it or not, atomoxetine appeared to give me instant side effects. I was tired, lethargic, tingling, and at one point, almost walked into the road. My brain always felt better for being rid of these intruders.

I was still nowhere near an answer to my ADHD problems, but I was hurt and upset when the clinic discharged me because 'Drugs don't seem to work for you, Tim.' This left me feeling abandoned.

I suggested to Katherine and the specialist that as none of the medications worked for me, I probably don't have ADHD. They both laughed at me.

Anecdotally, I have spoken with others that have late-diagnosed ADHD who have been unable to tolerate ADHD medication and have decided to live with the condition as they always have done.

However, I was now desperate for something to help with my low mood. There appeared to be no hope of ever feeling like my old self again. I was at the point of disappearing for a while, turning my back on those who depended on me, and finding a quiet and forgotten corner of the world to live in—I even considered that long swim out to sea once more.

I thought back to my first diagnosis and the psychiatrist's advice 'Take the medication and not just for one day, you will feel better!' I concluded that things couldn't get much worse and took a dose of the most recently prescribed short-acting methylphenidate. I think my acceptance that I required medical assistance finally helped as things became clearer almost immediately, and I could see myself and my behaviour for what it was. Although I'm aware that my brain isn't a hundred per cent, I was more productive, truer to myself, and at least able to function to help those around me and myself while somehow keeping my business afloat.

The clinic reversed their decision to discharge me and I was glad to be given another chance. I had the added bonus of a new ADHD therapist too. She was very pleased with my U-turn on taking the drug, and her personality was right on my wavelength. Later she confided that she 'probably' has ADHD too but had never been formally diagnosed. I often feel more comfortable in the company of those with the same condition.

When the medication initially took hold, it felt like I had been given a new pair of glasses with lenses that were too strong for my eyes.

Everything around me was now crisper and sharper. My eyes and brain felt like they were forced open. I could almost count the stones jumping from a shingle drive. The feathers of a starling perched on a branch were now in super technicolour that bounced and vibrated around my brain. However, the specialist told me this would be a one-off, and as I got used to the medication, I would lose this short-lived sensation and just feel better.

The methylphenidate certainly helped me to focus on the moment, be more engaged and perhaps a little more self-assured with those around me. They help to control my impulsive urges, too, so I managed to swerve a crazy bidding war on eBay for a twenty-year-old campervan three hundred miles away. However, there are downsides too. I know I'm not blasting on all cylinders, and the speed of my physical and mental reactions weren't quite as sharp.

My ADHD therapist insisted that I mustn't drink caffeine while on this medication as it can exacerbate side effects and spike blood pressure. But, of course, I couldn't resist and ordered a coffee at a garden centre café despite the warning from my wife.

'Timmy, you aren't meant to drink coffee with those pills!'

However, it seemed to give me quite a boost with the mix of caffeine and remnants of the methylphenidate that was starting to wear off after six hours, although I have never managed to replicate that feeling since, and of course, it's not advised.

For someone now taking five pills a day when until recently I took not a single one, the various pillboxes look rather similar, resulting in some predictable consequences.

For no apparent reason, my blood pressure had started to climb again and I often felt dizzy and nauseous. Katherine soon discovered I had been taking pills from a leftover rogue box of an SSRI rather than my blood pressure medication. They had both been thrown into a large, crocheted owl that also hosted any number of random items, including my daily medication.

When I updated my exasperated doctor on the latest escapade of starting yet another drug, he exclaimed, 'You do like to do things your way, don't you!'

I admire his fortitude and patience for prescribing tablets that I will refuse to take, self-prescribing others when he has instructed me not to, starting two courses of tablets when he has told me not to, and

119

asking me if I want to take a new medication to which I'll reply 'Yes' but with no actual intention of taking them as I might change my mind purely based on one of my preferred life mantras of 'always give yourself options.'

When it was first suggested that I might have ADHD, my doctor was a little sceptical, but I don't think he is in too much doubt now.

I should thank the mental health services in my area of the UK for persevering with me. It is an outstanding facility. However, it takes a while to get through the waiting list, and this, along with any negative issues, is purely down to a lack of funding, not the lack of skill by the practitioners or the quality of their care.

Methylphenidate is an ideal drug for my ADHD as it gets to work very quickly, and then within six hours of taking it, the effects are out of my system with no apparent withdrawal to deal with.

I'm pleased to have found a medication that I can tolerate, but I continue to inwardly wrestle with the necessity of taking drugs, endlessly contemplating whether methylphenidate stops me from being the true version of myself with all its flaws and potential benefits or whether it makes a more rounded and considered person. I change my mind about this almost daily, and I very much doubt that I am the only ADHD 'drug taker' who experiences this emotion.

There are days when I am more focused and feel better and others where there is seemingly no benefit at all. At times I consider the benefit more of a placebo than anything else. Although my ADHD therapist didn't agree and rattled off a list of improvements I had made and how much better I had been coping with the difficulties in my life.

However, while on methylphenidate, I miss being the real me, able to multi-task and have fast reflexes, the person who goes up and down the stairs three times or backward and forwards to the shops when if I had planned it, I could have done it all in one journey or being the person who jumps up and down in a supermarket queue wanting to floor the man at the front who takes forever to pay. Methylphenidate gives me an inbuilt 'count to ten' filter before reacting to a negative comment or dumping all my shopping in the middle of a supermarket and walking out when I can't face the queue.

While taking this drug, it has helped me focus on each chapter of this book, finding errors and re-editing. However, I doubt that I would have found the spark and flow required to tell my story in such an honest and raw way if my brain had been slowed from its normal free-flowing state by mind-altering drugs. Perhaps this sums up the pros and cons of my relationship with ADHD medication in one paragraph.

It also reminds me of the old-fashioned cassette players that were fitted with 'Dolby C' noise reduction. This facility would remove the unwanted hiss from the tape, but it also reduced some of the sharpness of the music. When I need to be on my best form and have my sharpest mind available such as making a work presentation, training course, or a media interview, the medication is likely to stay firmly in its packet.

However, when my accounts were due to be filed, and my mind was agitated and anywhere other than with the task in hand, I found a double dose of methylphenidate did the trick, and my year-end figures were duly completed in full that same day.

My intention remains to stop taking this medication, but only when I feel ready to. I'm still seemingly in denial. So, I'll take them for bad spells or as a quick-fix drug on a bad day, but the longer it goes, the better I feel. However, a part of me will always rail against the necessity of taking what is essentially a mind-altering drug. Furthermore, after taking them regularly for an extended period of time, I've noticed I am less inclined to get out of the house for exercise and feel a degree of dullness within me that I find difficult to accept, and one day I plan to find another pathway to keep the feel-good chemicals flowing through my brain that doesn't involve drugs.

As I write these words, I will only take methylphenidate when I feel the need to. I will reach for the packet in the way someone might use a remedy for a headache and take them for a few days, a week, or maybe a month or so until I yearn for the return of my sharper-free, thinking non, drugged mind to return. It is a cycle I'm yet to break, a work in process but one that I think works for me—for now.

Alternative Therapy 'Potions' for ADHD

Some while ago, Vicky asked me why I detested the thought of taking licensed medication but was still happy to buy and consume a variety of other options when I have no real clue what is in them. Perhaps I wasn't quite ready to admit I required 'proper' medication, and using something natural possibly had a less harmful effect on my body. I have since reconsidered and changed my view on this, but several remedies have anecdotally helped many people.

Rhodiola Rosea has been used in trials to see how effective it is in helping with the symptoms of ADHD. I understand it has some effectiveness in reducing stress, combatting fatigue, increasing mental performance and improving physical and mental fitness and resilience. My own experience of this herb was somewhat different. I purchased some from two sources and had two entirely different experiences. The first batch gave what I can only describe as a slight buzz and the second a slight dullness. There was a promise of the purest ingredients from the overly aggressive sales talk, and I should have taken that as a red flag. I found little or no positive lasting effect from my experience of consuming this product. Ginseng and ginkgo biloba are two other herbs that are thought to help with energy and focus. Both are in a daily multivitamin that I take.

Some years ago, I received tickets for a Norwich City football match that would celebrate their epic title-winning season. These tickets were extremely difficult to obtain. Katherine was away with her group of Brownie Guides, and I had woken up in a particularly low mood. I gave the tickets to a delighted friend and then drove to a quiet car park, trying to hide my negative emotions. I searched online for depression remedies and purchased St John's Wort, as this herb had some very good reviews. However, I found it difficult to tolerate and stopped taking the remedy within a week. It is essential to know these substances may have side effects and interact with medication, so always read the label first.

ADHD drugs can work highly effectively for many people. However, if they are not for you, there are some potential alternatives. The American website additude.com has a booklet about helping with ADHD symptoms more naturally, although please always check sources and suitability first.

Transcranial Direction Current Stimulation (TDCS)

I have used the Flow Neuroscience headset with some positive results for my associated depression. It comes with a mobile phone app full of helpful advice. Vicky and Alex, who both work in senior mental health roles, were diplomatically quiet about my purchase.

However, the more scientific family members were surprisingly encouraging. I'd initially kept it a secret, expecting a lecture on 'mumbo jumbo' and I felt encouraged by their support.

A low electronic current is sent into your brain via a headset that can be hired or purchased outright. It did seem to detangle some of my depression away from the ADHD so that I could tackle them one at a time, but I concluded that it was probably of no tangible benefit in the long term. In addition, I found the cost prohibitive.

Not everything has to be bogged down with scientific proof. Katherine was a *Reiki* practitioner, and I've experienced first-hand the benefits of her skills that can help the mind and body. However, when a friend and then a close relative rubbished what she did as just a placebo, it knocked her confidence, and she stopped practising for a while. But if something works, then it works, don't let anyone tell you differently. It is important to listen to the advice of everyone but always make your own decision and then own it, so the consequences of your actions are yours and yours alone.

I have tried various mindfulness and meditation techniques and even an expensive phone app. However, my ADHD mind and body couldn't stay still long enough to endure the painfully slow drawl of the app narrator, 'I'm going to count backwards from ten to one. Ten…nine…' But, I had already reached zero and became so frustrated with the slow tediousness of it all had twice told the recorded voice to 'fuck off!'

It was suggested the walking meditation app might work well for me, but it seems I was travelling too fast for it to keep up with my pace.

I once attended a mindfulness course on sugar addiction, but I couldn't wait for this boring session to end so I could run out and buy some chocolate. However, there are occasions, such as when I am at the beach or on holiday when I do manage to absorb everything around me and try to keep it as a snapshot in my mind. This is a new sensation for me and perhaps enhanced by the drugs that help my brain stay calm and to function better.

Katherine and I attended a series of tai-chi lessons. I was told to stop striking like I was kicking someone, and I grew increasingly frustrated with the slow teaching methods. I have also tried yoga as I thought it would help my mind and core strength for running. Unfortunately, I have the flexibility of the Tin Man and predictably got confused as the class stopped while a move was explained to me three times. There was also half an hour of inversion where everyone attempted to hang upside down like a bat, followed by some obligatory meditation, which became a form of *Kryptonite* for my ADHD brain as I would rather have run around the room or start singing.

Physical sports will usually give me a mental boost. I get so much positive energy and some of my best ideas while out running, but as I pass sixty, my body doesn't seem to correspond with what my mind thinks it can do, and I have taken up classes that I struggle to cope with. This leads to periods of injury, inaction and frustration with the inevitable low moods that follow.

Sugar

A number of studies have found a link between diets high in sugar and some mental disorders, as overconsumption of sugar triggers imbalances in certain brain chemicals. These imbalances can lead to depression and may even increase the long-term risk of some people developing a mental health disorder.

I had a terrible diet throughout my younger life, often resorting to Weetabix with a three-inch heap of granulated sugar for an evening meal and a chocolate bar or bag of crisps for school dinner.

As an adult, I would often eat in excess of 100g of sugar a day. This is more than three times the maximum recommended amount. Eating sugar would keep the buzz in my brain going, yet the inevitable dip would leave me tired and lethargic. I would often run to the local shop in search of a quick sugar fix. On one occasion, I purchased a triple packet of Jaffa Cakes as they were on offer and cheaper than a single packet—not great for curbing the temptation of a sugar addict! I started eating them before leaving the shop and got through the entire contents in less than ten minutes without even hurrying and didn't feel the slightest bit sick afterwards.

One therapist spoke of the stomach as a 'second brain' that is the same size as a cat's brain. He challenged me to give up sugar which I did, and as a result, I felt a positive benefit. I started to eat more protein and vegetables, and I believe I felt calmer as a result. I allowed myself to eat whatever I wanted on this diet, provided it didn't contain free sugars and the food was relatively healthy. It also helped to keep my weight stable. However, there is always a special occasion involving cake around the corner that can quickly derail any good intentions.

Excessive sugar, like many other addictions, slowly rots the brain and is a very difficult habit to break. There is seldom a straight road to recovery.

Alcohol

Whenever I drink more than a couple of units of alcohol, it has an adverse effect. Certain drinks, such as white wine, tend to lower my mood, so it is perhaps fortunate that I have never been much of a drinker. I'll admit I've been wasted once or twice, but that was a lifetime ago. I'll still have an occasional glass of red wine or a beer, and my daughter will make some high-octane cocktails for special occasions, but I can go for weeks or months without even thinking about it. Alcohol is expensive and contains so many calories that it makes dieting even more of a challenge while trying to lose weight.

Alcohol is an addiction far more likely to affect a person with ADHD than it might do for someone without the disorder, and your medical practitioner will have the correct information to help further with this.

Further Help and Guidance –

Ensure you do some research and consider all possibilities to help with your ADHD. Remember that you are unique, and something that works for others may not necessarily work for you and vice versa.

You may have to be in the right place mentally to try a new drug and potentially return to it at a later date, having first rejected the medication prescribed.

Your doctor or ADHD specialist should prescribe the most suitable drug for you based on your symptoms rather than routinely giving out the first one on the list. You may have to scrap and fight for the right help, so don't be fobbed off.

Cut out sugar and alcohol – If you can't cut them out, try and reduce them.

Exercise can help as it releases positive, feel-good chemicals in your brain. Try to find an activity or class you enjoy rather than doing something to punish your body.

Taking a good quality multivitamin and a daily dose of Omega 3 may help. Vegetarian and vegan versions are also available.

Enjoy your good days, never feel guilty about them, and don't have any expectations of feeling the same way tomorrow. It is sometimes like the weather, and you can't control it. Although for many being on the correct medication will almost certainly help.

Further updates on my quest for treatment can be found at www.timmacwilliam.com

CHAPTER NINE

Living With ADHD and What It's Like For Me

I have an overwhelming desire to jump on my chair and sing their name in the style of a Radio jingle. 'Music loving Peter Johnson!'

When I tell people I have been diagnosed with ADHD, they often don't believe me as they associate it with hyperactive children running around in circles and screaming. However, the reality is that it could be a relative, a friend or a colleague, or maybe even your own partner who doesn't necessarily display the classic symptoms of the condition.

I was told that having ADHD is like driving a Ferrari with bicycle brakes. For me, it feels more like I'm driving an automatic car that changes gear whenever it wants to. It also feels like attempting to complete a challenging jigsaw while additional pieces keep falling from the sky.

I understand the brakes analogy, particularly in an environment where I am expected to behave 'normally' and at least try to engage with my current surroundings. But, often, I want to jump, skip and run around, sing or talk nonsense. This juxtaposition can become emotionally tiring for the ADHD brain. However, since my diagnosis, I don't always feel the necessity to repress these feelings as they are part of me and it is who I am. I have ADHD, and I'm relieved to know there is a reason for the emotions that rush around my mind and body.

I just wish I had known earlier in life that it was OK to be me.

<u>Morning is Broken</u>

A new day began with the best of intentions. I was on a mission to lose weight and stood on the bathroom scales twice, but I became distracted both times and failed to record either result.

Once downstairs, I fed the two fluffy white kittens we had recently adopted, switched on the kettle, put away most of the items from the dishwasher, and then pulled some of the clean laundry from the washing machine that landed among some spilt milk on the kitchen floor. Before I got anywhere near the clothes pegs, I was hit by a wave of stressful realisation that I hadn't yet checked the morning work emails. While the computer was powering up, I heard the cats in their litter tray that I was asked to clean yesterday but failed to do so.

The computer was very slowly downloading a security update, so I departed my desk to empty the smelly old litter into a large black plastic sack leaving the cats temporarily without a toilet. However, before I could discard the litter, I noticed a ready-stamped birthday card positioned deliberately in my pathway to ensure even I couldn't fail to see it. I had previously bought one for a child in error and was sent back to the shop to exchange it. Within a few moments, I was heading towards the nearby post-box with the correct card in hand.

I had left the living room window open, but the wooden slatted blinds closed, assuming the kittens, awaiting their second vaccine and therefore, mustn't go out, wouldn't escape, but, of course, they have.

I quickly found Dolly hiding behind a bush in our garden. Meanwhile Charlie had made it to our neighbour's house where presumably he thought the identical back door was his own and believed that our bemused neighbour, still dressed in his pyjamas, was me.

'Excuse me, that's our cat! Would you grab him for me, please' I shouted over the fence, hopefully loud enough for him to hear but not to wake anyone else in our household who would view the cat escapade rather dimly.

On their return, our kittens continued to protest about my unfinished work, so I cleaned their litter tray before returning to my laundry duties.

The kitchen was now entirely filled with steam, and I could no longer see the work surfaces or the windows opposite. There was moisture running down every wall, cupboard, and door. The kettle, with the lid sitting nearby, had been violently boiling away for some time. I managed to unplug the bubbling cauldron at the wall socket moments before it ran dry, tripping the entire household electrical system

My phone pinged with a text from Katherine, now fully awake, asking if there was any chance of a cup of tea in bed.

'OK...' I replied, but not wanting her to be exposed to the growing mess or be unduly perturbed by the increasing catalogue of early morning mishaps, I continued, '... I'll just put the kettle on. I'll be there in a couple of minutes.'

I searched for Katherine's favourite mug but discovered the crockery that I had put away earlier was encrusted with rice and gravy, and many of the cups were coffee stained. A glance at the dishwasher control panel confirmed that I had previously failed to press the start button.

My attempt to separate the grimy crockery away from the clean succeeded only in polluting the area further as sour milk dribbled down the side of a cloudy glass. Dirty plates were stacked onto clean with sauce now sliding down the side. The only way forward was to completely empty the cupboards and restart the washing process. I began the task but decided this would have to wait as I was now running out of space with so many items piled high on every work surface.

The kitchen still resembled a steam room, but I couldn't open the windows as the kittens would immediately jump out again.

While the kettle was re-heating and I was still towelling down the moisture from the walls, my mind wandered back to the computer update and work emails. I returned to my desk, where I managed to complete the first two replies, when I heard yet another ping as a third email arrived, urgently requesting some important documents that I speedily edited and returned to my client. I was feeling pleased with myself that I'd got some focus today, and my mind was in the necessary work zone. The carnage elsewhere in the house having vacated my brain.

Ten minutes later, Katherine wandered into my office, having realised that her cup of tea in bed was unlikely to appear that day.

'Tim! What on earth have you done to the kitchen?'

Not every morning is quite so haphazard, but there is usually some degree of catastrophe resulting in varying amounts of broken pieces, both real and metaphorical, to pick up later.

The regularity of forgetting to put a lid on the kettle has become such an issue we now have a water heater that spits out one cup at a time and a hob that switches itself off when no pans are present.

Things will often ping in and out of an ADHD mind, so I was advised to keep a paper and pen with me to jot down my thoughts. These might be important tasks such as a new business idea or perhaps a present I had forgotten to buy. Latterly it has become something I want to include within this book. If I don't immediately record it somewhere, it will be lost through my sieve-like brain.

However, I have the worst handwriting of anyone I've ever met, so my scribbles are illegible, even to me. The notes app on my phone is the ideal replacement. But, it's not always readily available, especially in the shower, where a 'brilliant' new thought is so clear that I'm sure I won't forget it, but of course, by the time I am washed and dried, I will not only have forgotten about the idea but might also have forgotten that I had an idea in the first place.

While lying awake at night, I might have an avalanche of ideas and thoughts but cannot recall a single one the next day. Occasionally it might be something bordering on a 'Eureka!' moment. Still, as I had chosen not to wake the household and record my thoughts, any recollection of the idea had evaporated by morning, leaving only useless fragments from my imagination that disappeared along with the previous night's dreams.

There are times when so many things need to get done that my brain is overwhelmed and fizzes over. I have no idea what to do first. So instead, I make small movements in different directions, much like a child's toy running low on battery power.

In such cases, Katherine might ask me what is wrong as I seem stressed. I usually find the best way to explain it is with the answer,

'I've got too many tabs open and half of them seem to be frozen.'

During a conversation, countless thoughts and possibilities will go through my mind, but I may not have said a word in reply. So it may appear that I haven't been listening, am simply choosing to ignore them or can't think of the correct words in which to reply. This can result in them attempting to complete my sentence in something akin to an elaborate game of charades. On some occasions, I've already decided what their reply will be to the point that I had actually lived through the entire conversation and how it might unfold. However, ADHD often means a continually whirring mind, and I might also suddenly, rudely, and inappropriately blurt out my thoughts or interrupt them mid-sentence.

I'm obviously not the easiest person to live with, and life can get somewhat fraught when things go awry. It's like an endless game of trust and redemption, Snakes & Ladders.

One Saturday, I made the usual mistake of multitasking while cooking dinner and poured chicken gravy over half of the chocolate brownies my daughter had recently made. She took it quite well and wiped away the mess rescuing those that remained untainted, before telling me that I could only eat the cakes that had gravy soaking into them.

When I happily consumed all of the chicken-flavoured brownies, I was likened to a Labrador with special needs as, once again, I slid down the Snakes & Ladders board to square one.

Even during my school days, I would endeavour to multitask. While attempting to complete my American history homework, I was also engrossed in an England football match on the radio. Somehow the two had merged in my brain, and my teacher, when returning the essay, asked me what on earth Kevin Keegan had to do with the American Civil War.

Looking back through my life, I now realise that ADHD may have played a part in many of the mishaps I've encountered, including those described below.

Such as the day I had an appointment for a blood test. I hate blood tests and was frantically searching for my car keys, but due to the stress of the upcoming appointment, I could not find them, and with the spare set lost somewhere in the North Sea, I had no transport available. As a result, I was now late for my appointment and had no choice but to run the mile to the surgery. I needn't have hurried, though, as the waiting area had a massive backlog.

The thought of the impending blood test had made me somewhat agitated, and I began to march around the seats, shaking my arms at the thought of the needle slicing into my vein. I managed to calm myself a little and found a seat, but each time a doctor called for his next patient through the intercom, 'Peter Johnson to room five please,' I had an overwhelming desire to jump on my chair and sing their name in the style of a radio jingle, *'Music Loving Peter Johnson!'* I partially overcame this by digging my fingernails into my wrists and bouncing my legs around while the jingle was sung quietly under my breath. The person sitting next to me decided to get up and move.

On my return home, Katherine found my keys—they were in the fridge, obviously!

I once set fire to a wooden bench, having not realised or perhaps forgotten that a red-hot disposable barbecue tray would cause the bench to combust. I have since repaired the seat incorporating some of the charred remains for posterity.

On a visit to the Olympic Stadium in Munich, visitors were permitted to climb the famous glass-style roof and, despite the warning from my guide, 'This activity is not without danger,' I proceeded to joyfully zip wire across the entire pitch while shouting the iconic commentary line from England's victory over Germany '… and Heskey makes it five!'

A few years later, I was rather disappointed that no such adventure was permitted during our visit to the Olympic Stadium in Berlin. However, the steel wire gate that led directly onto the blue athletics track and green turf beyond had been left tantalisingly open, so I was tempted to run through the gate and across the pitch just to see how far I would get. I tried to distract myself by pulling my hair, but the urge to charge onto the hallowed turf where the famous Zinedine Zidane headbutt had taken place just a few years earlier had become too distracting. The sprinklers bursting into life only made the prospect of an adventure more alluring. Fortunately, the sound of a familiar voice approaching from behind halted any further thoughts of the escapade, 'Tim? Tim? Timmy! Are you OK, Darling? Shall we go to the gift shop now?'

While sitting in a favourite beachside café, my mind began to wander. I realised I hadn't re-ordered my regular prescription drugs, so I grabbed my phone and logged into the useful app our surgery provides. But my phone was slow and laggy, so I wondered if it was time for a new one and my focus shifted. I spent the next fifteen minutes looking through price plans for the latest mobiles, completely forgetting about re-ordering much-needed medical supplies. It wasn't until I got home to take my evening dose from a now almost depleted stock that I realised I had forgotten to complete the order.

People with ADHD love to think they can spot things others can't see, but it's not always the case. I was so excited by an apparent bargain on the easyJet website that I immediately booked a surprise family holiday. I then discovered the flights were departing from Stanstead but returning to Manchester. A cancellation and rebooking charge cost almost twice that of the original 'bargain.'

I am often told what a good judge of character I am and have a history of picking out bad apples when others initially think the person concerned is a good egg, including the nearby drug dealer, who most others thought was a lovely chap until their house was raided, early one morning, by the police.

However, if I am quite so savvy, I wonder how I once purchased a computer via an auction site that didn't exist. Rather worryingly, this is not the only such error of judgement I have made over the years. I attempted to sell a sports shop voucher online, but the minute I posted the advert containing the code, I realised my error and removed it, but the voucher had already been cloned and cashed in. I asked the manager of the large store if they could tell me who had effectively stolen £99 from me, but they couldn't or wouldn't due to their absurd misinterpretation of a data protection law that protected the perpetrator instead of the victim. I had a brief fantasy of throwing a shop full of expensive running gear out of the door and into the street, item by item, until they refunded me or the police were called, but instead, I meekly walked out and accepted my fate as a familiar wave of self-loathing and embarrassment swept over me. More recently, my sister-in-law asked me to buy her niece a £100 Amazon voucher as her bank card had been frozen. This was rather odd as I didn't think she had a niece. I'm sure you can guess the rest!

A rather tenacious police officer did track down the fraudster who sold me the non-existent computer, so at least I got that money back. Being conned is an awful experience. It leaves you feeling empty and violated. ADHD can amplify those feelings, especially when we boast about knowing better!

During the Covid-19 lockdown, I would easily become bored during family Zoom meetings, especially when everyone was talking at once. So rather than get involved, I would frequently disappear to hula hoop or balance on an exercise ball while the computer-based gathering continued. Katherine's family probably think I'm just a bit strange. However, I was still a little upset when she told one of her brothers about my ADHD diagnosis before I was ready. Although, I guess you can't write a book like this and keep it a secret!

When Vicky screamed that her eyes were stinging from the soothing eye drops that I had just administered. I belatedly checked the label and found that the bottle for eye drops looked remarkably similar to the one used to melt stubborn earwax. I really should have read the label first!

We had moved house when Vicky was just a few months old. The heating wasn't as it should be and her bedroom was often cold. So, I purchased some wall-insulating polystyrene to keep more of the warmth in her room. It's easy to put up, and it seemed to have dried in no time at all. I, therefore, ignored the advice to wait seventy two hours before pasting her Disney-featured wallpaper on top. The following day, we found Vicky still fast asleep but lying under numerous thin polystyrene strips glued to some Winnie the Pooh, Tigger, and Eeyore patterned wallpaper.

There are two people listed as 'Ed' in my email contacts. One is Edward Couzens-Lake, a mentor to me while writing this book, who offered endless support and encouragement throughout. The other employs me for food hygiene audits in three prestige hotels. The most sensitive chapters in this book talk about suicide, self-harm, and sex addiction. I can confirm that I am a big fan of the Gmail undo button that has come to my rescue on numerous occasions.

There were probably signs of ADHD throughout my childhood, including the long hot summer of 1976. On a weekend camping trip, everyone sensibly kept out of the sweltering heat and found some shade. Everyone, that is, except for me. I spent much of the day manically hitting a tennis ball against a wall in the full glare of the midday sun. When we arrived home, I complained that I felt sick and dizzy, but as I had probably been a hyperactive pain in the backside all day long, particularly on the fraught, baking hot journey home in my dad's Land Rover, there was little patience or sympathy from my family. I went to my room and passed out. Fortunately, my sister checked to see if I was OK, recognised I had sun or heat stroke, and poured cold water over me until my body cooled. After this scare, my mum bought me a sun hat for our following holidays, although it always seemed to rain from then on.

Nearly four decades later, the London Marathon was held on a particularly warm day, and I had predictably made a mess of packing my pre-race bag, forgetting the all-important sun hat. Since the problem in the summer of '76, I have struggled with any form of serious exercise in hot weather. I had trained hard all through a long cold icy winter and was now faced with running a marathon with the sun beating down on what felt like a mid-summer day. The crowds and the tall buildings all around reflected the heat back onto the course, making it feel even warmer. I wasn't going to stop or pull out of the event once it started. However, I knew, without a decent running hat, I was probably heading for sun-stroke and an intravenous drip, although I was hoping, somewhat optimistically, for this to be after I had crossed the finishing line.

As I approached the sixth mile, still pondering my ugly fate and already feeling some degree of discomfort from the heat, Katherine popped out from the crowd.

'Hi Darling, I've found your hat. Would you like it?'

Thanks to the foresight of my wife, I just about scraped over the finish line, but only just.

People with ADHD can often be made to feel stupid. We know we aren't, and perhaps that isn't the intention of those who made us feel this way, but we might still experience difficulties as a result.

For example, when I joined a swimming group for six weeks of coaching at an Olympic size pool. There was much to remember, and coordination was required for arms, legs, the number of strokes, and somewhat confusingly, keeping my face in the water to create a mini bow in which to breathe. The more it was explained, the more frustrated, forgetful, and panicked I became as the rest of the group progressed, leaving me back in the slow lane.

I begged the coach to let me skip this module for now and learn something else, but my plea was refused. So, for the next six weeks, the rest of the group learned sighting, turns, new strokes and cadence. None of which I was permitted to master. It was like an anxiety dream of being back at school, only this time it wasn't a pointy dunces hat but a swim cap with a capital 'D' written large.

As the course ended, I still had the most inefficient swimming stroke, which remained somewhere between a turtle and a sea horse. In reality, I would probably challenge the skills and patience of any sports coach.

I have also switched off during triathlon pre-race briefings, and as a result, I've travelled in the wrong direction, completed an extra circuit and swam additional lengths of a pool. Nowadays, I usually follow those in front in the hope they know where they are going.

Hoarding is symptomatic of ADHD, and I try so hard to throw stuff away. Books, records, clothes, and running gear are all in a pile to give away before changing my mind and storing them once again, 'just in case.' I was given a beautiful new sports bag as a gift which I love. But I already have several other sports bags, none of which I will be discarding.

The author of the self-tidying book may have found her match should she ever visit our house, particularly as my daughter is possibly even more of a hoarder than I am. I told her that I had been offered £25 for a box set of old Beatles cassettes. 'No Dad, keep them! This is what lofts are for,' she protested.

Those with ADHD, are seldom good listeners.

'Timmy, I do love you, but I wish you would listen.'
Katherine said this to me over twenty years ago, upset and exasperated by my apparent lack of attention or interest.

I don't think anyone has ever completely got used to my switching off when they are talking to me.

Even if I am fully interested and engaged, my mind will often drift off somewhere else. I'll really try to stay engaged, but all too often, the voice will become a background noise like rain on a flat roof as other more pressing thoughts intrude into my mind.

I can see the hurt in their eyes when they eventually recognise their words are falling on deaf ears, and they think I do not care, but I do. I really do, and I receive another small wave of shame each and every time this happens.

Teachers would throw chalk at me and shout, 'Listen!' colleagues would see me drifting off during a work event and ask,

'Tim, are you still with us?'

I was regularly asked to take minutes for a safety meeting that would likely be more a work of fiction than an accurate description of the latest trip hazard. Such was my wandering mind.

I was advised during a training course that 'He who asks a question feels a fool for a moment. He who never asks a question feels a fool forever.' In my case, this simply isn't true.

A teacher at school had spent nearly half a lesson explaining rules to students for a game of rugby about to take place on a cement playground. The main rule was that you mustn't tackle, which he repeated several times before asking if there were any questions.

'Can you tackle?' Was my predictable query, to which the teacher rolled his eyes to the heavens while the rest of the class groaned.

Our family enjoyed a regular camping holiday on a farm in Dorset, coinciding with the annual sheep shearing event. We attended the obligatory talk given by the head shearer, who probably told everyone multiple times that his demonstration would start the next day at 9 am. When he asked if there were any questions, no one raised their hand except for me. I enquired what time the shearing would commence.

There was an audible mixture of tutting and laughing aimed in my direction. I was embarrassed and wanted to forget the episode, but inevitably I was teased. My brother jokingly told me how proud the entire family was of me for asking such a stupid question. My dad became quite tetchy.

'Weren't you listening? He must have told us the start time a dozen times!'

'I didn't hear.' was my rather weak explanation.

'You should try and pay more attention!' he replied rather crossly.

Sometimes it isn't failure to hear. It's a failure to remember information that was given only moments earlier.

Vicky was part of a large school concert. All the parents were packed into the sports hall, with countless more craning their necks at the back of the room for a better view of their child. The head teacher clearly instructed the sizeable gathering that the next student would play two pieces of classical music on her violin but asked us not to applaud until both had been completed. I know I heard the words spoken, but the instruction had simply popped out of my head as I took it upon myself to break the silence by enthusiastically applauding immediately after the first piece of music, to which no one else joined in.

I was probably being rather optimistic in hoping nobody saw or realised it was me.

'Hey, Tim, was that your impression of a seal? I'm surprised no one threw you a fish,' remarked another parent with just a little too much scorn as we left the building.

I was fifty-eight years old before I read my first piece of fiction from cover to cover. Prior to that and my diagnosis of ADHD, the books that I owned were mostly ornamental and gathering dust on a shelf.

I might, perhaps, get through half of an interesting biography, a book with advice on radio presentation, or a football history yearbook, but that was about my capacity for the written word.

I would usually lose interest after a few chapters, sometimes after only a few pages, quickly becoming impatient with the storyline. The words became meaningless as my mind wandered off into the distance, with names and plots soon forgotten. My brother would light heartedly tease that 'Tim read a book once but didn't like it, so he never read one again.' I wondered why I never had the capacity to read a novel of any description. I have since learned that many people with late-diagnosed ADHD have had a similar experience.

The discipline of sitting still and committing to reading a chapter of a book was a challenge in itself. On rainy camping holidays, it would drive me mad to see my parents engrossed in the latest Georgette Heyer novel while I was desperate to run on the beach and didn't care that it was raining.

Due to her M.E., Katherine had found it ever more difficult to focus on printed words, so she asked me if I would like to read to her. I found a half-price paperback on a rack while queuing in the local post office that I bought purely in jest based on the title of *The Mum Who Had Enough* by Fiona Gibson.

I knew Katherine had read many in-depth novels and listened to audiobooks that were read by professional narrators and accomplished actors. I feared that she would soon become frustrated with my amateur efforts, and I would become embarrassed by my choice of a rather simplistic book and amateur reading skills.

I needn't have worried. Katherine loved the book and adored our bedtime reading. I was being relied on to complete the book, so there was no option to give up halfway through, and I enjoyed being a narrator as it fed my inner show-off and apparent neediness to please.

If I ever get confused about a book's plot or forget names, I will ask Katherine to remind me, and we often stop to discuss various alternative plotlines. We have since completed dozens of books, and it's opened up a whole new world of discovering favourite authors and contemporary titles. We have even managed to wade through the occasional dreary stinker without giving up and have created our own mini-book club.

There are times when ADHD has left me unaware of what I've actually said or done. People may be upset or offended and I have no idea why.

On a day trip to London with a group of work friends, I was 'off the lead,' being generally silly and larking around. Everyone was involved as we moved out of the tube station into a bustling Oxford Street the week before Christmas. I was excitedly walking ahead a few paces, thinking of the next funny comment or lark.

I felt a small random shower of liquid over the back of my neck and face. I assumed it was just a few spots of rain, but my friends had all stopped messing around and were now staring at me disapprovingly.

'What?' I have absolutely no idea, but I'm given judgemental looks by all. These are pre-Katherine days, so I have no guardian angel on hand to save me from myself.

'That poor man!' A female colleague exclaimed loudly with an exasperated tone.

'What poor man?' I reply, dumbfounded.

It seems I had been charging around and bashed into a homeless man knocking his drink out of his hand in the process. I didn't hear him swear or notice him chase after me; I only felt a gob of phlegm against my neck and the remains of his cold tea that he had thrown at me now trickling down the side of my face. I was oblivious to my apparent act of random violence and felt completely mortified.

The guy had spat at me, and it was far from a pleasant thing to do, but I was in the wrong. I tried to find the man to apologise and buy him another tea or give him some money, but he had disappeared back into the throng and was nowhere to be seen. My friends just tutted and moved on with cleared minds and made a joke about it, but my day was now effectively over as my sensitivity kept the incident spinning and replaying in my mind for several days.

I'll often rush to the front of a queue like a hyperactive child as I want to get there before the line gets any longer or someone barges in.

When I first started dating the emotional wasp, I had a misguided thought that men should always pay. So, on our trip to London, I bought the train and theatre tickets and then pushed in front of her to pay for the tube tickets. I hadn't realised I'd done anything wrong, but I was aware her mood was beginning to simmer, although I wasn't sure why. As we travelled further down the escalator to the platform, I leaned over to her, smiled then asked tentatively.

'Is everything OK?' I soon wished I hadn't.

'Let me pay my own fucking way, will you!' she snarled from the moving metal stair directly below me. 'I've already told you twice!'

The aggression in her voice and face was too much for me to deal with. It was about 11 am, and the show we booked started at 8 pm, but I was so shocked and taken aback by the hostile response I was unable to recover, remaining quiet, distant, and sulky for the rest of the day.

Am I too sensitive? Probably. It's rejection sensitive dysphoria. There is more about this condition in chapter six.

Even as a small child, there were often issues with my behaviour.

'How can we ever take you anywhere when you behave so badly?' scolded my father.

Our mealtimes could be torturous. My parents would insist that we sat up straight, held our knife and fork correctly, didn't talk with our mouths full and chewed every piece of food before swallowing. I would try and speak but couldn't get myself heard above my elder's voices. My sister always stood up for me, and her high-spirited efforts occasionally ended with being smacked and sent to her bedroom.

I'm adamant that when I have children, we won't have any such ridiculous Victorian-style rules; in fact, we aren't going to have any rules. Not surprisingly, this wasn't a successful piece of parenting on my part. Whenever we ate out, things were knocked over or spilt.

Katherine would become annoyed and embarrassed as I entered into my clown act.

'It's like having three children, not two!' She would scold.

I think she had a point. Although this not-uncommonly delivered comment often stung me, as I just wanted everyone to be happy.

Whenever asked to do something, I'm like a Greyhound fresh out of the traps. I have to do it there and then, or I will forget and the task simply won't get completed. Sometimes I will get unnecessarily agitated at the slowness of the instruction of what I am being requested to do.

Katherine had asked me a couple of times to clean the bathroom floor as she struggled with her mobility.

I'm told, 'It's OK. You don't have to do it now.' But, two days later, Katherine is on the bathroom floor cleaning the tiles.

'Sorry, Darling, I just forgot.' ADHD people are sometimes branded lazy, but things often just slip our minds.

'It's OK, it doesn't matter,' she replied, but it really did matter, and my mind burned with annoyance at my inability once more.

Why Me?

I'm often asked what caused my ADHD, and there are many answers, although none are conclusive. This may be because the condition is probably still in its infancy as far as serious research is concerned.

Most ADHD appears to be hereditary, although I don't remember my parents or grandparents having the condition.

When I was born, the cord was wrapped around my neck, and I was apparently a 'funny shade of blue.' It was only due to the skill of the midwife that I survived without serious incident or injury. There is a possible link between a lack of oxygen at birth and ADHD, although it's doubtful whether this was the cause in my case.

My mother suffered from epilepsy, which I understand can potentially be passed down to a child as ADHD. The two conditions are often found co-morbidly, particularly in children. The drugs given for epilepsy at the time were also thought to be a possible link.

Further Help and Guidance -

Carry a pad or notebook, or if, like me, your handwriting is illegible, have the notes app open on your phone handy.

Understand that the problem isn't your fault. It is a neurological condition, so please don't beat yourself up. I have learned since my diagnosis that acceptance is the key to a more settled life.

If you have a late-in-life diagnosis, try not to grieve for lost time. Instead, look forward, not back, and think of your diagnosis as a motivation for your plans.

It's difficult enough carrying ADHD with you, but if the people in your life are disapproving or putting you down, it can be worse, so wherever possible, surround yourself with those who appreciate, accept and love you for who you are.

Remember, you are clever, not stupid, but you do have ADHD, and being different from others should be celebrated, not hidden or something to be ashamed of. Eat well, exercise and be kind to yourself.

The website www.theadhdfoundation.org.uk is a source of excellent information and support.

CHAPTER TEN

Your Troubles Aren't Always Out of Reach On The Beach

Family members now insist I go through a pre-sea entry check
of emptying every pocket.

———————

People with ADHD are known to continually lose or misplace their belongings. I lose things all the time. It usually doesn't cause too much concern, but today I have lost my two-year-old daughter on a crowded beach in Suffolk, resulting in an ice-cold electric shock of terror slicing through my brain and down my spine.

The atrocity of James Bulger's shocking abduction and murder had recently been in the news headlines. The horror of the story kept me, like many other parents, awake at night. The fear this incident invoked created a nationwide rush to buy child leads. A short plastic curly rope with a Velcro handcuff that could be attached to the wrist of a child and their accompanying parent.

In reality, one hasty tug either way and you were left with a piece of plastic minus a child.

I had been particularly vigilant that day, holding my youngest daughter close to me among the crowds. There was no way I would let her go, and I certainly didn't think I would need a child lead. But, somehow, I had lost my concentration, and she had vanished into the brightly coloured throng of beachgoers. I quickly found a wall with a higher vantage point to see if I could spot her, but it was like looking for the proverbial needle in a haystack. I frantically asked anyone I passed or bumped into if they had seen her. But, all I got in return was a disinterested shrug or a brief shake of their head, with others just staring right through me. By now, my brain was completely focused, even amidst the horror of the unfolding nightmare. ADHD minds are supposedly good in a crisis, as the thought process is so fast, and a solution can often be found extremely quickly. This situation was a true test of that particular theory.

I described what she looked like to anyone who would stop long enough to listen.

'Her name is Victoria, she has short light brown hair and is wearing a brightly coloured orange and yellow cotton dress with matching shoes, she is two years old!'

The panic rose in my voice with each person I asked. However, it was like describing any number of kids on the crowded beach dressed in bright colours that day. I was about to move on from yet another shaking head to the next person when a lady with an Italian accent shouted from the nearby ice cream stand.

'Sir! Sir! Your daughter!'

'Yes! Where? Have you seen her? Where?'

'I think she is maybe sitting on your shoulders.'

'What?' I replied, now stunned and confused.

She offered me a wry smile.

'A little girl is sitting on your shoulders.'

Vicky looked down at me with a bemused look on her face clutching onto her teddy with one hand and the sleeve of my t-shirt scrunched into the other. She was no doubt wondering what on earth was going on.

'Is that her?' continued the lady from the ice cream stall.

'Ah yes … thank you!' I'd forgotten I'd lifted her onto my shoulders for safekeeping.'

Thankfully I didn't lose Vicky that day but losing essential items on the beach became an unwanted speciality of mine through the years.

A perfect mid-summer day by the seaside was about to hit the rocks. I had lost our car keys somewhere on the wide sandy beach at Lowestoft. Katherine was still frantically trying to find them.

We had been through every bag numerous times and retraced our steps back to the ice cream van, the coffee shop, and the toilets. Much to my shame, our two small children, aged five and three, were helping with the search, furiously digging little holes with their tiny plastic spades. It was a big day in football, with the 1994 World Cup final due to kick off in an hour. I really wanted to be home in time for the match, but it's doubtful we will be there for kick-off as I knew exactly where the keys were but, at the same time, not exactly where they were. I had realised, with some horror, a full fifteen minutes ago but, as yet, hadn't found the courage to let my family know.

I had been rehearsing how I might break the news in the most tactful way possible.

When I was instructed to search a rubbish bin full to the brim with insect-infested ice cream wrappers, lolly sticks, snotty tissues, nappies, and poorly tied bags of dog poo, I finally cracked and decided to share my guilty secret.

'I've got some good news and some bad news,' I began.

'The good news is that I know where the keys are.'

'Hooray!' Exclaimed the girls, jumping up and down and waving their spades victoriously in the air.

'Really...' enquired Katherine, not quite yet managing a full smile '...where?'

There was a long pause while I was subjected to the gaze of three pairs of expectant eyes. Two sets were innocently hopeful they would soon be off the now chilly beach, but the third pair looked a little more concerned as the silence lingered on.

'Well, that's the bad news,' I eventually managed to share, 'they're in the sea.'

'You'd better be joking!' Katherine might as well have had steam coming from her ears, such was her rage.

I was immediately ordered back into the waves to find the keys. I knew it was an entirely futile act, but it would have been rather unwise and probably unsafe for me to deny the animated request from my wife in her current mood. The tide was retreating at a pace, with the keys presumably well on their way to the Hook of Holland by now.

The keys had, most probably, dropped out of my swim shorts a couple of hours earlier when I was throwing the ball into the waves and then diving into the foamy surf to make Peter Schmeichel-like saves as the ball bobbed back towards me at various speeds—just like any normal grown adult.

'They really need to make those Velcro fastenings on the pocket a bit wider or fit a zip.' I half-jokingly suggested trying to wriggle out of the blame as I broke the news the keys were not to be found.

'Or you could leave them in the bag!' came the not-unreasonable retort.

Public transport wasn't an option, and no one was able to rescue us late on a Sunday, so we had little choice but to spend a fortune on a taxi. The driver wouldn't allow me inside his vehicle with my wet sandy shorts resulting from the key search, but I had no dry clothes left to wear. Finally, Katherine reached into her bag and handed me a pair of her pink lycra cycling shorts that I forced my way into. It was my only option.

I sat in the passenger seat of the taxi. Katherine and the girls now squeezed into the back. Each time I turned around or looked in the mirror, hoping for a smile or a hint of forgiveness for putting Katherine through another, as yet undiagnosed, ADHD nightmare, I was met with a stony unforgiving stare as she tried to keep up her silent annoyance for the entire journey. Still, I'm sure I could see glimpses of the pretence in her eyes and the effort it took her not to crack and return my smile when she looked away.

As we arrived home, our neighbours looked up from their gardening duties and silenced their noisy mowers to say hello. I returned a hasty greeting and marched past. They seemed unperturbed as they observed me, resplendent in what was seemingly one of Katherine's pink undergarments, smashing a brick into our front door and climbing through to locate the spare keys. My young daughters were apparently already familiar with our erratic lifestyle. They took proceedings in their stride, rushing upstairs to find their noisy McDonald's Happy Meal World Cup toys for the match and didn't understand why I had to travel back to Lowestoft.

I was really hoping to change out of the uncomfortable pink lycra shorts for my return journey to the coast as they weren't designed for men and certainly didn't leave much to the imagination. In addition to that, the chafing had become somewhat uncomfortable. But Katherine still appeared livid and wouldn't allow it.

'No, the taxi is waiting, the meter is running, go now!'

Further argument was still seemingly foolish as I was virtually shoved out of the house.

When I had taken a few steps towards the taxi, Katherine called after me.

'Tim! … I like your bum in those shorts.'

I was relieved to hear my wife's familiar laughter again as she closed what remained of the front door behind her.

Over the next decade, a wallet, a phone, and three additional sets of keys were lost on the beach or in the sea. We would have been stranded on one occasion, but Mary, my sister's partner, lent us her tiny Fiat to get back home. I had now added my mobile number to the key fob, which helped when they were found and handed in by someone searching the beach for treasure with a metal detector while, on another occasion, a friendly female PCSO, who often stopped to stroke Pebbles, knocked on the door.

'I think these are yours?'

Family members now insist I go through a pre-sea entry check of emptying every pocket.

On a cold winter's day, I had taken Pebbles for a long walk on a stretch of Norfolk beach between Overstrand and Cromer. There was rain in the air as we headed back, tired and hungry. Fortunately, I had her dinner in my car.

I felt into my pocket for the car keys but could only locate a hole where they had fallen through to become yet another victim of the tide.

I called a taxi company to pick up the spare keys from our house and bring them to me, but no one would be home until Vicky returned from school. She also had to find £60 from somewhere to pay for the taxi. Meanwhile, I had no money or food, but at least I could get the dog some water from the public toilets. Pebbles kept taking me back to the car as if she thought I couldn't locate it.

I decided to make the best of my time while waiting for the minicab and found a plastic bag floating around in the wind and filled it with litter from the beach. Passers-by seemed to assume I was homeless and probably searching for half-eaten sandwiches. Pebbles found some chips, so at least she was no longer starving. I had a tiny glimpse of how homeless people might feel, being rejected and judged by those who look the other way as they walked past me.

It's not the first time I've been given such dark looks. On a morning dog walk, I would often pick up litter and put it into the nearest bin while Pebbles would eat the remainder of the previous evening's takeaways dropped on the ground. One morning, I found two empty beer bottles, so I picked them up before they got smashed and took them to the bottle bank.

I was unshaven, wearing an unusual winter combination of shorts and an old coat walking with my dog holding empty beer bottles. Meanwhile, children were on their way to school. Some of them I vaguely recognised from Katherine's Brownie group and gave them a cheery hello.

At this point, I realised I was on the receiving end of some rather dark and disapproving looks from parents, with one even taking their child across the road to avoid the dodgy homeless-looking guy who was seemingly drinking beer from a bottle at 8.30 am.

My daughter had told the taxi driver that a man with a dog would be waiting for the keys in an empty car park in Overstrand. It was now pouring with rain and descending into something like the final scene from *Back to the Future 2*. I was relieved to finally get home that evening but proceeded to play a risky game for the coming months, as we now only had one set of keys, and the cost of replacing them was exorbitant.

Soon after and without any prompting, my car breakdown company offered me unlimited replacements for lost car and house keys, all for the special price of just £6 a year. Now that sounded like a bargain! However, I doubt they realised quite what they had let themselves in for.

CHAPTER ELEVEN

Put Your House On Brexit

'You won't let him do this will you, Mum?'

People with ADHD are known to enjoy taking risks, often without any apparent thought of the consequences.

I've tipped a week's wages into a fruit machine and tried to reclaim growing losses of failed 'certain' bets on football matches that quickly became a growing spiral of debt. So, I won't risk even a tiny flutter for a bit of fun as it isn't contusive with an addictive personality or my all-or-nothing outlook on life. I have now locked the door on the temptation of gambling and thrown away the key.

However, in the Spring of 2016, I planned to make a considerable amount of money very quickly.

It was a surefire way to pay off the remainder of our mortgage and probably have plenty of change to spare. I was genuinely excited by this idea and hopeful I would persuade Katherine too. This is the 'positive' side of ADHD, seeing an opportunity while others can't or won't take the risk. That's what I like to think, anyway.

The United Kingdom was about to vote on whether to remain in the European Union. I had absolutely no doubt that the residents of the UK would decide to stay put. I reasoned that it would be just like the Scottish independence referendum or the vote for a change in the election system that the Lib Dems failed to win.

I was certain the result would be a landslide in favour of remain. But to misquote Winston Churchill, 'A lie can get halfway around the world before the truth can get its pants on.'

I planned to find every penny we had, empty every bank account, max out every credit card, apply for further credit cards and max out those too, but the really big money will come by re-mortgaging the house. I had made some enquiries and it was possible.

I would then gamble our entire monetary existence on this 'surefire bet.'

The 2016 referendum is merely a formality. In early June, experts predicted the chances were 82% of remaining, and the betting prices were receding as the vote became more of a formality.

'This is literally a licence to print money,' I pleaded to Katherine with growing impatience. 'Every day we dither, the lower the amount we will win.'

'You need to think outside the box', I snapped. I was genuinely mystified and a little annoyed that she wouldn't agree. To my mind, this was a simple and perfect opportunity.

Katherine pointed out that we had overspent recently and had a mortgage, loans, and debts to pay. I'd also had a recent dip in income, but I wouldn't back down.

'Why are you always so negative? This will wipe away those debts.'

Both my daughters were also very sceptical and thought my idea bordered on lunacy.

I eventually made a concession to leave the mortgage but still max out the credit cards, but there was still too much negativity from the rest of the house.

'You won't let him do this, will you, Mum?' pleaded Vicky.

Throughout our relationship, Katherine will usually hop aboard my surfboard of crazy ideas and dreams, even in rough seas. She even agreed to invest a chunk of our pension in barrels of whisky! But there were too many rocks and sharks in this particular ocean for her and I grumpily backed down. The credit cards had also been removed from my wallet and hidden until June 24th at the earliest.

To prove my point and show my family what they would have won, I scraped together about £150 from somewhere and gambled it on the 'certainty' of remaining that would give a very modest amount in return. But, unfortunately, in my haste, I had inexplicably placed the bet on leaving the EU. I then had to spend considerable time contacting the betting company's customer services to change the bet again. If I hadn't, I realised I would have won about £500, but in the end, I lost £150.

However, in the grand scheme of things, it wasn't quite as bad as losing £150,000 and, with it, the house, everything inside and possibly even my marriage.

The following day while I drove my daughter to the airport for an early flight, we listened with growing horror to the Brexit results as they came in.

There was so much angst at the result in our household that opportunities for freedom of movement and work in Europe would now be flushed away for the sake of some false promises and fanciful dreams, so the fact that I almost compounded it by losing our family home was seemingly forgotten among the general woe.

I thought I had got away with it as I said goodnight and turned out the lights when I heard a familiar, softly scolding voice coming through the dark.

'Well, we still have a roof over our heads then! It's a good job you married me.'

CHAPTER TWELVE

You're An Embarrassment!

I've reached the point where I'm not certain what I will do next.

To celebrate our wedding anniversary, I booked tickets for *West Side Story* at The Theatre Royal in Norwich. The production was sold out on the actual day of our anniversary, so I booked a performance for the previous evening, September 11th, 2001.

This date is now etched in history and referred to worldwide as 9/11, the day terrorists flew two passenger airliners into the twin towers in New York and one into the Pentagon. Another crashed into some fields in Pennsylvania.

The shock waves of the tragic event still reverberate to this day.

Like most of the world, I had been glued to the TV and radio throughout the day, watching events unfold. The media coverage was wall to wall and it was also fascinating how the broadcasters were coping with this massive unexpected news story. Simon Mayo had recently swapped duties as a music DJ on BBC Radio 1 for a more serious role presenting rolling news on BBC Radio 5 Live. I doubt he expected such a baptism of fire, but he coped with it admirably while more seasoned journalists were seemingly overwhelmed by what was happening.

I was unsure whether a trip to the theatre was now appropriate, and I would much rather have sat in front of the news channel than go out for a jolly musical that evening. Katherine was also doubtful and had asked me several times if we should stay home, but I didn't want to let her down. We had paid for some decent tickets in the posh seats and had both been looking forward to a rare night out together, so I found some long trousers and we set off.

Once in our seats, the overture began and went on and on and on.

I've never had much patience with overtures since, as a small hyperactive child, attending my dad's amateur dramatics society operas. I couldn't work out why they didn't open the curtain. 'Be patient, will you!' my exasperated father begged me.

I would be aching for the interval so I could run up and down the aisle and eat sweets. Maybe an ADHD version of musicals could be produced '*sans ouverture?*'

Attending this performance on 9/11 was, of course, a mistake. I'd been affected, like many, by these horrific events, and I was in no mood for this musical. I wanted to be at home with my family, watching the news unfold. Katherine was also concerned as two of her cousins were New York cops that day.

Hopefully, this will be a short production—but it isn't.

The overture was never-ending. The thoughts were getting louder in my brain by the second, and keeping still in my seat became a real battle. My legs were bouncing around underneath my seat like an agitated Jimmy Connors waiting for an opponent to serve. Nearby seats were now starting to shake from the movement.

My thoughts persisted. 'Please get on with the show so we can go home…'

But the overture endures.

'La, La, La, La, La La America; La, La, La, La, La La America…'

'Ugh! Just get on with it! Get on with it! Just get on with it, will you!'

I believe the slang term 'shart' was popularised in the 2004 film *Along Came Polly* when a character in the movie 'followed through' when passing wind with the inevitable messy consequences.

I'm not sure what the exact word is when a thought escapes your brain and out of your mouth, but I fear this may have happened as several people in the adjoining rows and the steward standing by the nearby fire exit were giving collective death stares in my direction. There was plenty of accompanying tutting and shaking of heads.

I tried to pretend that I was not the guilty party, animatedly joining in with the mildly outraged theatregoers searching for the culprit, with *Mr Bean*-style tuts, my eyes searching for the phantom culprit. However, the attempt to lay blame elsewhere was futile as the house lights were still shining down, and Katherine had already outed me.

'Tim!'

Great! So now everyone knows my name too. Mental note to self, never do a bank job with Katherine.

'I knew we shouldn't have come,' my wife tersely informed me.

'Shh!' responded a man several rows in front, his neck twisted round 180 degrees like a demented eagle owl.

I was tempted to stand on my seat and shout to the growing number of affronted masses, 'Oh, just fuck off, will you!' but Katherine had my arm in a death grip with her fingernails digging straight into my wrist, and I was well aware of the damage they might cause, so I decided against any further affray.

The steward at the door continued staring at us, and I wondered if we would soon be asked to leave.

To date, I've never been thrown out of a football match, let alone a theatre, but I have had some issues with security on the Centre Court at Wimbledon.

To gain entry to the All England Club, I had stood, jumped and bounced around in a queue all day with Vicky under the hot sun. At the very moment we entered the grounds, the tennis stopped, and the rain set in for the rest of the day.

We then noticed the sign on a wall that stated, 'Strictly No Refunds.'

The roof on the Centre Court was closed, so at least there was some play going on-and those leaving for the day gladly gave up their tickets to others nearby so they could enjoy the Centre Court experience for a set or two. However, it seems this isn't actually allowed, and the tickets are meant to go back for re-sale, which involves yet another queue on the other side of the grounds.

ADHD and queuing are seldom happy bedfellows.

When we hurriedly approached a couple of departing spectators to request their tickets, a portly middle-aged steward dressed in an ill-fitting sea scout uniform jumped in and threatened to evict us with such force that it reduced Vicky to tears. A blind eye had been turned to the smarter, better-dressed people who were allowed to request tickets with no questions asked, but those weather-beaten plebs dressed in shorts and soggy rain macs were given short shrift.

The hours of queuing, the rain, the inverted snobbery, the selective bullying and now witnessing my daughter reduced to tears on what was meant to be a lovely day out was just too much. I followed the man as he stalked away in search of his next victim.

'Are you proud of yourself, reducing a young woman to tears?' I shouted, repeating the words three times. My voice grew angrier and louder than the last until I had not only his full attention but also that of a growing number of other would-be spectators, all ready for a sideshow in the absence of any tennis.

There is a point where we all snap. I hate confrontation, partly because when I lose my temper, I can really lose it. For someone with ADHD, my breaking point is actually quite high-unless it's a member of my family being upset and bullied. Then, the red mist will descend rather quickly.

I had reached the point where I wasn't sure what I would do next as the uncontrolled rage began to fizz in my brain like a shaken bottle of cola. Part of me actually enjoys the sensation of entering my 'out-of-control zone,' but another part of me also knows it can be dangerous and loathes it.

'Leave the area, or I will have you removed,' came the pompous reply.

'Come on then! Let's see if you can throw me out!' Was my instant retort.

The steward was a little taken aback. The man he had assumed was such a soft touch and easy to deal with had now become a slightly unhinged potential physical threat.

Fortunately, Vicky has inherited her mother's ability for de-escalating such episodes and having gathered herself once more. She grabbed my arm and said,

'Come on, Dad, let's get out of here.'

We had taken in our stride, being inadvertently stranded on the wrong side of fences and a horseback police cordon while a smoke bomb had been thrown in our direction at Portman Road prior to the play-off semi-final between Norwich City and their bitter rivals Ipswich Town. But, somehow, we were out of our comfort zone in the serene backdrop of the centre court at Wimbledon.

Whenever I lose my temper, blurt out something inappropriate or perhaps try for a cheap laugh, I'll often instantly regret it and the trouble it may cause, although when trouble does strike, it isn't always of my own making.

Close to an ancient university entrance in Cambridge, I moved aside to allow a man walking the same narrow pathway to get through. I expected a nod, a smile, or a thank you but realised a split second too late he meant harm as he craned his neck towards me and spat directly into my face. Was he angry, unhinged, on drugs or just didn't like my face? Who knows? But he continued past at an ever-increasing pace. I decided to follow him while thinking of some form of retribution. Should I approach him and ask him to apologise, drag him from behind onto the floor, or just hit him? I was once told that when you are attacked, you become the attacker, not the victim but perhaps that isn't always the wisest reaction. Judging from his behaviour, he was possibly dangerous. Could he pull a knife on me? If I did manage to floor him and he hit his head on a hard stone pathway, or I shoved him into some oncoming traffic, I would be the one spending time in jail.

After fifteen minutes, I stopped following him, calmed down and walked slowly back to the college where I was employed for the day. I'm annoyed at my cowardice and ashamed of being a victim. Wrong place, wrong time, there should be no such thing. I knew people at the university well enough to share my trauma. They were mostly sympathetic, but one individual told me with bravado how they would have performed a citizen's arrest.

Some years later, I recounted this tale to a self-defence instructor. I asked how I could defend myself against this kind of attack. A punch to the throat, maybe? But his reply was just to walk away, and if someone wants your wallet or phone, give it to them and leave the scene quickly. This allows everyone to get home safely. He then asked, 'Do you want to be happy and safe or proved right, get revenge, then someone gets badly hurt?' He advised that it is always better to get away in one piece without any physical violence, even if it leaves your pride shredded.

I've tried all kinds of classes over many years that I initially enjoyed, thinking this might be something I would be good at, for once, before rapidly losing interest or heart, usually because I couldn't remember a move, try too hard, then panic, doubt the validity of what I'm being taught or lose my concentration. I would misunderstand an instruction and hurt someone or be sent flying across the room. Learning the moves in Japanese and Korean as part of a class was never likely to be a winner for someone with ADHD.

Once back home, frustrated, annoyed and feeling stupid, the kit was hastily thrown into the loft and forgotten.

At a class learning knife self-defence, the instructor asked me to throw the knife back to him, which I did instantly and obediently from about five metres away.

There was an audible gasp from the rest of the class as the knife twisted and turned high through the air towards him, akin to a scene from *Crouching Tiger, Hidden Dragon*.

He made a drama of attempting to catch the weapon before it finally dropped to the floor in front of him, causing his cloak of calm demeanour to temporarily fail.

'I said don't throw the knife! Give it to me carefully. Handle first like everyone else does!'

'Sorry, I thought you asked me to throw it.' I replied. Unfortunately, I had missed the all-important 'don't' bit of the sentence. '...you almost caught it, though,' I continued, perhaps unwisely.

I'm not sure why he was so perplexed, as the 'blade' was only made of soft rubber.

In my late teenage years, I took a course in football refereeing and passed my level three exam. After that, I bought all the kit—whistles, cards; stopwatches; flags, and every other refereeing gadget on the market. Even back then, I would think to myself, 'What is the worst that can happen?' I couldn't have imagined it would be quite so awful.

During my first game as an official, I predictably lost concentration. I gave a goal that didn't go in, awarded a penalty that clearly wasn't a foul and refused another spot kick for a blatant handball. I then played less time in the second half than I had in the first. Not surprisingly, the players and, moreover, the parents of the junior football teams weren't impressed and didn't hold back in letting me know their feelings.

My first game as a referee was also my last and the kit was never used again.

Frustration and impatience in life are common traits of ADHD. Jobs, hobbies and often relationships. 'It's unbelievable you haven't gone off with other women,' said Katherine. It's the one area where I have managed to buck the trend.

'When you win the jackpot, why keep on playing?'
In reply Katherine just rolled her eyes.

The Wimbledon episode was perhaps karma, as I should have been thrown out along with Katherine the previous year. We had tickets for No. 1 Court, but late in the day, I had dragged my wife to Centre Court while a steward hurriedly let ticket holders through the gate as the players changed ends. So we briefly flashed our ground passes and dashed up the stairs and into the stands.

'Timmy, we shouldn't be doing this,' said Katherine, now rather concerned

'It's OK.' I assured her there were always plenty of spare seats available this late in the day.

Except for this day, there weren't any, not even one. The stairs were then secured with a purple cord by security, and we were left stranded, caught like rabbits in the headlights.

'Oh my God!' exclaimed Katherine in a panic.

Roger Federer was about to serve at the start of the third set. The umpire was now demanding stragglers, including us, to take our seats '...quickly, please.'

I was about to grab Katherine's hand and make a dash for the exit when the mirage of two spare seats appeared nearby, and we hastily dived into them. But, of course, they belonged to someone else who had probably nipped out for some strawberries and cream, so they would more than likely be returning any minute to reclaim their seats.

I quite enjoyed the jeopardy, although our heart rates would have made an interesting graph each time the players changed ends and

163

hordes of people were allowed back into the stands. 'This is them, they are coming our way... we're in trouble!' Katherine fretted each time someone came anywhere near us, but thankfully, they all walked past and sat elsewhere. Fortunately, Federer got the job done quickly, and Katherine gave a great sigh of relief as we left the scene. To see Federer at his pomp for a set was a sporting memory to treasure, even if we did risk being thrown out in disgrace.

The feeling of unease was similar on 9/11 at the Theatre Royal in Norwich as we both stayed frozen in our seats, wondering if we were about to be evicted.

Fortunately, the interminable overture ended, and the curtain rose to a sea of colour, with just enough light for me to see the look Katherine was giving me. I was obviously going to be in big trouble later.

During the interval, Katherine suggested we go home, but I never liked to leave early, so we stuck it out to the end. When we returned to the house, Katherine regaled the episode to our girls, who were still glued to the news channel.

'You won't believe what Dad did.'

But they can believe it quite easily. ADHD isn't a permanent get out of jail free card with a built-in excuse to do what you want, but I was often treated like an unknowing fool, subjected to tutting, rolled eyes and barbed comments, even from those close to me.

I continued to deny anything was wrong with me, and diagnosis was still decades away. In the meantime, there is seldom any attempt or understanding of my behaviour. Only a handful of people, and a Labrador, have ever seemed to fully accept me as I am.

I knew my behaviour could be silly and eccentric, although I was often viewed as an embarrassment. This would frustrate, humiliate and hurt me as I was forced to repress my feelings and actions almost daily, adding to the inner turmoil and resulting low moods.

CHAPTER THIRTEEN

Driven to Distraction

*'I expected him to get out of the car and cancel
the driving test there and then.'*

———————

How on earth does someone with ADHD pass their driving test? Well, I can recommend a rather agreeable route in the north of Scotland. However, there were quite a few bumps along the way before I eventually acquired the precious certificate of driving competence.

I had carefully brought my vehicle to a halt in the left-hand lane on the approach to a large roundabout in Rickmansworth. Abiding, at all times, the best I could to the laws of the road as written in the highway code. At that moment, there was an almighty crunch from behind as the car was shunted forward. My passenger shuddered and screwed up his eyes whilst I put on the hazard warning lights, engaged the handbrake, and turned off the engine. I exited the car only to be confronted by two rather 'tipsy' women alighting their Mini Cooper, which appeared to have rather ineffective brakes. My passenger addressed them before I could.

'This gentleman is on a Ministry of Transport driving examination.'

The two women in question failed to keep a straight face and dissolved into fits of laughter, that laughter soon joined by my own, quite hysterical accompaniment. However, the driving test examiner remained stony-faced and decided to bring an end to the proceedings. So my fifth driving test ended with the same result as the previous four, as he coldly informed me.

'I'm afraid you haven't reached the necessary driving standards required.'

I was rewarded with yet another certificate of failure.

My previous driving tests had involved varying degrees of misfortune. I'd misunderstood instructions or suddenly pulled out into heavy traffic. I have gone through more driving instructors than I have therapists. Yet, I could apparently drive perfectly well. I knew I should pass, but things usually went wrong on my test days but admittedly, not quite this badly. Driving instructors said they had nothing more to teach me other than to concentrate long enough to get around the test route. My failures became a laughing stock and a millstone around my neck, a stressful mountain of an issue to climb that seeped into my everyday life.

On some test days, I became so nervous and distracted I struggled to focus or even read the number plate correctly in order to prove that my eyesight was good enough. I was ready to give up, unable to deal with the endless failure, but I also desperately wanted my full driving licence. The emotional wasp scolded, 'Get on with it! you can't be a Womble all your life.' I guess I should thank her for the kick up the backside that kept me trying.

The towns for my tests were all different. Chertsey, Aldershot, Watford, Reading and Guildford. They may sound like part of an unlikely train route in the South East of England, but the next stop was to be in the north of Scotland, where I would attempt once more to finally lay the ghost of driving test failure to rest.

My instructor was local to the area and told me that people think it's easy to pass a driving test in that particular outpost of Scotland. However, many still fail because they get caught out by the ever-changing speed limits on the roads that lead into Ullapool. It was good advice, so I almost forgave him for his phone call on the very morning of my test to glibly advise that he had double booked me and I was on my own.

Fortunately, I had purchased an ancient lime green Vauxhall Viva for £150 the previous week, but it was starting to leak petrol. The examiner turned a blind eye to the state of the rusty heap and gingerly stepped into the passenger seat, whereupon the car instantly lurched down towards the pavement. I expected him to get out of the vehicle and cancel the driving test there and then, but instead, he said with a smile, 'OK, let's go.'

There was one very long hill the instructor had warned me of, which was 30mph for the entire stretch, one that led steeply down towards Loch Broom. It felt like it should be at least a 50mph limit, something every other driver on that road seemed to agree with as they repeatedly tailgated, flashed their headlights, or loudly hooted their car horn and, in one case, overtook me on a blind bend. Meanwhile, the examiner was delicately perched on his seat to stop the undercarriage from scraping on the road, willing me, it appeared, to keep to the correct speed.

We eventually reached the bottom of the hill and somehow got around the test route in one piece. Other than stalling the engine on my three-point turn, everything else was textbook, or so I thought, and after some brief consideration, so did the examiner. With a broad smile, he informed me.

'That is the end of your driving test, and you will be pleased to know you have passed.'

I was so excited that I immediately wrote out the form for my full driving licence. The emotional wasp said my writing on the form was so bad it probably wouldn't even reach the destination. But it did.

Passing my driving test was a load off my mind. I subsequently got an avalanche of cards from relatives who were as relieved as I was. The whole thing had been on my mind for years and had a sapping effect on my confidence, from being the butt of their many jokes. I continued to have stress-filled dreams for many years after, waking up in a cold sweat and believing I had failed yet again.

Although, there were probably times, as you will read later in chapter eighteen, when it may have been better for the safety of other road users if I hadn't passed at all.

CHAPTER FOURTEEN

Walking The Line

I really wanted to scream at them. 'Get out of my fucking way!'

———————

An everyday activity that most people can easily manage, especially British people, is the ability to queue politely. However, to those with ADHD, queuing is not such an easy task. For me, it can feel like an electric current is running through my body, internally screaming and shouting with every imaginable expletive, fantasising about some form of physical retribution to the person at the front of the queue who is taking forever to pay. To a normal person, of course, everything is just fine.

As a child, I remember hopping and spinning around in a Post Office queue and being told on more than one occasion to 'Bloody well, stop it and stand still!' usually by random old people in front of me.

It didn't get much better in my teens. My mother asked me to help her shop in a large supermarket. I snatched the grocery list from her grasp and instructed her to stand at the checkout counter while I speedily grabbed everything from the list. The plan was for me to arrive simultaneously with the shopping at the very moment my mum was at the front of the queue and ready to pay. That was the plan, anyway.

'I think I'll do the shopping on my own next time' were her thoughts on my queue avoidance as we made our way out of the store, with very few items on the list having made their way into her bag.

The queues at the Bayeux Tapestry exhibition also proved too much for me. While others studied every exhibit in detail, I put Vicky on my shoulders and gave her a camera with the instruction to take photos. We ran, giggling, through the masses of people as flashes from the 35mm camera went off from above my shoulders. We finally made it to the exit door and the highlight of the tour, namely the gift shop, to be met with a large red sign in English that stated.

'No Running, No Carrying Children, No Flash Photography.'

They really should place that sign at the entrance, not the exit.

Decades later, following a fraught work meeting in Suffolk, I journeyed to Southwold on the promise of some 'me time.' I intended to go for a long run but only got through a mile before my knees started to protest.

The autumn weather was still warm, and I tried some mindfulness by taking in the sound and sight of the waves, but I'm often hopeless at being able to relax and struggle to master any kind of meditation as my brain span around like a fruit machine.

I had already made a string of stupid decisions that day by parking at the furthest possible point from the town and wearing shoes without insoles resulting in blisters. I had also jumped onto an inviting stretch of beach right next to the 'Danger! No Access To The Beach' sign. I couldn't reach a suitable pathway from the forbidden beach, so I was forced to walk on the shingle with the seawater around my ankles. I trudged towards the pier before climbing a wall behind some multi-coloured beach huts.

The fence rail above the wall was lower than expected, so I had scraped my knees and shins on the rugged cement surround resulting in two large grazes with blood seeping through and angrily offered up a torrent of foul language, for which I quickly apologised to a very nice young family who were just out of sight, relaxing in their beach hut. They politely lied to me, insisting they didn't hear a thing.

My mind was now rather agitated. I had left my phone in the car, and I was concerned about potential missed calls and emails. My shoes were still sloshing with seawater as I yomped past the pier to the busier part of the resort, determined to get a boost from a caffeine and sugar rush. There were four tea shops in different parts of the esplanade, all with various post-Covid lockdown control measures with which very few seemed to comply. My own family members are at high risk if they catch the virus, and despite my ADHD, I'm always careful with distance, masks, gels and hygiene.

There was an unexpectedly long queue at the first kiosk, so instead of waiting, I walked to the next cafe, where I was confronted with a slightly longer queue. I strode on to the next one, but the queue was still too much for me to deal with. This ridiculous pattern of behaviour continued for a full frustrating self-inflicted twenty minutes. I wanted to push in at the next place on the grounds that I'd actually been waiting longer than anyone else.

I'm told they have a fast-track system to help people with ADHD at theme parks in parts of America. So perhaps a treadmill queuing option would be a good invention for those that can't stand still.

I could see from a distance there was no longer anyone waiting at the tea bar next to the pier, about a hundred metres ahead of me, so I upped my fast walking into an urgent jog. As the kiosk came into focus, there was still no one there, and now running, I searched anxiously around for any rivals who might pip me to the post. It looked clear, so I dropped my pace a little while deciding what I might choose to drink. At the very moment I arrived at the counter, a middle-aged couple appeared from nowhere and reached out in front of me towards the counter.

I really wanted to scream at them. 'Get out of my fucking way!' But instead, I stepped back, smiled and politely said, '…after you.'

With just two customers ahead of me, I decided to stand and wait, but one of the cafe employees had gone for their break, and the young woman left serving on her own was moving so slowly it appeared *rigor mortis* might set in. If I had someone with me, I would stay and queue for their sake, but I was now bouncing on my toes while giving myself a pep talk to stop and wait. I breathed in deeply and tried to focus, visualising that Katherine was with me. I wondered what she would say to keep me in the queue? Perhaps something along the lines of,

'Tim! Don't be stupid! There are only two people in front of you. Stand still and wait.'

The people I had politely let in front of me took an age to read the blackboard menu and, after some deliberation, ordered a decaf americano and a latte with toasted coconut. This is Southwold, after all!

I tried to convince myself that it wouldn't take long, but it did. As my impatience grew, I visualised putting the man in a stranglehold and had to stop myself from jumping through the kiosk window to help the woman serving to move just a little faster. Finally, with an audible groan, I gave in to my frustration, left the queue, and lurched twenty yards away before managing to halt, berate myself and turn back towards the kiosk, by which time three more people had speedily joined the others waiting in line. I swore loudly and stomped away.

Eventually, I found the boating lake tea shop where there was no one waiting. When I was asked by the lady serving behind the counter where I was going to sit, I literally could not make up my mind. It was both frustrating and embarrassing.

My symptoms had recently deteriorated. This was probably because I had started taking the ADHD drug atomoxetine, which resulted in some difficult side effects. Within a short time, I had stopped taking them, but my brain was left feeling rather bruised at having been messed around with once again.

I found a seat and waited for my drink to arrive, I really wanted to check my emails, but my car and, therefore, my phone were still too far away for me to quickly nip back and retrieve as I would probably miss the person delivering my tea tray. The order took much longer to arrive than expected to the point where I was prepared to get up and leave without receiving the expensive scone and cup of tea. Finally, I decided to cut my losses and head home. 'Me time' isn't always fun time with ADHD, as I proved once more how useless I can be while on my own and looking after myself.

Not being in control of a situation on the road can be challenging for someone with ADHD to deal with, so a hold-up, a traffic jam, or a lengthy queue for petrol can be almost unbearable. I've heard it likened to a form of claustrophobia. Trapped in a queue with no way out or ability to leave the situation.

'Fuel' if you think it's over.

The Prime Minister of the day, Boris Johnson, has instructed the residents of the United Kingdom not to panic-buy petrol, but as we are seemingly a nation of fools, there is indeed a surge of panic buying, and a week of forecourt chaos ensues.

I had already decided I would not join in with this nonsense and had driven past a small queue of just three cars on the first day of the crisis—big mistake! There was soon no fuel to be had anywhere, and queues for the occasional delivery stretched on forever. Things became so fraught that police officers were called to petrol forecourts to keep the peace.

Within a week, I had just a thimbleful of diesel left in my tank, but I also had an urgent meeting with a client in the Midlands. In order to refuel, I dragged myself out of bed at 6 am and walked to the nearest petrol station, where the manager, whom I am on nodding terms with, told me in a hushed voice that a delivery was arriving at 9 am. I rushed home and, at the allotted time, returned to the growing queue that had already stretched to more than fifty vehicles. The garage didn't want everyone to immediately know they had re-opened with the potential chaos that would ensue, so the bright red lights that displayed the ever-increasing price per litre were left blacked out. This caused a woman in a convertible driving very slowly in the opposite direction to troll every driver in the queue, informing them that the garage was still closed and they should stop blocking the road. At least half of the people complied with her deception, but thanks to my earlier inside information, I stayed where I was and, for once, patiently waited my turn, although the cost of refuelling approached £100.

The thought of an endless queue for diesel almost resulted in a knee-jerk decision to buy an electric car, but there was now seemingly a very long waiting list to buy these too.

CHAPTER FIFTEEN

Let's See If That Is A Pointless Answer?

The presenters don't usually laugh at the contestants,
but they did that day

———————

Pointless is a popular tea-time quiz show that is broadcast on the BBC. Vicky is a huge fan of the programme, so she applied for us to appear as contestants, and within a few months, we were at the studios, ready to record our two episodes.

Multiple recordings are made during the day, so contestants may be required to wait around for several hours before being called. We were told that we must stay in the green room for the entire time but, not surprisingly, decided to escape and completed an entire loop of the doughnut-shaped television centre, during which we found the comedian Jon Culshaw wandering around rehearsing his various impersonations of *Dr Who*.

I can never be sure of much on these occasions, but I know from a lifetime's experience, no matter how much I practice or rehearse, that I will make an idiot of myself or mess up. This is not a negative thought, it is simply a fact, maybe from a childhood filled with disapproval. On the few occasions I have done something well, it is usually after a scorched earth first attempt.

We are contracted to record two episodes. If we don't complete them both, it will completely mess up the continuity of the broadcasts. In the first show, we successfully navigated the opening round and were told to stay silent while they changed the set. I couldn't stay quiet, and at this point, even Vicky lost patience with me. Later, I asked for a drink of water and promptly spilt it down my trousers.

The recording came to an abrupt halt while I was marched to the presenters changing room, where I was subjected to five minutes of a high-powered hair drier directly onto my wet groin.

I had already annoyed the production team by taking photographs during our rehearsal, having missed the strict 'No Photography' sign. On my return, I smiled and then made an ill-judged comment to lighten the mood. This was only met with tuts from the audience and death stares from those on stage.

In the second round, I was asked by co-presenter Alexander Armstrong to name any Daniel Day-Lewis film. But I have no idea who he is. So I considered making up a fictitious answer, such as *Then There Were None* or *Midnight Cowboy,* as even though I knew they would be wrong, I probably wouldn't be ridiculed. Still, I wondered if he did a voice-over for an animation film, so I decided to take the risk.

'Pocahontas.' I finally answered.

The presenters don't usually laugh at the contestants, but they did on this occasion, as did most of the audience and our opponents. I was laughed at and ridiculed, so everyone had their revenge on the idiot incapable of even drinking a glass of water. We were duly dumped out of the quiz, having had a total nightmare in round two, and considered escaping the building before our second performance but couldn't find a suitable exit. Fortunately, we had more success in the second show and actually won the whole thing, receiving little glass trophies but, alas, not the financial jackpot. We recognised everyone from the green room when the shows were finally aired. Frustratingly, if we had appeared on the previous show or the one immediately after, we would have known the *Pointless* answers required to win several thousand pounds.

I was stopped in the street for many weeks after the quiz was shown on BBC1, referencing in particular, the first programme when I gave that ridiculous answer to the question about Daniel Day-Lewis, which resulted in the all too regular scoff of, 'Pocahontas!' What were you thinking?' Social media was similarly unrelenting.

'Make sure you watch tomorrow's episode', I would reply, knowing there would be at least some redemption to be had.

During this time, my obsession with running led to an Achilles tendon injury. It even hurt to walk, and any form of exercise, often the best natural remedy for my mental health, wasn't currently available. My injury was so bad that I could barely take my elderly dog for a walk.

Pebbles was also unwell, and now it seemed she was incontinent too. I had already been advised that her time was up, but I had refused to accept it. Her condition was sometimes so bad that it was difficult to know when something had 'dropped' from her backside or not. I knew I would have to make the difficult decision soon so she didn't suffer anymore, and my brain was in constant turmoil.

I was jolted out of the doldrums by a woman screaming at me from her gas-guzzling diesel estate with two kids in ill-fitting 'Tweedledee and Tweedledum' school uniforms, smirking from the back seat.

'Oi! Are you going to pick that up?' Her shout was so loud the people in a nearby bus queue literally jumped in shocked unison. I managed a mumbled apology in reply. I know it was irresponsible, but I just didn't see it, and I should have done better. I feared the rejection sensitive dysphoria would set in, so I tried to erase the episode from my mind and decided not to mention it to anyone.

However, on my return home, I found my name was all over local social media for not picking up Pebbles pile of poo. I knew I was in the wrong, but this woman was a rabid troll. I managed to stay calm, and it helped that a large majority of the growing online mob understood and appeared to take my side. Seemingly defeated, the troll moved to another social media site to stir things up further. Fortunately, my daughter followed to destroy her exaggerated tale once more.

I will always try to forgive, forget and move on, but it isn't that easy with an ADHD mindset, and I still occasionally find myself dreaming of a suitable form of retribution—involving dog poo!

A couple of weeks later, I spotted another woman heading towards Pebbles and me. I can hear her shouting but can't make out the words. I feared she was another dog poo vigilante. I felt victimised as I would always make a point of clearing up dog mess that other pet owners fail to pick up on a daily basis. I would often remove rubbish and bottles and regularly clear up junk from various Norfolk beaches to stop the sea from becoming polluted and causing harm to wildlife. I wonder how many of these self-righteous keyboard warriors have ever done this?

A few years earlier, I would have said, 'Let's go, Pebbles!' and we would have broken into a run and disappeared over the horizon to avoid the conflict. But my dog is old and riddled with arthritis, and I can barely walk due to my Achilles injury.

Finally, the now exhausted lady caught up with us, panting more than Pebbles with the effort. I steadied my brain for the conflict and the damage it would cause to my mental health. Whenever I have a clash, it usually stays with me for days. I smiled and took a deep breath. I'll either roll over and apologise for whatever apparent misdemeanour I'm guilty of or will tell her to get lost.

'I need you to settle an argument I'm having with my husband,' the breathless woman ordered.

'What is that?' I replied, still fearing the worst,

'Were you, or were you not on *Pointless*?'

Much to her joy, I confirmed that I was. 'Yes!' She exclaimed triumphantly and with that, turned and strode happily away.

CHAPTER SIXTEEN

ADHD On The Radio

As he got closer, I realised with horror
that I had completely forgotten his name

Broadcasting wouldn't be the first career that jumps to mind for someone with ADHD, but there are many highly accomplished and successful broadcasters with the disorder.

As a young child, the big annual Christmas film was meant as a treat for our family, one for us to sit down and enjoy together. *The Great Escape, Oliver!* a James Bond film or whatever that year's TV blockbuster might have been. However, for me sitting in the smoke-filled room felt like a form of torture. I would continually walk in and out of the room, annoying everyone, especially my dad, who'd shout, 'Sit still, Timmy!' I would then search out an old transistor radio, go to my room and tune through the various radio stations from far and wide.

I liked the radio as you could move around and do stuff at the same time as you listened and never had to sit still.

I told my careers teacher that my dream job was to work on the radio and I wanted to be a DJ. He responded by advising me the electrical hire company Radio Rentals were looking for Saturday staff. This was about as much help as anyone got from their careers advisor in the 1970s.

As a teenager, I decorated two entire walls of my bedroom with rejection letters from virtually every radio station in the UK. Some were personally handwritten or typed, while others were just a photocopied scrawl. I even received rejected demo tapes from other wannabe DJs that were returned to the wrong address.

Today those hoping to get into broadcasting rarely even receive a reply, although I doubt whether there are enough radio stations left in existence to cover a bedroom wall.

While I was still waiting to be discovered, I volunteered for hospital radio in Ascot. Prior to each broadcast, DJs would visit the various wards and chat with the patients to get their record requests before returning to the studio and playing their favourite tunes.

In the maternity ward, a young woman asked for anything gentle for the baby she had just lost in childbirth. She then asked me to sit and talk and we chatted for some time. I just wanted to hold her hand, stay with her and somehow, in some small way, make things just a little more bearable. Her ability to elocute the depth of sadness at that time and the total admiration of her strength and bravery have never left me. This was also the moment I fully understood when you talk on the radio, you are talking directly to one person. Radio is the most personal and powerful medium of communication. It is also the best.

In the early 1980s, the local commercial station in Reading, Radio 210, offered me some unpaid work. I was asked to give post-match reports for Isthmian League side Wokingham Town FC for their away travels.

My brief was to give all the key match details in precisely one minute, but first, I had to find a working telephone box. In the dimly lit back streets of towns such as Walthamstow, Harrow, Bromley, Slough and Dagenham, this was a task in itself.

After the final whistle, I would immediately go to a pre-located phone box and stay there until the studio called me, wait for my cue then begin my report. This often resulted in a tetchy queue of people waiting outside. On one occasion, I was mid-way through my report when a man decided I had been in the phone box quite long enough and barged in, demanding that I hang up. In my panic, I held out my hand to stop him but only succeeded in face-palming him, and he staggered back through the open door. Unfortunately, as he did so, I dropped my barely legible notes in a puddle of stagnant smelly liquid that had been deposited on the phone box floor.

I now had to ad-lib as best I could, but it bore no recollection of the actual match, the details of which had now evaporated from my mind. I fear I may have even got the final score wrong. But, with my panicked fantasy report now complete, I hastily thanked the studio and pushed open the heavy iron door of the phone box, proceeding to outrun the disruptive guy, who was still recovering from his sore nose, and head back towards the floodlights that were still shining in the distance, providing a welcome, safe haven.

I fully expected to be fired by the radio station the next day, but no one appeared to notice and nothing was said. Was anyone even listening, I wondered?

I decided that I should confess to the head of sport that I had messed up and apologised, but he was quite upbeat about it. 'Good work Tim, most people would have hung up and pretended the line had gone down.' I hadn't realised that was an option! In reality, I wonder if they had anyone else lined up who would volunteer to file non-league reports from East London for no payment or safety money. It also ensured that the radio station kept its commitment to the local non-league sports scene. So, I was asked to carry on.

Having a live show on the first day of broadcasting on Future Radio in Norwich was a dream come true, and I always felt at home in the studio, a place where many others probably felt a degree of stress.

How can someone with ADHD present a three-hour radio show with multiple guests and features going on throughout? I've wondered this myself, but it seems those with ADHD often make good broadcast journalists, and as mentioned earlier, there are plenty of examples to be found. The speed of thought, multitasking, and asking questions that others might not dare to are all plus points. However, I couldn't always absorb a guest's answers as their words sometimes ricocheted off my brain like water from a dry sponge.

When broadcasting live from our mini stage during an outside broadcast at The Royal Norfolk Show, we had booked the BBC F1 presenter Jake Humphrey for an interview which he happily agreed to do, providing we agreed to include the Break charity he was a patron of. I was told, '…he can come over right now,' so I was instructed to keep the microphone open and verbally tread water for a minute or so.

As he approached, I realised with horror that I had completely forgotten his name. There was no option to ask anyone as the microphone was live, so I frantically wrote scribbled messages to those around me asking, 'What is his name?' But only received blank looks in response.

Nausea rose in my stomach, and we handed him a microphone as people gathered around to watch. Although I started the sentence still with only the brick wall of embarrassment ahead, fortunately, by the time I had got to the end of 'Welcome our next guest…' my brain finally decided to re-boot from its nightmare freeze-and, just in the nick of time '…to the stage Jake Humphrey.'

It isn't the first or last time I would forget a name while live on air.

Later that day, two Norwich City football legends, Paul McVeigh and Iwan Roberts, were on stage with me. It was a perfect scene with the mobile radio studio behind us and a growing crowd in the foreground, all on a perfect summer's day. I spotted the official photographer at the back of the crowd and allowed my ego to imagine how good this photo might look on my office wall.

Later I was shown a close-up of the photographer's work that contained just Iwan Robert's face.

'Sorry Tim, I left the telephoto lens on.'

I was stopped near our studios in Norwich by a gentleman who advised me they had been enjoying a particularly in-depth film review on Radio 4. Then they heard me speak, so they immediately switched channels. I am still unsure as to whether this was a compliment.

Charles Clarke was the local MP and Home Secretary when he came in for a *Desert Island Discs* style show to play his favourite tunes and talk about his life.

Prior to his visit, there were plenty of jokes flying around, including his eclectic choice of tunes. Unfortunately, I mistakenly sent one of the less complimentary replies to his secretary and received a rather cold reply. 'I think you may have sent this in error!'

Oops! Fortunately, Charles saw the funny side.

The security in the country was very tight for politicians at that time following the 7/7 bombings, and I'd had a call from the Home Office Protection Unit telling me in a rather chilling voice that they would be

'...watching me the whole time.'

I wouldn't see them, but they could always see me. As a result, we did have some light-hearted off-air conversations on how a high-ranking government official might be 'taken out' while live on the radio. I am quite sure the security services were listening in but obviously didn't take our musings too seriously, as no SAS-style interruption was made.

A few years later, I invited the leader of the opposition into the studio during a visit to Norwich for an important by-election. David Cameron sent his gaggle of assistants armed with their high-tech Blackberry phones to list all the questions that I would ask, so he would have a decent answer and not be flummoxed, to which we obediently complied. But, once the red light came on, I simply forgot this was the agreement and proceeded to ask him a whole bunch of other questions he had no idea about. Our listeners had demanded to know what he would do about poachers and otters stealing fish from the local waterways. I asked him what he admired about Gordon Brown, and we then talked about his son, Ivan, who sadly had recently passed away. To his credit, he completely opened up more honestly and sincerely than I'd heard him at any point before or since.

The Blackberry-holding minions had now gone a weird shade of purple and had apparently been giving me the cutthroat gesture to curtail the interview for some time, but guess what? I hadn't noticed.

'God, that was brave,' the afternoon DJ said to me later.

I broke the news first that Doris Day had sadly passed away. It turned out to be a worldwide exclusive.

While covering the breakfast show for the regular holidaying presenter, a colleague called in with the sad news that the legendary singer had passed away.

Minds were quickly focused, and a hasty obituary was put together within a couple of minutes. This radio station was known for playing edgy music and giving Ed Sheeran his first break when he won the annual talent contest called 'The Next Big Thing.' Unfortunately, we could only find one Doris Day track. This was the not entirely appropriate Deadwood Stage, and proceeded to play it with the hope that we wouldn't be thrown into the car park by management for completely veering away from the station's typical musical sound.

Throughout the morning, I continued to announce her death and asked listeners for their memories of the singer. However, the story wasn't being covered in our national IRN news service, social media, or seemingly, anywhere else on the planet. So, did we have an exclusive? Apparently not. Ms Day was alive and well and continued to sing for several more years. I have never found out whether this was a deliberate 'stitch-up' or a genuine mistake, but either way, it's the one news story I definitely 'broke' first.

Alarmingly, this may not be my worst-ever radio faux pas.

The regional leader from the National Trust was making a rare on-air appearance and was rather unimpressed when I twice referred to him as the leader of the 'National Front', and yet another brain malfunction led to me ask the owner of an award-winning garden centre that had recently developed a new variety of clematis to describe her '...unique clitoris.'

I was offered a series of programmes playing show tunes on BBC local radio. However, this wasn't a genre of music I was particularly familiar with, but I gladly accepted the role. I then proceeded to do my homework and purchased a CD collection of '301 Showtunes' that I played continually on a long trip to Scotland driving my family almost mad in the process.

I've played a record twice in the same show multiple times and even the entire playlist for the next show that contained the DJ's carefully hand-picked specialist music. I was mortified, although he was more upset than angry, as it left him with nothing to play. I've also spilt hot drinks over the studio control desk at the BBC and local radio. I probably didn't see the sign 'No Food or Drink in the Studio'—I have ADHD.

I've forgotten to press the record button a few times on the mobile equipment when out in the field. Although, I have only been brave enough to admit it twice, the first with the local Norwich City FC newspaper reporter who threw a complete hissy fit and the other with Sir Bobby Robson, who smiled and said, 'No problem, son, let's start again.' He was probably the nicest and most interesting person I have interviewed, and he would have spent all day talking about his passion for football had we not been interrupted by his agent.

Another time I had the most powerful hour of content with a former professional footballer who had been on the brink of suicide with details so graphic, I wondered if we could even use it. However, this time it was the failure of the computer software that the radio station had recently installed rather than my pilot error that meant I listened back to an hour of silence.

As my growing depression rode along with the still unknown ADHD, I made a particularly ill-advised decision to record an interview with an elderly gentleman living with dementia. It was done with good intentions, and I was hoping to raise funds and awareness for their charity, but it was also a misjudgement. His wife was apoplectic with rage and a complaint was made against me.

The following week I took the station off the air.

I had lost interest and been going through the motions for months, finding it difficult to get motivated and bickering on air with regular contributors. However, on this particular day, I had a rather engaging guest talking about ghosts who inhabited Norwich—I used to get annoyed if people ever likened me to Alan Partridge, but now, I realise it was probably a compliment!

I played a record mid-way through the segment and then continued with the interview. But a problem had seemingly developed as everything now sounded rather strange in the studio. My guest's voice had become distant in my headphones and there was a weird echo when I spoke. Most alarmingly, the big red 'On Air' sign remained unlit. Something was clearly wrong, but as not to alarm my guest, I carried on without missing a beat. A few minutes later, the station manager barged into the live studio to ask if everything was OK as the emergency playlist was currently going out on air due to prolonged radio silence. I blamed the transmitter or some such nonsense, but in reality, I belatedly realised that I had simply forgotten to fade up the studio microphones. Finally, after so much silence, the transmitter kicked in and played some random music.

I decided to take an extended break and returned the following year to broadcast live from the new city centre studios, but I felt like a zombie and couldn't get my enthusiasm back. It probably showed with my ever worsening on-air performance.

When it got to the point that even Katherine was listening to Jeremy Vine rather than my show, it was obviously time for me to take a complete break from broadcasting.

It probably seemed like I was being difficult to management, but this wasn't the case at all. I was struggling badly with some mental health issues, and I had no idea why or how to deal with them.

Unsurprisingly no one really got it and why would they?

Some months later, I asked to return, but a new regime was in place. They wanted me to re-apply and attend a training course that I might have once written and presented myself. I really couldn't be bothered and took it as a sign that I was no longer valued or wanted.

I would love to return to the airwaves again one day as, despite the large number of cock-ups I've included in this chapter, I'm sure there must have been occasional moments of acceptable broadcasting amongst the dead air.

One morning I leapt out of bed and dashed out of the house. I had forgotten to post a package, and it had now become urgent to send.

I hadn't shaved, I was wearing a top with food stains on, my hair was a total mess and I probably smelled. The guy in front of me was moaning about the referee cheating Norwich City out of a goal the previous evening. When he had gone, I jokingly enquired to those around me,

'Is this where you come each week for some post-match counselling?'

A man stared at me and then announced rather loudly,

'I know that voice! You're Tim MacWilliam from Future Radio.' Others in the Post Office all looked up, and a cringingly awkward conversation began. I had actually left that radio station some months ago.

I look a mess even by my standards and could have done with a hole to fall into.

CHAPTER SEVENTEEN

ADHD and Social Media – Friend or Foe?

My ADHD has often hair triggered an instant response
to posts that I disagree with, sometimes quite aggressively,
and then I wonder why I have been 'unfriended.'

———————

A couple of local journalists with varying degrees of ego and self-importance became involved in a public spat regarding an insignificant local news issue. Neither would back down, and the public conflict rumbled on for some time, much to the amusement of message board voyeurs.

Many weeks later, one of the journalists who still seemingly couldn't bear to be wrong decided to keep the spat going with some rather unkind comments on a message board. A reply was made suggesting this was unnecessary and he should move on. Wise words that I felt should be rewarded with a click on the 'like' button.

The affronted ego not only took the time to find a list of people in the small print who dared to like this comment but proceeded to follow me on social media and take me to task for apparently siding with his opponent. He may have had a valid point on the initial topic but behaved like a fool by continuing to fan the flames of the disagreement.

I felt forced to agree with his view. I wish I hadn't caved in to keep the peace, but the alternative was to start my own lengthy spat over an argument that wasn't even mine. As a result, I felt compromised by this bully and my own self-worth diminished.

Although, If I hadn't wasted my time searching on a toxic message board, I wouldn't have noticed their simmering battle. But you should always be allowed the freedom to make comment without fear of retribution from a media bully. I was tempted to get further involved, but a walk outside cleared my head, and when I returned to my computer, I decided to leave the group completely.

If someone has this much of a fragile ego, it is probably best to avoid them and click 'unfollow.'

You don't have to have an opinion, and surely it is better to walk away than risk getting involved in an argument over something that, in the bigger picture, probably doesn't matter. After all, a thought is just a thought, not necessarily the truth.

Off The Ball City

I had recently been tipped off by a senior colleague at Soccer Sight who suggested that the football club were monitoring my social media posts. I was liable to lose my position as a match-day commentator for the blind and partially sighted if I continued to express anything controversial regarding Norwich City.

The club had recently changed their season ticket policy, and not everyone was particularly happy with the decision.

I simply tweeted, 'I predict a U-turn.'

I'm fairly sure the club didn't read my tweet and couldn't care less what I thought, but if you can't be trusted to comment on social media and your employer wants that much control, I think you need to question what the reasons are. In reality, this was more faux importance of a self-appointed supervisor over-egging their position than the football club playing 'Big Brother.'

As someone with ADHD, I'm liable to ping off a message without much thought, and I dislike unnecessary petty rules or being overly controlled. It is one of the reasons I took a step away from social media, but I would much rather quit a position than live without the freedom to express a view.

There is further jeopardy in doing things too fast and clicking on the wrong web page, such as when I searched for the source of a specific ADHD medication only to find the words had somehow appeared on the condolence page of a local resident who had recently passed away.

Of course, if we didn't have social media, we would all miss it, and there are numerous advantages to this modern-day phenomenon.

When French police told a pack of lies about Liverpool fans misbehaving at the Champions League final in 2022, the evidence of posted videos and photographs would show the reality of unnecessary police brutality and incompetence, resulting in formal apologies and changes being made to those in charge.

Social media can be life-saving, reunite lost relatives and find stolen pets, help to bring criminals to justice and be of massive value on matters that might otherwise be ignored. It is also a lifeline for less mobile people and gives a voice to those who might not otherwise have one. Yet it can also be horribly toxic and a massive time stealer from other, more important matters. As a result, I find social media easy to love and loathe in equal measure.

There is seemingly no subject that won't cause a row, fake or otherwise, and I wonder how long it would take, after logging on to a favourite social media platform, to become irritated, upset, or annoyed by a deliberately controversial message posted purely for a reaction.

It may be an abusive opinion, a provocative point of view to get people to 'bite' or from a narcissist who has millions of followers, an attempt to deliberately antagonise, a vile display of animal cruelty, or someone in the public eye who doesn't realise they are arguing with a 'bot.' Perhaps it's a piece of cut-and-paste misinformation or the football fans who never stop bickering.

I guess we are all guilty of showing off on social media to some extent but there is perhaps a point when this becomes more a need for attention seeking.

'Look at silly old me having a swim in the sea in January and doing a snow angel dressed in my bikini. I'm so crazy, aren't I?' all followed by numerous emojis.

A Facebook friend may post a photo of their perfect family on a beach in an apparently idyllic lifestyle, carefully given to deliver a pang of jealousy or a feeling of failure in others. But, of course, they may well be covering up for their own failings, and what is viewed online might be concealing a life of misery, but that is another story.

A colleague put a photo of her teenage daughter on Instagram proudly declaring how lovely she was and promised this photo had absolutely '…no filters.'

I have learned over time that irony doesn't travel well via the type written word, as I have been occasionally branded rude and arrogant following an intended self-deprecating comment that was taken literally.

Having seen the line-up for a Norwich City match at the start of a new season, I instantly pinged an intended jokey comment about the team's chances of success that year. But, unfortunately, the joke was misunderstood by some, and after the Canaries won the match in some style, I was ripped apart by the club's head of media on Facebook for all to see, duly receiving a large custard pie in my face.

Looking back now, I've posted nonsense, had arguments and many nasty spats where ADHD has hair triggered an instant response, and then I'm left to wonder why I have been 'unfriended.' I have seen first-hand the damage that overexposure to social media can do.

'Is there anything better than the first day of Goodwood?' one ex-Facebook friend posted.

'Yes! One where horses aren't going to needlessly die' was my instant, terse and probably unnecessary reply.

Our bitter public quarrel lasted for several days, with my prediction of dead horses sadly coming true. The feud ultimately descended into comparing a horse's death to the human rights of those building stadiums in Qatar for the World Cup and suggesting I shouldn't watch football in a stadium where people had died building them.

During the pandemic, there were acquaintances I had known for some time that I assumed to be entirely rational. However, they began posting bizarre messages suggesting Covid-19 was the fault of 5G masts and gave absurd conspiracies about Bill Gates controlling the world through the vaccine rollout. I know of people who refused a vaccine because they decided the opinions on social media were more reliable than science.

Conspiracy theories are not just confined to social media.

My radio show had a crisis. Every one of my guests had cancelled. This had never happened before, although I quite enjoyed riding the challenge of the situation.

While searching for anything newsworthy to fill the air time, I announced that it was the birthday of Neil Armstrong, the first man on the moon.

'Oh! You don't believe that do you?' snorted my producer into an open live microphone.

'Of course I do! I replied.

So began a particularly lively show full of conspiracy and counter-conspiracy theories from contributors and listeners. Alarmingly, by the end of our time on air, opinion was divided almost fifty-fifty.

It seems people will only believe what they want to believe in the 'post-truth' era.

In recent years, speech-based radio has become more driven by the style of social media. As a result, broadcasters are making their political position clear to the left or the right. One radio station employs hosts that swing from one extreme to the other, with just a three-minute news bulletin as a buffer between them.

I don't have a strict political allegiance, but it seems many do to the point where they would vote for a shop dummy provided it wore the correct colour of rosette. Unfortunately, we live in a time of name-calling, insults and slogans as a substitute for proper debate.

'Compassion for the conned and contempt for the conmen' is the regular mantra of James O'Brien, a well-known mid-morning radio presenter, and I'll admit that I share some of his opinions. But, if your viewpoint happens to be the extreme opposite, then, just along the radio dial, there are daily broadcasts just for you. It seems the public are less likely to want balance in their news these days, instead tuning in to whatever they want to hear and shouting 'fake news' at reports that contradict their own beliefs.

Whatever your political viewpoint, and even if you agree with the presenter and every caller, other than the occasional conspiracy theorist who can barely string a sentence together, the radio station of your choice may soon become an angry echo chamber. There is probably a limit before it might adversely and perhaps unknowingly affect your mental health.

The day after the Brexit result, I went on an ADHD fuelled social media rant. I was rewarded by a large photograph of a crying baby posted to my Facebook feed with the line, 'I love democracy until I don't get my own way, boo hoo!' My tormentor added a cheeky message that he would be allowed an Irish passport which meant his family would still get the freedom of movement throughout Europe. I considered so many replies that I would almost certainly have regretted and possibly resulted in having my account suspended, so instead I just unfriended him.

Mindless web browsing is clearly a modern-age problem and shouldn't be an escape from the real world or life goals. When I challenged a friend to stop reading the endless nonsense on their timeline as it was seemingly annoying them so much, they said that, in reality, they actually enjoyed it. If you realise that you are having fun beneath the annoyance, it's OK, but I wonder, at what point might it become a potentially unhealthy obsession?

Sometimes the most challenging thing is to say nothing at all. You don't have to have an opinion or feel compelled to agree while those around you are spewing out their opinionated nonsense, both online and in person.

Some well-known tweeters have a month off from their account; others get their partners to change passwords so they can't access their accounts over the weekend. They often report feeling better as a result.

It's tempting to follow the antagonists who are sexists or racist bigots or people who believe that the earth is flat and the Royal Family are lizards or that 5G is spreading Covid-19. However, when you decide to engage then it is wise to choose your battles carefully. It may be sensible to block, unfollow, or report a matter if the content is offensive or potentially harmful rather than enter an unnecessary toxic row that others may view and join in with.

If we find social media annoying, upsetting, or a time stealer, it is best reduced or avoided altogether so the ensuing arguments with 'bots and idiots' are avoided.

I think it was Richard Branson who said,

'The simple fact is that nobody ever learned anything by listening to themselves speak.'

One acquaintance of mine doesn't read the news or engage in anything political whatsoever.

She has never voted, didn't get involved in Brexit and doesn't have an opinion or seem to care. They view these issues as being out of their control. Her social media never expresses an opinion or asks you to sign a petition. Instead, it's pictures of the countryside, beach, or her running along the coast.

However, this seems to irritate and annoy other people who think she is derelict of her moral duties and seek to pick a fight. Compare this with the juxtaposition of someone who 'doom-scrolls' from the moment they wake, so they live with the anxiety and fear driven by too much misinformation, thus becoming concerned and angered by almost everything they read. I wonder which is the better way to live?

A friend once lamented that when he took his grandchildren for an exotic and expensive African safari, they spent more time playing games on their mobile phones than they did looking out for lions. I told him they should leave their phones at home, but he laughed out loud at my suggestion. However, I have found that having some enforced time without a mobile phone stuck in your hand is rather cathartic.

In September 2019, my ADHD had recently been diagnosed, and everything was starting to make sense. It was now obvious and a relief for those close to me to know there was a reason for the ups and downs they had endured for so long.

I booked a holiday in Rhodes to coincide with our wedding anniversary, and Katherine bought me a copy of the book *All Dogs Have ADHD* as a present.

Katherine's health had not been good recently, and it gave me a chance to focus all of my attention on her as we enjoyed a beautiful week together. I'm even let loose in guiding her wheelchair over the cobbled streets of our chosen sun-kissed Greek island.

On the last day of our holiday and while Katherine was resting, I enjoyed a run through the sprawling hotel complex intending to jog around the pool to the beach. There was a shady shortcut via a narrow outdoor corridor between the swimming pool, the closed bar, and a storeroom where I literally bumped into the woman in charge as she was busily stocking up before opening. I had seen her most days of our holiday, a rather formidable-looking Greek woman. She is quite overt and sociable and seemed to enjoy flirting with the younger, well-hung men in Speedos who frequented her bar for much of the day. I apologised for our near miss, smiled and then tried to run past, but she held up her arms to stop me from leaving the scene as there was clearly something else she wanted.

'You! You are an amazing man!'

I was completely stunned and said nothing, now regretting my chosen shortcut as she continued with a crazed smile while staring passionately into my eyes.

'A lovely man! I look at you every day,'

I was obviously in big trouble and started to weigh up my options for escape. I was certain she had seen me with Katherine and must realise that I am married. So, I wondered, what on earth was she playing at? There were plenty of younger better-looking guys available at this resort who would be more than happy to spend time with her long into the night and well into the following morning, so I had no idea why she would choose me.

This lady was quite feisty, and it had become a little disconcerting to have her animatedly stare into my face at close quarters, her toned arms wildly flapping and seemingly about to proposition me physically.

It felt somewhat reminiscent of the comedic television advert for Hai Karate aftershave that was last seen in the 1970s, featuring an infatuated woman driven wild by the scent of the male perfume where she jumps on a man wearing the product who, although a karate expert is still powerless to fend off her amorous advances. But all I smelled of was sun cream and sweat, and I wasn't laughing. I wondered if I would literally have to fight her off and what the correct etiquette was to deal with an over-amorous 'cougar' as I don't believe this was included in the self-defence class I attended, but if she goes for me, I might be able to restrain her. I'm pretty sure I could outrun her if only I could get past in one piece without the situation getting completely out of hand.

My other escape route was to simply jump into the pool that was right beside me and swim away, but it was being cleaned by one of those electric robot machines, busily hoovering up any remaining dirt from the corner of the deep end, plus I was wearing my expensive new running shoes that the pool chemicals would ruin. However, it looked to be the best option available for my safe escape.

I took a deep breath and projected my best incredulous and slightly annoyed tone that I hoped would convey an utterly disinterested attitude towards her while my heart pounded at the impending confrontation.

'Come on, seriously!' I finally managed to spit out. My arms were held out wide to keep the distance between us while I tried my best to hold her intense gaze but immediately failed to do so.

I was about to break into an emotional plea that I am married and love my wife, but before I could open my mouth again, she continued.

'Yes, seriously! I watch you every day!'

Her arms were still whirling in circles.

'The way you look after your wife, it's amazing! The way you care for her. Oh! and how you protect her!' She exclaimed.

'Every day, you find the perfect place for her by the pool. You are always by her side. You make her happy, I see you, you love her!'

'Oh…' is all I could manage to say, somewhat relieved I had avoided a potentially awkward bout of submission wrestling, but she continued without pausing for breath.

'Every day, you go through all the ice creams to find one without gluten. Then, when she goes into the pool, you help her into the water and swim just behind in case she drowns. Every man should be like you!'

She had become slightly emotional by this point, proceeded to pick up a crate of beer and quickly disappeared behind the closed bar shutters.

I was tempted to go back and get my phone with the audio recording app and ask her to repeat what she had said, as absolutely no one would ever believe me.

However, I had left my phone in the UK. On purpose too!

It is liberating to be away from the ball and chain of the constant unnecessary and irrelevant messages and the temptation to answer emails or worry about missed calls. Do we really need to send daily updates via social media or text colleagues at work?—No.

After the first couple of days, I'm always glad that I did. I don't miss the worry of losing my phone either and can concentrate fully on the present and the people I'm with, and probably have a better holiday as a result.

I'm asked why I don't take it with me and leave it switched off. The answer is that I would be tempted to use it and read work emails that I don't wish to know about.

I wonder if my friend's grandchildren will ever get another chance to see lions in the wild or go on safari again or whether the new high score on their mobile phone game will always be more important to them.

There are, of course, many plus sides to social media, and for most people, the positives outweigh any negatives.

But it's important to make technology work for you in a constructive way, like, for example—promoting a book about living with ADHD.

CHAPTER EIGHTEEN

Staying Out Of Jail

I grabbed the batteries from him and ran out of the shop, the alarm sounded once more, but this time I didn't stop.

Twenty-five per cent of all people currently in prison are thought to have undiagnosed ADHD. As yet, I've avoided arrest, but I have had a few near misses, and my life could easily have taken a wrong turn. My first experience of criminal life started when I was just eight years old and led my exasperated father to cry out loud.

'What if he becomes a Juvenile Delinquent?'

I could hear his raised and prosecuting voice from my upstairs bedroom, where I had been ordered to stay until further notice. My sister, as usual, was doing her best to give a case for the defence.

I had been caught red-handed, stealing a chocolate bar from the local corner shop.

I'd successfully stolen from the same shop on my way home from school the previous two days but had run out of luck on day three.

The first occasion was entirely accidental as I had absent-mindedly wandered out of the shop, engrossed in *Striker Magazine* and had simply forgotten to pay.

As no one had noticed my inadvertent theft, I wondered if I could repeat a similar act the next day, so I deftly placed a brightly coloured pink chocolate bar inside my school coat and promptly left the crime scene. This was so easy! I went to school and bragged about my exploits, telling those who would listen that I could steal anything anyone wanted. I even started taking orders. So, later that afternoon, I strode confidently into the shop with my list and reached for a Mars bar on the far side of the counter.

I couldn't have been more obvious had I worn an eye mask, a stripy top and carried a bag with 'swag' written on the side.

A shop assistant who vaguely knew my family stood before me, blocking my exit with her arms folded and a highly disapproving scowl on her face.

'Put it back, Tim.'

I hastily did as I was told and was instructed never to return to the shop ever again. I departed with her next command still ringing in my ears and audible to everyone in the shop.

'If you don't tell your mother what you've done, I will!'

I trudged home with the weight of the world on my shoulders and duly told my mum.

The shame and numbing horror of being caught stealing that day still occasionally haunts me, but perhaps it stopped me from becoming a career criminal. The only thing I had deliberately stolen was a pink chocolate bar priced at two and a half new pence, and I can confirm it tastes as bad as it sounds.

The crime wasn't to be easily forgiven or forgotten. Every shopkeeper on the parade seemed to know about my theft, including the butcher, who was the father of a classmate. This led to exaggerated news of my escapade rapidly spreading through the school. I imagine it was uncomfortable and embarrassing for my mother too. Whenever we entered nearby shops in the immediate aftermath of my theft, she was given disapproving looks, having apparently raised her son as a criminal.

It was many months later when my brother entered the same shop. By then, I had assumed the whole thing had been forgotten. But, it seemed from the moment he passed through the doorway that he was under suspicion and overheard the shopkeeper instructing, with some apparent venom.

'Keep your eye on him. He is going to nick something just like his little brother did.'

The first thing I knew was James angrily marching out of the shop and straight into my face to spew out his shamed anger. I realised even then it must be a real challenge being related to me, and I sometimes felt detached from everything and everyone around me.

In my teens, I was so desperate to complete my World Cup football sticker album I would spend my dinner money on packets of them only to be rewarded with ten stickers I already had. I took offence to wasting my money and felt conned. So, I felt almost entitled to occasionally pick up two packs of stickers and fool the elderly shopkeeper into assuming I only had one. I was eventually caught out and ordered from the shop. The owner, who my friend knew, pointed straight into my face advising those in the shop to 'Beware of him!' as if I was the evil character Damien from the horror film *The Omen*.

Now, many decades later, as an 'entirely honest' grey-haired adult, there are still issues to be negotiated when shopping.

Those with ADHD are often in a tearing hurry and don't always wait for a receipt. Unfortunately, this has almost proved costly a number of times.

On one occasion, I bought a couple of cheap T-shirts at a large supermarket. I didn't want a bag, so I headed for the exit, remembering, just in time, that I also needed to pick up a few groceries, so I quickly gathered those items together and went to the next available till. I was about to pay when I was asked if I was going to buy the T-shirts too. 'It's OK, I've already paid for these,' I replied.

I expected that to be the end of the matter and was taken aback when the cashier asked for a receipt, which, somewhat predictably, I could not find. A nearby store detective overheard, and a little too briskly entered the scene.

He was already giving me the 'Stay still and stay calm, sir' talk as I began to get a little annoyed by the thinly veiled accusation of shoplifting. So, I marched them over to the till, where I was served by the jolly lady with red hair just fifteen minutes earlier. However, she didn't remember me even though we had a laugh and a joke that I was wearing shorts in mid-winter.

I dropped everything onto the floor and searched for the receipt, but I couldn't find it. The security guard suggested we go upstairs to the office and discuss matters more formally. Instead, I requested they check the till roll, but this was refused. The guard now put his arm on my shoulder, that I forcibly pushed away.

Things were about to escalate significantly, and a small crowd had gathered, although they all pretended not to be looking. I manically checked my pockets once more, and with some relief, I found the crumpled receipt and the show was over.

On another occasion, my car required an urgent service, but the battery in the electronic key fob had gone flat, so I couldn't get into my vehicle. I had a hundred things to do and now this. I ran to a nearby supermarket to buy the tiny circular battery and, to make things quicker, used the automated till, refusing the offer of a receipt. However, there was some kind of barcode on the packaging that required removal. So, as I ran out of the shop, the alarm sounded, and I heard a security guard shouting from the other side of a brightly coloured cereal display for someone to stop and realised he meant me.

I considered running faster for the high jinks, but I thought better of it and returned.

'Can I see your receipt?' He asked flatly.

'No, I didn't get one.' I quickly replied

We returned inside, but I was in a hurry and ran ahead. Fortunately, no one else had yet been to the automated till, and we were greeted by the words 'Button Cell Battery £2.10' displayed on the screen.

'There!' I said triumphantly.

'I suggest you always get a receipt, sir,' the out-of-breath security guard informed me.

'Why do we have the option? How could I prove that I had bought the item without a receipt?' I replied rather crossly.

'That's nothing to do with me, sir.'

It appears that I should have scrubbed away the security code that sets off the alarm before leaving the store.

I grabbed the batteries from him and ran out of the shop, the alarm sounded once more, but this time I didn't stop.

For the sake of the problems ADHD might cause It's always worth the few seconds to get a receipt.

I don't like this particular supermarket and try to use a different store whenever I can.

However, it isn't always possible, especially as Katherine had already booked a Christmas delivery. After the food had been unpacked, I found the security tags had been left attached to the bottles of alcohol. This meant they could not be opened. Fortunately, my daughter found a YouTube clip on how to remove them.

The following month I dutifully returned the tags to the store.

Upon entering the shop, the alarms sounded and once again, I found myself face to face with the same perma-irritated security guard. I handed him the tags and tried to leave, but he blocked my exit as he wanted to know where I had got them from. 'They were left on bottles from a delivery a few weeks back,' I explained.

'We don't deliver from this store, sir,' he replied.

Clearly believing I was a returning shoplifter, he asked me to stand in a corner while he radioed the manager. I was made to feel like a thief rather than someone kind enough to return their property.

The manager duly confirmed that the tags were probably from his store, but as deliveries come from elsewhere, perhaps the alcohol 'might' have been stolen. I remarked that it would be rather stupid of a thief to steal alcohol and then return the security tags.

I was fed up with being made to feel like a fool, so I pushed past my two accusers and left the store with a ridiculous pang of unnecessary guilt gnawing away inside me. I was a little disappointed they didn't follow me outside as I would have felt somewhat justified in 'losing it' had they done so.

I decided I would most definitely never go there again!

Yet, I was forced through necessity to return back to that nightmare of a supermarket one last time, during the pandemic, for a 'click-and-collect shop.'

A rather elderly gentleman was parked next to me, but the spaces were narrow, and he proceeded to scrape his vehicle along the entire length of my car. He couldn't see or hear what had happened and didn't even realise there had been any damage.

There was no point in my causing a scene or an upset. I hate unnecessary conflict and reminded myself that I might get to his age and if I do, I hope someone will be as forgiving and understanding as I had just been.

Although, I am yet to meet anyone who agrees with this particular piece of forgiveness. Perhaps I'm not kind at all, just weak.

Dodging Bullets on the Beach

People with ADHD often have poor organisational skills and may go headlong into a project without proper planning, and that includes me.

Take, for example, a well-intended week on the Isle of Wight to raise money for charity that could easily have left me on a manslaughter charge.

In previous years I had walked along the East Anglian coastline and much of the South Coast without too much of a problem other than inadvertently venturing into an open prison wearing the same high-visibility clothing the inmates wore. Having a Labrador with me probably helped with my explanation and speedy release, although the guards declined my request for a charity donation.

The Isle of Wight walk looked a doddle, a case of circling the island's coastline on foot. However, it wouldn't be as straightforward as the map suggested, as some of the beaches and footpaths had recently become inaccessible due to coastal erosion that had changed the landscape.

I arrange these walks to raise money and awareness for those who suffer from M.E., a condition that has hit my family particularly hard and has little proper understanding, help, or funding. The money I raise will assist with important research and, one day I hope a potential cure. It's also an excuse for me to spend days walking on the beach and become an exhibitionist on the local media outlets who follow my exploits. As always, my golden Labrador, Pebbles, has joined me on the expedition, with various relatives coming and going during the week to assist or walk part of the route with me.

On the second day, as I walked along with my sister Alex and two of her children, we approached some large red flags with 'Strictly No Entry – MOD Property' and 'Live Ammunition Being Fired' warning signs.

To double back would add a further ten miles to our walk that we really couldn't afford, and besides, surely those signs weren't meant for us. The sound of bullets being fired was quite distant to our untrained ears, so we agreed to plough on through some rough terrain, but the further we went, the more trouble we found. It was only a mile of MOD land that we were required to negotiate, but I hadn't reckoned that the shallow stream we expected to hop across was, in fact, a deep and sizeable estuary.

We either had to dodge back through live bullets and boggy fields, losing an entire day of walking in the process, ending the day exactly where we had started, or we could swim across. Unfortunately, neither was a viable option.

Bizarrely a rescuer came into sight in the form of a man furiously rowing a small boat towards us, all the while shouting his displeasure in our direction. As he arrived on shore, we received a full-on lecture about health and safety. I declined to tell him about my line of business.

'They are firing live ammunition, for God's sake! What on earth are you thinking?'

With the situation becoming ever more desperate, I asked him if he would kindly take us across in his rowing boat to safety, but he refused 'point blank' and barked instructions that we should return the way we came and hope we wouldn't be caught trespassing—or shot presumably.

I produced a very soggy banknote from my coat pocket and enquired, 'What about if we gave you some money?' To which he readily agreed and suddenly became quite the charming tour guide. We were promptly taken across to the opposite bank, where we alighted straight into a mass of brambles and a steep muddy hillside, but at least we were no longer being shot at.

The next day things got even worse.

A communication mix-up led to me being trapped on a beach with my dog and two teenage children.

The exit stairs from the beach highlighted on the map had been washed away by high tides the previous month, so we continued our search for them in vain, assuming we had misread the chart. I had a vague idea the high tide was starting to ebb but, to be honest, wasn't completely sure as the water began lapping against our feet, with the occasional rogue wave now threatening to cover our ankles. I couldn't trust the tide, so I found a route away from the beach. But, immediately after we arrived on our apparently safe ledge twenty feet above the water, Vicky sank to her waist in mud and appeared to be in danger of going under. I managed to grab hold of her arm and somehow pulled her out. Unfortunately, it later transpired I had broken her arm in doing so.

I thought we could negotiate our way up to safety, but the sea mist had rolled in, and the climb had become impossible. The extra height had at least given me one bar on my mobile signal, so I phoned Katherine to request the coastguard be called, but she was one step ahead, and they were already on their way. Vicky, now suffering from hypothermia and in severe pain, was safely winched up the cliff while the rest of us were guided back for a walk of shame through the ever-thickening fog, retracing our footsteps back the two miles to safety. Fortunately, the RNLI were on a training exercise nearby and seemed quite happy to have a live incident to attend.

'If in doubt, always go back the way you came,' advised our guide. Why hadn't I thought of that?

Early the following day, I looked down at the vast sheer cliff edge to the narrow beach and realised we had been very fortunate to escape.

The shame for one young relative was too much, and he wanted nothing more to do with the shambolic project. I now wondered about quitting too, such was the overwhelming feeling of disgrace, but there was no escape as a local radio reporter had now doorstepped me for details of the charity walk but also to enquire about our near miss. They asked me rather pointedly how I felt about putting my young relatives and members of the RNLI at risk. My desire to become an exhibitionist on local media had come true. I guess I should be careful what I wish for.

We spent much of the night at the local hospital. The x-ray seemed to suggest a hairline fracture, but this was inconclusive. Vicky was told she would not be allowed to continue the walk or go bowling the following evening while she was in plaster, so she decided her arm probably wasn't broken after all, duly ripped off the itchy dressing and pronounced herself cured.

'That's really going to improve your mother's mood,' I laughed, ever the responsible parent.

I somehow managed to complete the walk on schedule, but this dreadful episode is often recounted at family gatherings as a jolly tale while I squirm with embarrassment, putting on a smile while dying inside, but still thankful we'd all, somehow, got off the island safely.

A Head-On Problem with the Law

It is thought that adults with ADHD have a higher risk of car accidents than those without the condition. I think of myself as a responsible and careful driver these days, but, as the following passage suggests, this wasn't always the case.

I had escaped my workplace for a few hours to take Katherine for her antenatal hospital appointment. Our second child was due any day, and I was really excited about becoming a dad again. However, en route to collect my wife, I had decided, rather stupidly, to make the journey a little more exciting.

I had stopped my Renault 11 two hundred meters from a humpback bridge on a quiet lane in the open Norfolk countryside and rewound the cassette tape to my favourite part of a tune, then put my foot down on the accelerator. I planned to get the full-on feeling of butterflies in my stomach as I flew over the bridge and the song boomed out from the car stereo.

There is never any traffic here, ever.

Except for this day when two other cars, nose to tail, loomed into focus on the very hump of the bridge. Brakes screeched as the vehicles moved in slow-motion horror. Then, finally, the red Nissan crashed into the back of a Mercedes that smashed straight into me.

The Nissan driver, understandably distraught, was stuck between the other two vehicles but somehow managed to force his way out of the car.

When the police arrived, they carried out some skid tests, after which they informed me that I would likely face prosecution. The message was given in a friendly but matter-of-fact way. Meanwhile, I could see people in the queue of traffic now forming behind the accident, I knew a number of them and would have appreciated a friendly face, but they all looked the other way.

Very fortunately, everyone walked away from the accident without a scratch. However, three cars were written off. I was given six penalty points, a heavy fine, and another fine for failing to update the address on my driving licence. It was yet another task I had put off or just forgotten to do.

When Katherine arrived at the scene, I apologised. There is now the realisation that I could have left her without a husband and our young child without a dad.

'And what about this one!' she replied, dramatically gesturing towards her heavily pregnant bump, having now missed a very important hospital appointment. Shame and stupidity engulfed me once more.

What the hell is wrong with me?

That weekend was my Birthday. James very kindly gave me a portable television and a comedy birthday card addressed to the 'Renault Wrecker.' Then, to further lighten the mood, he suggested we locate what remained of the car and syphon off any leftover petrol, to which I declined. Victoria was born eleven days later, fortunately, with both parents still on the planet.

Decades later, I took some advanced driving lessons. One lesson took place on the very same country lanes as my accident had. My instructor told me always to drive as if a mother pushing a pram or a horse rider were on the other side of a bend or a humpback bridge.

The thought of what might have happened that day still haunts me.

————————

Football Hooligan!

I've attended hundreds of football matches and, to date, have never been arrested or thrown out, having become quite adept at staying out of trouble even when it was all around me.

At one match and while still in my teens, hordes of Portsmouth fans jumped over the low cement wall of the South Bank terrace at the former home of Reading FC. They ran over towards the home supporters who had been forced into the Tilehurst End, at which point many of those around me started to run in fear for their safety. I had just turned fifteen years old. Standing with my friend, we were caught like rabbits in the headlights as we witnessed a scene similar to that from a movie where the enemy had launched a surprise attack.

If Michael Caine had been there, he might have advised, 'You zig and I'll zag.'

We decided to join the retreating stampede and run when the man next to us, in the style of a strict dog trainer, ordered us to 'Stay!' And then quickly continued to suggest the hooligans would run past us if we all stood together as they'd always chase the moving targets first. We had literally five seconds to decide before the pitch invasion reached its intended target, so we agreed to stay put. The angry mob duly ran past us just as our wise guardian had predicted, searching for those moving targets to kick and punch to the ground.

My friend that day, Paul still follows Reading home and away and is a regular at almost every England international match around the world.

When Russian ultras violently chased and attacked England fans during the 2016 European Championships, it was his turn to give the same risky instruction to 'Stay!'

Happily, he let me know the advice continued to hold up well. 'I always tell them, never run as it makes you a target.'

In the 21st century, it's not quite as necessary to have your wits about you at football matches, or so I thought.

Over forty years on from the Pompey pitch invasion during an end-of-season night match that was also being shown live on television, Norwich City scored a very late equaliser against Sheffield Wednesday with almost the last kick of the game. The goal virtually assured Norwich City's promotion to the Premier League and was possibly the most dramatic moment of an unimaginably exciting season at Carrow Road. Such was the drama, when the goal was scored via a spectacular free kick, one of my colleagues began to hyperventilate.

After the high-octane finale to the match, a few Wednesday fans who may have had one beer too many were pushing and shoving just outside the exit. There was a lot of shouting from a couple of huge lumbering guys dressed in blue and white striped shirts. Still, far scarier than the two men was their companion, a rather inebriated woman, screaming like a banshee and physically going for anyone in her way.

I'd survived all kinds of crowd trouble on packed terraces as a teenager throughout the 1970s and 80s, and this was nothing in comparison. I could easily have evaded the scuffles and then walked away, and I certainly should have done!

But instead, I decided to stay and watch events unfold. Better still, I thought I'd take a video as Vicky would no doubt find it amusing.

A few seconds later, I notice the banshee looking straight at me through the camera phone screen.

'He's fucking well filming us. Get him!'

'No, I'm not' was my instant retort, delivered with all the conviction of an athlete who had just been caught doping.

'Give me your phone!' she screamed before leading one of the huge lumbering guys towards me.

Fortunately, an even bigger police officer in a fluorescent jacket jumped in to shelter me. He quickly considered if I was part of the problem and whether I, therefore, needed arresting, decided against it, and then forcibly shoved me into the mass of Norwich fans heading towards the car park. I pulled up the hood on my coat and got out of there before the banshee or any of her mates could follow.

I was really hoping that didn't look quite as bad as it seemed and no one noticed, especially anyone I might know. Moments later, my phone rang. It was the Soccer Sight supervisor.

'Hey, Buddy.' His voice is as cheerful as ever.

'What on earth happened there? Are you OK?'

A fug of annoyance, shame and disbelief now descended upon me. I'd made yet another ridiculous error of judgement that could have resulted in potentially being badly beaten up and having my phone stolen.

It's another incident in my collection of awful memories that will forever make me cringe with embarrassment. I'm seemingly unable ever to learn my lesson.

But that is what living with ADHD can entail.

CHAPTER NINETEEN

Breaking Up Is Hard To Do

*'I had rocked the boat once too often and now
it was seemingly about to capsize'*

———————

Behavioural problems associated with ADHD can result in difficulties with relationships. You don't have to search very far to find anecdotes about how difficult it is to live with someone with ADHD. But imagine what it's like to be in a relationship with a person yet to be diagnosed with the condition, so there is no apparent rhyme or reason for their challenging behaviour.

Any marriage is likely to have its highs and lows, and the key to a decent relationship is communication, but after twenty years of living with Katherine, we had virtually stopped talking and become too immersed in our separate worlds. We are now just going through the motions of our marriage, wondering if this is how it will always be.

Neither of us could understand how or why it had come to be like this. We no longer talked and we seldom, if ever, dated. Even if we did laugh, it was rarely together. We hardly ever said goodnight to one another, let alone share any intimacy. I didn't say goodbye when she left for work, and when Katherine returned, I was apparently not interested in her day. My undiagnosed ADHD was causing ever more issues for her to deal with. I hated the way things had become, but, at the same time, I was doing nothing to help and was just hoping that the problem would somehow go away.

A rift such as this is seldom, if ever, entirely down to one person, and Katherine knew this too, but she still had no idea how to reach out to me. Yet, deep down, I realised it was mostly my fault for drifting along with home life while my mind was frequently elsewhere. We were both silently screaming and desperately willing the person we currently lived with to leave and the person we fell in love with and married to return.

Dealing with grief can be a particular struggle for those with ADHD, and it now appears that I hadn't fully come to terms with or grieved properly for my mother. Prior to the ADHD diagnosis, Katherine believed the bereavement had caused me to become depressed, but it wasn't something that I recognised and petulantly swiped away the notion. Meanwhile, I had thrown myself into a new project.

I had become heavily involved in a local radio station, something I'd always wanted to do but never dreamed I would have the opportunity to fulfil. I spent all my spare time preparing, presenting and producing shows. I was sometimes up all night texting other radio presenters, including single women who shared my passion for radio, but it was nothing more than that. However, I remained oblivious to how inappropriate this was or what Katherine might think.

I had spent decades as a one-man band running my own business. So, it was refreshing to work with a pool of enthused and talented people who shared my passion for radio. I'd been starved of this kind of interaction for so long and immersed myself fully into it. I was valued for my radio work and spent more time on this part of my life than anything else, including my family life, which started to suffer as a consequence. I never thought it would affect my relationship with Katherine, and I didn't seem bothered that it had.

My dad had done something quite similar after his own mother died. He didn't have ADHD, but he became obsessed with hobbies and other people that he believed needed him more than his own family, causing rifts that were never properly healed, and I seemingly hadn't learned from his mistake.

My radio projects also deflected the constant tide of stress I felt while running my business. It was another reason why I focused on a hobby that I misguidedly thought might, one day, be a new career.

I was asked if I would be interested in filing non-league football reports for a local commercial radio station. It would be quite a time-consuming project involving long-distance travel away at weekends. Katherine said she was happy for me to be achieving my dream but was somehow distant with her comment, the sorrow palpable behind her smile, and I knew the further damage it had the potential to cause.

I decided to turn down the work long before the offer fell through. The radio station was taken over by a larger organisation soon after and no longer exists. However, (spoiler alert) my marriage does.

At that time, I held an arrogant certainty that however difficult, distant, absent, or moody I became, there was absolutely no way Katherine would ever leave me as I, misguidedly, believed that she had more to lose than me. However, it seems she had been making tentative but detailed plans to leave me if things continued to deteriorate. Apparently, I would keep the dog, but the cat would stay with her. She had been looking for accommodation, including a nearby Buddhist centre to live. Do Buddhist centres take in cats? I wondered.

We continued to wade through the daily toxic household air for weeks. Katherine had the summer holidays away from her job at a nearby school, so she had no escape from the situation. One morning I found her sitting miserably alone in our conservatory and asked her, rather tersely, what was wrong.

People with ADHD have a self-destruct button. It's partly a kind of sick thrill to see how far you can push things before they break. Although I fully doubted we would ever confront our situation properly, so it came as a shock when Katherine requested that we do.

'I feel sick, we need to talk!' Katherine had tears in her eyes.

'Why?' was my childish reply.

Things simply had to change, but I continued to hold the absurd pretence that nothing was wrong. In reality, of course, I was acutely

215

aware of our growing problems. We finally agreed to talk but had to get out of the house to do so. 'Me and Dad are just going for a drive,' Katherine called out to our teenage girls, who remained oblivious to the potential upheaval they might soon have to endure, both on the sofa watching endless episodes of *Friends* or *Sabrina*.

My behaviour had been akin to continually challenging someone I viewed as weaker to a fight but never dreaming for a moment they'd agree to one. So, when they do finally run out of patience and square up to do battle, there is the realisation that I had completely underestimated their ability, and I was now very likely to get a pasting. They are past breaking point, so the option to apologise and back down no longer exists. I was told never to fight someone who is calm and silent while you are raging as they are coolly thinking of a plan to deal with you. I had rocked the boat once too often, and now it was seemingly about to capsize.

Katherine was the person I needed most by my side that day, but as I looked over, she sat in the opposite corner as my opponent.

The hairs stood up on the back of my neck at the magnitude of what may be about to happen.

My mind was now racing so fast, everything was a blur, and nothing useful was feeding back to me in return. It felt like a snowfall that actually contains unlimited brilliant colours, but the brain cannot cope with them all, so all you see is white.

We sat in our car, parked among acres of beautiful South Norfolk countryside that now, many years later, host hundreds of soulless, ugly houses, many of which are without a garden or even a parking space. We talked but didn't say much, the last thing either of us wanted was to separate, but I suggested it twice, almost choking on the words as I continued to play a nuclear game of *Russian Roulette* with our marriage. Katherine looked away and refused to respond both times.

It must have been really scary for Katherine, too. I was no longer by her side, a place I had always promised to be, and if I could somehow wade through the toxic sludge presently clogging my brain, it was where I wanted to be. But, I had pressed the ADHD self-destruct button and was seemingly about to drive her away.

Katherine's usual tactic in this situation would be to engage me in some kindergarten-level reverse psychology along the lines of, 'OK, If you don't want to talk and don't value me, then I'm leaving you.' She would find some bags to pack, make a coffee and read the paper while I was left flat on my back and floundering.

I would immediately come to my senses and jump on her like an emotionally needy Labrador and say something along the lines of,

'I'm sorry I was being stupid; my mind is all over the place at the moment. I just can't cope with life right now. Please don't go.'

Or the dam in my brain would have burst open, and I would dissolve into tears. Katherine would have instantly melted and found it impossible to resist the urge to reach out to me.

Although I'm assuming quite a bit here, would she still want me back once I was free from whatever demon was holding me down? There may be a chance that I had caused too much damage. Countless others would, no doubt, have headed to the solicitors and estate agent long ago to begin a new life, and the choice to re-kindle our marriage may no longer be mine to make, the opportunity to save the situation gone, and our world about to change forever.

But the stakes are seemingly too high for her to risk any reverse psychology today, and Katherine stayed deep in thought without saying a word.

Would we have reached the point of discussing a potential separation if I had an ADHD diagnosis years ago? I doubt it, and it's a crisis that may have been avoided if I had the correct help when it was first required. But now the undiagnosed symptoms had taken the form of a large marriage wrecking ball.

I'm not sure what would have happened if we had parted that day. Well, I think I do know and it is quite terrifying.

This was a life-changing, sliding doors moment, and I imagine an alternative reality might have played out like this.

It would have taken a day or so for me to process and understand what had happened, resulting in an overflow of emotions, guilt, self-loathing and a total inability to cope.

Katherine as the stronger person, would have made a point not to cave in first and already started to plan with thoughts of making a better life for herself. But simultaneously, every cell in her body would have wanted nothing more than to return to my side and make our relationship work.

However, my requests would most likely be denied, with the hurt still raw. I would be left alone to dwell on the mayhem my misguided behaviour caused.

I had found her breaking point, and the consequences now lay heavy upon me.

Lost, hopeless, frightened, and ashamed that I had needlessly succeeded in pushing away the only woman I have ever loved.

'What the fuck is wrong with you!?' It would be my turn to ask the question.

My ever more frantic attempts to make contact, just to hear her voice and beg her to come back, would be left unreturned on the advice of those now keeping her safe with well-meaning but short-sighted and damaging advice.

'Don't go running back to him. Give it time. Let him stew a bit longer. Be brave. You can do better than him.'

After a few more days without a reply, my efforts to contact her would start to diminish, and Katherine might wonder why she hadn't received a message, perhaps becoming concerned enough to send a text of her own just to see if I was OK.

There would only be silence in return and, presently, a knock on the door of her temporary home with two police officers staring glumly from the doorstep.

Her husband was now a statistic from an untreated or unknown mental health disorder that led to a breakdown in communication of a relationship that was never meant to end.

A grieving wife, a life destroyed, and never knowing the part ADHD and its toxic outriders had to play. The first sympathetic voice with the continual mantra would begin.

'I'm so sorry for your loss. Is there anything I can do?'

Fortunately, back in the real world, Katherine was the very epitome of the Bruce Lee bamboo, stronger than an oak tree. She simply refused to break, and this horrible episode had just proven further that we are only ever likely to part when our hearts stop beating.

The world felt clearer, like a storm had blown away the dying embers of an overbearing heat wave, and we both breathed a huge sigh of relief. I held her in my arms and told her that I was sorry, and I had never stopped loving her and never will. We were virtually inseparable for weeks afterwards.

There are twelve male suicides in the United Kingdom every day.
Samaritans 116 123

Many years later, we were forced to spend a few weeks apart for reasons that had nothing to do with our own relationship. It was difficult, but we both coped really well or so I thought, until Katherine phoned me in floods of tears, telling me she felt completely overwhelmed with the situation and was no longer able to eat and unable to cope with being apart from me, describing herself as lovesick.

I thought of the unimaginable, sickening hurt and damage I might have caused to so many people had the doors slid open slightly differently a decade earlier.

Once more, I was humbled and slightly confused about the depth of Katherine's love for me. If you know your partner has ADHD, it can be difficult, but if you don't, it is likely to be even more challenging, and it is remarkable that we got through it together.

I gave myself an endless torrent of verbal abuse for being so foolish and reckless. I'm never letting this happen again. I postponed every work appointment I could for the next two weeks and all radio commitments for the foreseeable future. We needed time away together. Our girls remained unaware of the drama but are quite happy to be given free rein of the house for a week. Pebbles stayed with our kindly neighbour, who buys her favourite dog treats and lets her sleep on his bed.

Meanwhile, I booked a holiday that I had found at a bargain price on eBay.

You always took a risk in booking a holiday from an auction site in those days, and most people I told responded with an alarmed 'You did what?'

There was no guarantee the cottage in rural Cornwall actually existed, but Katherine seemed so relieved and happy to have her marriage back on track that she didn't seem to care, as we headed off more in hope than expectation with a vague plan of buying a tent if required. Fortunately, we managed to find our way to the allotted outpost via, quite possibly, the most potholed road in Cornwall to a beautiful and remote spot with only a few nearby chickens strutting around for company. Our holiday turned into a perfect second honeymoon.

Have you ever wondered whether your partner is satisfied with their sex life? To find out, buy them a bottle of beer!

In a pub or restaurant, I'm very likely to finish my drink first, then I will get bored or distracted, so I'll start to peel the label off my beer bottle. There is an urban myth such behaviour means you are dissatisfied with your sex life, although for me, no doubt, it's just another ADHD thing.

While in a quiet Cornish pub, I pointed out to Katherine in a rather self-satisfied and probably needy way, 'Look, I don't rip the labels off the beer bottles anymore,' only to be floored by her wide-eyed response, 'Good! Neither do I, not for now at least…'

Our first honeymoon, decades earlier, wasn't without significant drama either, and Katherine might have returned home a widow had she not found a way to quell my hyperactivity. The jeopardy made all the greater that we had travelled without insurance, as surely we wouldn't need it, would we?

Our plan of two perfect weeks on the Greek island of Zakynthos didn't quite turn out that way. I had a terrible throat infection, with the effects seeping ever deeper into my body as each day passed. We planned a boat excursion to swim near an area known locally as the Blue Caves. I was already running a high temperature that was alarming Katherine, but the symptoms came and went, so I was determined my illness wouldn't stop us from enjoying our day. That year was the hottest summer in recent Greek history and caused over a thousand fatalities on the mainland. Venturing out into the blazing midday sun, even fully fit, took some considerable effort.

'Timmy, you aren't well, you need to rest,' pleaded my gorgeous new wife.

'Let's go out. I'll be fine,' I smiled, but clearly failing to convince either of us.

'You are so tired, darling. Please rest, you need to sleep. It is so hot today. We can go tomorrow or the next day.'

'It's OK.' I replied, 'I'll be alright once we get there. Honestly, let's go. Come on, or we'll be late!'

I attempted to stuff some swimming gear into a bag, but the pain and the symptoms of the infection kept taking over. Every time I spoke, it was like swallowing a piece of coarse sandpaper, and it was ludicrous that I even wanted to go out, yet I was insisting we didn't waste our day or our deposit even though I'm sure they would have let us re-book for another day.

I wanted to prove that I was strong enough and refused to give in.

Every time Katherine asked me to rest, I bounced around, trying to convince her that I was OK, but I was met with a continual gentle refusal until she put an end to the impasse.

'But I'm tired today! It's so hot out there! I would like to stay in and rest for a while. We don't have to go out every day, do we!'

Katherine looked at me, slightly hurt that I hadn't considered her feelings, but she also knew that I had walked straight into her trap, and my resistance was now at an end.

'Oh, I'm sorry, I wasn't thinking of you,' I croaked. Any remaining argument now evaporated. She knew I would do anything for her, and the truth was that my body was desperate for a very long rest, and furthermore, my brain could no longer withstand her unique style of mental jujitsu.

Katherine has developed her mindful martial arts more skilfully and subtly through the years, keeping hold of me when much tougher challenges have threatened to overwhelm us and avert a potential catastrophe.

She will understand and calmly agree while giving an alternative point of view, patiently helping me to realise the bigger picture and the part

I may have played. Thus, defusing the anger, hurt and emotion until we find a way forward and somehow solve the problem together.

This is all delivered with a simultaneous flood of love and understanding that I'm left overwhelmed and powerless to resist, with my only remaining conscious thought … 'God, I love this woman.'

That day in Zante, I required every ounce of energy to fight the infection, so I obediently laid beside her on the bed and slept well into the next day.

With her new husband safely asleep and happily protected from himself for a while at least, Katherine moved out onto the balcony with her book and a well-deserved bottle of Ouzo.

And it was just as well Katherine persuaded me to stay in bed that day, or there was a possibility she would have returned home a widow.

The island on-call doctor said it was one of the most severe cases of a poisonous throat infection he had ever seen. If I had gone on the trip and jumped from a boat into the sea, there would have been serious consequences leading to possible sepsis, a condition that would quickly become impossible to treat.

We eventually made it to the Blue Caves on condition I wouldn't jump in, but Katherine knew the temptation would be too great long before she heard the splash that signalled her hyperactively restored husband had disappeared into the water.

Antibiotics are truly amazing. I had a potentially life-threatening infection only a few days before, and now I was happily jumping into the sea. When we returned to our hotel room, it was my turn to persuade Katherine to stay in bed but for an entirely different reason.

I wanted our honeymoon hotel to be as close to the shoreline as possible. I pictured something beautiful on the sandy beach close to the gently lapping waves. Instead, we arrived at a damp and squalid hovel reeking of sewage. The rusty pipes leaking from the toilet were broken, with suspect liquid seeping under the door. There was dirt and sand everywhere and a bin full of used toilet paper. The sheets were a strange hue of brown, and there were a couple of small lizard-type creatures gadding around the bedroom floor. Not the most romantic environment for the first night of our honeymoon. My sore throat had started to kick in, and the squalid environment undoubtedly added to the worsening symptoms.

'What do you expect from the Simply Greece brochure?' the holiday rep said later, refusing any further help or support.

Many months afterwards, we did get some financial compensation, but what price can you place on a lost week from your honeymoon?

The previous year we'd arrived on the island of Kos to be told, rather worryingly, our accommodation was still being built. However, we were given a huge upgrade, complete with flowers and fruit on arrival.

I've had some of the most overwhelming and intense feelings of my life with the love I have for Katherine, but I don't remember any fireworks, a bolt of lightning, or an arrow from Cupid's bow landing in my heart when I first fell in love with her. It was more like finding a favourite piece of clothing that fits so perfectly and feels so wonderful, secure and comfortable that you put it on and never want to take it off.

We had booked our trip to Kos only a few months after our first date, and it felt more natural than impulsive when we stopped to look in the window of the only jewellers on the island where Katherine's eyes lit up at the sparkle of one particular engagement ring. So, we went in and bought it there and then. Later that day, realising I had neglected to provide a suitably romantic proposal, I went down on one knee among the shallow waves of the Aegean Sea under a perfect blue sky and asked Katherine to marry me.

The previous day had been somewhat less romantic when the island was hit by rough seas deemed too dangerous for any of the official tourist boats to travel across to the nearby islands. Undeterred, I found the owner of a boat named *The Nisyros Express,* who was prepared to risk the crossing but warned it might be rough. It was a total misjudgement as halfway across the seas appeared almost to boil. With hindsight, I wonder if ADHD had led to my foolish insistence on making this dangerous trip that unnecessarily put Katherine in danger.

When the crew stop laughing and start to look worried, you know you are in trouble, and when a particularly large rogue wave hit the side of the boat, we very nearly capsized.

My emotion was compounded as I was now powerless to protect Katherine. There were life jackets but no lifeboats as the vessel was so small. My mind was racing for any possible way to keep her safe if the boat did go on its side. ADHD minds are meant to be good in a crisis, and this was another true test of that particular theory.

Fortunately, the raging sea eventually abated, and the crew members later took turns holding a cardboard bowl for Katherine to be sick into, albeit with limited success.

We limped towards the tiny harbour where we stayed and waited long into the evening until the sea was deemed safe enough for our return. While we waited for the seas to calm, the captain's brother took us to what was apparently a volcano, although I would never have identified it as such. We bounced around in the back of his open-sided truck next to some sacks of cement and a monosyllabic couple from Wales for company. I made a mental note to book the official tour next time.

These two days were perhaps typical of the rollercoaster life that lay ahead of us.

On our return to the UK, there was little surprise at our rapid engagement. The only person as thrilled as my mum was Katherine's boss, who reckoned he knew before we did and had considered running a book as to whether we would return from our holiday engaged in order to make a tidy sum of money.

So, other than almost capsizing and potentially drowning my fiancé on our boat trip to Nisyros, the time in Kos was idyllic, but eighteen months later, on our honeymoon, things were not quite as perfect as I had hoped. The holiday company were useless, and we had used a large amount of our spending cash to move from the smelly beachside hovel to the four-star Hotel Australia with its lovely owners, who were very sympathetic to our plight and welcomed us like friends.

We didn't want to use the remainder of our spending money, so I produced my newly acquired Access credit card to be sure we could afford to pay for the hotel on departure. They smiled and readily agreed, although a warning should have sounded when I realised that I had shown them my organ donor card by mistake. One of us had clearly misunderstood.

'We don't take cards' was the stark message when we checked out the following week.

There was a distinct look of hurt on their faces when they found we couldn't pay, and it must have felt like a betrayal. I promised I would send them cash, but it was met with a disbelieving shrug of the shoulders, and our former friends just walked away from us. We left without a goodbye.

The hotel owners had been so kind, even arranging the doctor and the urgently required medication for my throat infection that may have saved my life. They had little choice but to take our word for it but clearly didn't believe us. Once back in the UK, I quickly sourced the correct amount of Greek drachma plus a bit extra for their inconvenience. I packaged the money in a large white envelope, sealing it with a ridiculous amount of Sellotape and enclosed a long letter of thanks with the hope we would return one day.

There was no reply and as much as we tried, we couldn't find any information on whether the cash had arrived safely. I fear the money was probably stolen somewhere en route, and we are yet to revisit our honeymoon hotel.

CHAPTER TWENTY

Let's Talk About Sex ... Addiction and ADHD

There is a specific reason why adults with ADHD are more likely to struggle with this kind of addiction than those who don't have the disorder.

I'm not a betting man (ADHD and all that). But, if I did gamble, I'd wager that virtually every man who reads this book has looked at some form of pornography in their life. Furthermore, a growing number of those men will have or may soon be struggling with a porn-related problem, even if, at present, they don't realise it.

A study on the website Psychology Today found that 97% of men have viewed online porn, 94% had done so in the previous six months and 82% were regular viewers, and this is assuming that everyone on the survey was telling the truth. So, unpalatable as it may seem, there are dads, grand-dads, brothers, boyfriends and husbands, including those in any number of highly responsible roles such as teachers, pilots, politicians and priests, all regularly watching porn.

Of course, they probably do so secretly, and I very much doubt will be announcing it to the world.

'My family are going to read this!'

This was Katherine's initial shocked response before realising the importance and depth of the issue. She then had to spend some considerable time persuading me to keep this chapter included when I had decided to - most definitely - cut it from the final edit.

Yes, they probably are going to read this, and I would refer them to the paragraphs above.

I've been called brave for openly discussing suicide, grief and self-harm. Subjects that are no longer taboo, but the writing of a battle with this kind of addiction is still a step too far for some. Perhaps things are beginning to change, particularly amongst the younger adult generations who tend to discuss these matters more openly.

Addiction affects an ever-growing number of men and women and has the potential to destroy lives. It could have destroyed mine if I hadn't read the warning signs.

Compulsive sexual behaviours often happen because of negativity in a person's life. They may begin for reasons that include boredom, loneliness, lack of sex, abuse, stress, a disinterested partner or no partner at all, health issues, rejection, or just feeling unloved. Yet, there are many people in a loving and seemingly healthy relationship who slide towards the abyss of addiction and that includes me.

However, there is a specific reason why adults with ADHD are more likely to struggle with this kind of addiction than those who don't have the disorder.

The natural 'happy drugs' dopamine, serotonin and oxytocin that are released before, during, and after sex are not easily retained by those with ADHD, and they drain away through our sieve-like brains very quickly. This is why people with ADHD are more likely to be addicted to sex or porn, or both. Dopamine is the biggest culprit, as it's essentially a craving drug that fuels a sense of wanting and seeking beyond what a person is normally satisfied with. Those with ADHD already have an addictive mindset, we were born with it, and this can lead to a heap of further trouble.

I tried to convince myself that I was purely addicted to the dopamine 'drug' as it is a slightly more palatable thing to admit to. After all, I'm a feminist, I have two daughters, and I'd never seen the attraction of mainstream porn sites. But I was probably only fooling myself. All I knew was that whatever was happening to me was detrimental to my physical and mental well-being, and when I looked in the mirror, I was not the person I wanted to be, although, to be entirely honest, I never have been.

Yet, there are in-depth articles and TED talks available online from highly accomplished business people who are now completely open about how their addiction began, the effect it had on them and their families, and how they overcame it. Interestingly, they now look to help and even inspire others from their own experiences, and this, in some way, is what I hope to do within these pages.

I worked at a small private bar for six weeks. They paid extremely well but couldn't keep hold of their staff for very long and I soon found out why.

There were all-night gambling sessions, female escorts and regular stag nights. Once a week, there was a 'strip night' and I was asked to welcome the female artists at the staff entrance. Both had young families at home and were practically dead behind the eyes at the prospect of their night's work ahead. Nevertheless, they somehow managed to paint on wildly happy faces and a pretence of enjoying the endless groping from the drunk and debauched men in attendance.

Following their act, I served the women tea while they recovered and asked them if they ever enjoyed their work. 'I enjoy the money' was the reply. 'Do this once a week or work for hours every day behind a bar, what would you rather do?'

I didn't answer as I highly doubted anyone would pay cash to watch me strip off!

I was earning double the standard rate, but working at this club for six weeks probably merited a long service award where drinking sessions would go on well into the small hours of the morning. This is where self-proclaimed 'alpha males' would brag and joke about their various sexual exploits, followed by a decidedly awkward game of 'truth or dare.' At this point, one of the men admitted to his lifelong sexual fantasy that involved *The Wizard of Oz*. Thus, whenever this man got to the point of no return in bed, he would involuntarily shout out.

'Surrender Dorothy!'

This, not surprisingly, had proved to be a relationship ender for him on a number of occasions.

A therapist told me the route to some mental health issues can start with unwanted sexual fantasies that first develop when we are just eight years old and are then further influenced and reinforced when puberty is reached. I doubt this man realised a trip to the cinema would cause him a lifetime of embarrassment and unwanted thoughts.

There is still relatively little professional help available for porn and sex addiction, which can result in potential difficulties with relationships later in life. The current generation, who grew up on fast fibre technology, may be storing up a tidal wave of problems for themselves and, potentially, the image and well-being of women.

When one image isn't enough, a person may search for more extreme viewing, so when it comes to making love to a real living and breathing woman, there isn't enough stimulation or excitement present in their brain. It seems men in their forties and fifties were more able to recover from 'Porn Induced Erectile Dysfunction' (PIED) than younger men, as they had spent the majority of their life without broadband or were, perhaps, attempting to negotiate a wank via dial-up while someone else waited to use the phone.

Of course, porn is not exclusively a modern-day issue. During the mid-1980s, a flamboyant work colleague invited Katherine and me to a house party where he suggested the assembled guests might enjoy his selection of VHS video tapes. These were mostly German porn films. Our host then requested that Katherine, fluent in German, translate for the audience, who grew ever more uncomfortable with the entertainment on offer. The film involved an everyday office scene that descended, for no apparent reason, into an impromptu orgy. Three guys, each with a foot-long penis, took their turn with the same woman who, clearly and quite understandably, didn't appear to be having such a great time, proceeding to spit out the resulting contents of her misadventure towards the camera.

There was a collective 'Ugh!' in the room, except for Katherine, who took it in her stride and laughed. Did this really need translating, I wondered? For the sake of everyone involved, I really hope they managed to film that scene in one take.

The video proved too much for many of those assembled who decided to leave the room. A change of channel was subsequently requested, and belatedly, a recording of *Top of the Pops* was found. Never has Simon Bates looked more attractive. Full-on porn apparently made our Italian friend happy, but did he ever stop to consider the woman in the film and the real-life scenario of producing such content? How did she end up doing this for a career? Perhaps she answered an advert for an acting job, thinking she might have a part in a movie. It is even possible the women and men are being abused and forced into filming these scenes.

Self-esteem issues can also manifest from porn films where men and women compare themselves to those on view and don't measure up either physically or in the actions and reactions involved with what is happening on screen. A quarter of internet searches are thought to be porn related, and the industry is estimated to be worth nearly $100 Billion.

Porn and sex addiction is an ever-growing modern-day problem, especially amongst young people who need help and support instead of a cloud of shame and embarrassment from something they find unmentionable. Remember, this is an addiction, just as gambling, alcohol, or drugs might be, and it shouldn't be seen as a judgement of someone's morals. You only realise you have an addiction when you try to stop.

Some years ago, Katherine and her group of friends would meet up for coffee mornings and discuss a variety of subjects. One such topic was why men wanked and what it was like for them. I may have been the only partner who answered the question honestly. I told her that it was like eating a bar of chocolate instead of having a proper meal which, the following week, she bizarrely decided to relay back to the giggling women. If you are living solely on a diet of sugary snacks, junk food, and soda, then you aren't going to be particularly healthy, and it may lead to significant problems, but I guess everyone enjoys a chocolate bar and it shouldn't be demonised.

Of course, the issue isn't just confined to men. It is a girl thing too...

The newspaper and magazine section of our local bookshop was often left unsupervised. In my late teens, It gave me all the time I needed to check out the football results and reports without fear of being interrupted and asked to pay or leave the shop.

I found myself standing next to a young woman of a similar age to me who was fully engrossed in a bodybuilder magazine, nodding with approval and biting her lip as she carefully flicked through each shiny page of bulging male muscle. Then, as she came out of her secret world of desire and, realising I had seemingly noticed her choice of reading material, a little red-faced, she giggled and then put the magazine back on the shelf.

After a moment's hesitation, she turned back to me and whispered, 'I just love big muscles,' then grabbed the magazine back from the unsupervised shelf and ran out of the shop, out of the shopping mall and off into the distance.

Although this young woman may have risked an embarrassing shoplifting offence, it seems likely that accessing soft porn in the early 1980s was probably far less risky or harmful than it is today when virtually anything is freely available online 24/7. The Independent newspaper reported that one in three women viewed porn every week.

With the conscious and unconscious negativity fired at kids with ADHD, it's no wonder that many grow up with crippling low self-esteem. As a twelve-year-old, I felt self-conscious, ugly and awkward.

This wasn't helped by having huge sticking-out ears that I still haven't properly grown into.

I once asked a barber if he would cut my hair in a style that would cover my ears. His reply was not particularly sympathetic.

'What do you think I am a magician?'

The entire barbers' shop roared with laughter, but my cheeks were so red from embarrassment I could have combusted and almost wished I had.

My teenage years were a nightmare. I would never even consider asking a girl on a date as the potential rejection and ridicule would be too much to bear, let alone the horrors of ever bringing her home to meet my family. Anyway, I knew full well that no girl would ever want to date me, although I once received a Valentine card from an apparent mystery admirer.

Aged fourteen, I was given a Playboy magazine with an attached calendar for Christmas that I unwittingly opened in front of my entire family. Fortunately, I had become rather adept at laughing away my frequent embarrassments by then.

The calendar in question depicted women having sex with their portly middle-aged boss in different areas of his office. Each photograph seemed ghastlier than the last. None of the photos in the calendar seemed at all pleasing or anything approaching a 'turn-on.' I found the whole thing horrible and couldn't work out what the appeal was. Maybe there was something wrong with me.

The Recovery Village website states the main difference between sex addiction and porn addiction is in their names. Sex addiction is an inability to control urges to perform sexual acts. Porn addiction is an inability to control urges to view pornographic material. I'm not sure whether I fell into either category, but I knew whatever was going on needed to stop. If I had known about the link between ADHD and addiction, It would have at least helped me to understand my situation better.

However, an advocate for a well-known UK mental health charity told me they had seen for themself how people with ADHD had been accused of using their disorder as an excuse for addiction. This accusation is both unfair and untrue. To compound matters, people without ADHD had also claimed to have the condition as an alibi when being discovered so their partners might forgive them.

I spoke to a female therapist about my ongoing issues and how I could overcome them. I thought getting her perspective would enable me to quit before the problem got further out of control. I was looking for advice on how to stop, perhaps a rebuke or something to scare me of the risks I was taking. Anything to hold on to and halt my ever-downward spiral.

But rather than offering advice on how to quit, she became a little wide-eyed and smiled.

'Nothing wrong with that, it's perfectly normal. Just carry on. Ooh, sounds great, enjoy!'

I guess she thought it was helpful to let me believe that my behaviour wasn't wrong, unusual or any different from that of countless other men in the world and maybe it wasn't, but it felt like she was advising a potential alcoholic to have a few more drinks and loosen up a bit.

The material I looked at wasn't full of degrading acts or naked flesh, far from it, and I wondered if I could acquire a get out of jail free card here because what I was viewing wasn't porn in the sense that it is usually regarded.

However, when I contacted Paula Hall, the Founder of The Laurel Centre, one of the UK's leading sex and porn addiction therapy centres, for some further accredited research, she told me that anything which is viewed with the intention of causing sexual arousal is classified as pornography, regardless of what the actual content might be. Their clinic has seen many people who have become addicted to what might be called 'mainstream porn,' such as that found on most popular porn websites. However, they had also worked alongside many whose addiction has been to a genre that others may not consider pornographic and might not be arousing to other men at all.

As my therapist seemed so blasé about my issues, the vicious cycle of craving for a fix of dopamine followed by its hastened exit through my brain continued unabashed.

I tried to kid myself that there wasn't a problem, but the alarm bells started to ring very loudly when I began to malfunction in bed. I couldn't engage, I couldn't finish, I'd even fake it (not easy for a guy!), or I would avoid the potential for failure altogether by telling Katherine I was tired or didn't feel well. These are all likely signs of this kind of addiction.

I eventually found the courage to speak with a qualified sex therapist. He tried to reassure me that I wasn't on the scale compared with some of the heavy stuff he often dealt with. Initially, he didn't agree that it was an addiction at all until I pointed out the physical and mental effects were having on my life and these really couldn't be ignored. Of course, the role ADHD played still hadn't been properly considered or dealt with either.

Porn is one of the most searched things on the internet, but there are also tens of thousands of searches each day for those seeking help with porn addiction. This is because it's affecting millions of people in so many ways, but unfortunately, it is still taboo.

As my own problem grew, I looked for further help online, and I was surprised at what I found. A whole brotherhood of support for all ages.

Countless men in turmoil, all going through some horrible problems. Lives destroyed, careers ruined, relationships ended, many unable to cope, most feeling isolated with their own perceived nasty secret. Yet, they all needed help, not the judgement and shame often thrown their way and, quite possibly, in some cases, by those using the issue to cover their own difficulties.

I found tales from young men still awaiting their first real sexual encounter who were already suffering from porn-induced erectile dysfunction, many of them desperate for help but scared to ask and with no idea of where to find it.

The main feeling of sex or porn addiction is often shame. This is one reason why it is so secretive. However, when you are in the company of those also experiencing the same turmoil, there is no judgement, only understanding, help, or even respect given for any progress made. Not all of the information and advice on these forums is sound, but it's an example of how deep the problem has become.

I read through several message boards for help, although I wasn't brave enough to join in with the discussion. It was pretty much a wall of support except for the occasional and inevitable internet troll, who goaded those trying to come to terms with their problem.

'Enjoy your prostate cancer.'

This was in response to an apparent scientific study that suggested an adult male should have twenty-one ejaculations a month as this may help ward off prostate cancer. However, there appears to be no definitive proof of this as yet and further research is required. Either way, I doubt it could be used as a legitimate excuse for viewing endless porn.

At home, we had reached the point where Katherine, quite understandably, seldom wanted to be intimate as I had become ever more distant and difficult. I doubt whether she was getting much out of it whenever we did have sex and was probably relieved when it was over. Thankfully, she was still oblivious to my problems, although they were becoming ever more difficult for me to cover up or ignore.

It was probably thanks to a spam email that found its way through to my inbox that finally made me realise I had a potentially serious problem developing. The email threatened me with blackmail, quoting an old password and telling me they had recorded videos of both myself and the material I was viewing. So, if I didn't pay them a very large sum of money in Bitcoin, they would share this video with my entire address book, which, apparently they had also hacked into.

I didn't have any Bitcoin handy, but I did stay awake well into the night, checking how real this threat might be and changed every one of my passwords.

In reality, of course, they didn't have a video of me or access to my address book, they got my password along with countless others from a wider historic data breach and it's just another scam. But, this was the wake-up call I needed and if I wasn't already addicted, I now realised that I was well on the way to being so.

I don't know how or why it started, but It had become a vicious circle that was now a danger to my relationship with Katherine and wider family life. I'd become increasingly moody, secretive, difficult, sullen and irritable, often upsetting those around me. I had become so full of inward self-hatred and loathing during this time that it polluted everything in my life with a downward spiral of anger that I couldn't stop.

Occasionally, a day or two's progress would be made, then a bad experience or an upset would release the demons to send for copious amounts of soothing dopamine, quickly followed by an even bigger dose of shame that further added to my ever-darkening mood. There were moments when the question of whether I was worth more dead than alive crept into my brain.

The first step to beating an addiction is to admit you have a problem. Things had to change and I knew I needed help. I promised myself that I would stop, but it was like promising to go on a diet while eating a packet of chocolate biscuits, enjoying the sugar rush but then regretting it, feeling dirty, and promising to do better tomorrow.

Katherine would have made a brilliant detective as nothing much gets past her. She was obviously aware that something wasn't right with me and hadn't been for a long while, but she had no idea what it might be. I was often secretive and would disappear without any explanation. I had to be careful, and it was a constant strain wondering if I had covered my tracks successfully, but the longer things went on, the more risks were taken and the more likely it was that she would find out, but at times I didn't care as my mind continued to slowly rot away.

I knew I was being a shit person and a shit husband.

I was asked to work out of the local area for a while, and on the morning I left, I decided today was the day things would change. I'd made this statement in my mind many times before and failed, but I was determined it would be different this time. I hated what I had become, what I was doing, and its effect on those close to me. Katherine was hurting too, and she deserved better. I planned to make some progress towards getting clean, and then I would tell her everything.

It's better to have control of the situation and tell your partner these issues on your own terms rather than be found out and forced to admit it with the fallout and feelings of betrayal and deeper shame that would likely entail.

However, you can't beat porn addiction 'single-handed' as it will need help from someone who is understanding and experienced. Talking to a therapist may be the safest route, and you will receive non-judgemental, clear, and independent advice from them, although finding one to whom you can speak openly and who is on your wavelength may take some time.

With the advent of online meeting software such as Teams and Zoom, you can talk with any therapist in the world without the fear they are known to you or a friend or that you might bump into them in the street. If you do talk to a therapist, there is no point unless you open up and tell them everything. It isn't easy and may take some time, but they are there to help, so if you can't, won't or don't, it's essentially a waste of your money.

If you choose to tell a trusted friend or relative, they may not appreciate having to share the burden of your addiction. In reality, I doubt many people do actually keep a secret. This runs the risk they will tell at least one other person, usually their partner, who will then tell at least one other person, and so it will go on, with the details quite possibly exaggerated each time. If you are really unlucky, your admission may end up being the talk of your workplace or perhaps on social media.

Telling your partner about addiction is brave and potentially a huge gamble. It can be life-changing for good or bad, but once you examine the possibilities, there is really no choice, as you will need your closest ally on side to help find a way safely through this difficult maze. It also allows them an opportunity to leave the relationship, even temporarily, while they have their own time to consider the matter properly.

Either way, honesty is the best policy and it's what I've decided to do.

As my progress began in earnest, I managed to stay clean for several weeks and felt ready to face Katherine with my news. The timing had coincided with my working away from home for a prolonged spell, and I had already started to shed a few of the toxic cobwebs that had been clinging to my skin and eating into my soul. My mind was starting to clear and I was sleeping better. Katherine was a regular guest star in my dreams, and I can't wait to see her. I'd already told her there was something important I needed to share.

However, I'm still anxious that a residue from the self-inflicted problem will remain, and I wonder how capable I might be. I have read many tales of people who take months to recover from this form of erectile dysfunction and others who are still waiting.

We finally managed enough space and time to book a Bed & Breakfast near to the coast with a large covered jacuzzi in the garden. Our room had a beautiful view of the countryside. It was well stocked with posh fizzy water, piles of fluffy white towels, and a bowl of Katherine's favourite fizzy heart-shaped sweets, with a different cheeky love message on each tablet.

I doubt that 'Your husband might have PIED' was one such message.

It was such a beautiful setting that it seemed a pity I was about to tarnish our perfect weekend with my shameful admission.

We had a romantic evening followed by an even more romantic morning. To my great relief, everything was in full working order, and I had the love of my life back in my arms once more.

I was as sure as I could be that Katherine would understand and want to help, but I didn't want to take anything for granted. I also knew she might be annoyed and upset, perhaps even deciding this was the last straw for our relationship. I then had to remind myself that once I told her, if she couldn't deal with my news, there would be no 'undo button' to click or any way back. When the time finally arrived, I almost lost my nerve, but my mind was overwhelmed by so many mixed emotions, and I just blurted the words out ADHD style while she was still wrapped around me. Hardly romantic, I know.

There was a split second where I could see in her eyes that she thought I was joking. This turned into moments of shock and confusion while my admission sank in.

When she found her voice, the words were caring, loving, kind and reassuring. Once again, I was completely humbled. Katherine seemed relieved to know the reason why I'd been so quiet, distant, secretive, irritable, and ever more difficult to live with in recent times. All she wanted to do now was help.

However, a partner is likely to blame themselves and wonder where things went wrong; Katherine inevitably asked, 'Is this my fault?'

'No! Absolutely not. This is completely down to me.'

I didn't confess to get absolution or unload guilt. I tried my best to reassure her and told her there was absolutely no reason to take any blame, but I was annoyed with myself that I hadn't understood she might feel the need to share some of the responsibility. It is essential for any admission of this kind that you own it absolutely and completely.

Over the coming weeks, we talked more than we had done for years. Things continued to improve each day, and it felt like the sun had broken through the clouds. I was starting to feel human again, and the world was now a brighter place. I noticed people and places I would have previously walked past in a depressive fug while craving the next dopamine hit.

There was a moment soon after when I held Katherine in my arms and told her how beautiful she was and how much I loved her. We were both completely taken by the moment and abandoned all other plans for the rest of the evening. Afterwards, I held her close and told her how much I loved her over and over again.

'Oh, where has this Timmy been?' She asked with a sad longing.

It's one of the nicest yet saddest things I'd ever heard her say to me. I was glad to be on the road to recovery and to hopefully become a better and nicer person, but I was also overwhelmed with the sadness, loathing, guilt and shame that I had been such an endlessly horrible person to live with. I hadn't even realised for much of the time the full extent of how bad things had become and the increasing risks I was taking or, of course, that unbeknown to anyone that ADHD had significantly contributed to the growing problem.

I still carry the shame of this episode, but having put it into words, I now realise just how challenging this kind of problem is for anyone, let alone someone with ADHD, and there is an element of pride among the indignity that I found the strength to kick it. However, it was later pointed out that no one beats an addiction as you are only ever in recovery one day at a time.

As with any addiction, the journey ahead is unlikely to be straightforward, but as there is now a growing social acceptance with more help and understanding available, there is a far better chance to tackle the problem successfully.

My admission could have gone one of two ways. If Katherine had reacted badly, I might have died from the feeling of disgrace, and our marriage would be over, but happily, she responded better than I could ever have imagined, and we developed a renewed and extraordinary emotional bond with a rarefied level of honesty between us.

While on our way to a family event in Essex. Katherine and I were chatting about my recovery, and this led to a conversation about our intimacy. For the first time in our marriage, we openly discussed our fantasies. Katherine became so involved with our fun new world that she suggested we either leave this conversation until later or leave the motorway at the next exit and find somewhere quiet. Unfortunately, or perhaps fortunately, the next exit was for the M25, and there was unlikely to be anywhere suitably quiet. However, this may have saved us from arrest and being disowned by our families.

Even though I had seemingly tackled the problem and we were behaving like young newlyweds, I was worried that an episode of erectile dysfunction might strike. So to be prepared, I'd made an impulsive online purchase of some ridiculously expensive Viagra, a drug that was first used to help blood pressure but was found to have a rather positive side effect.

'Why?' Was Katherine's doubtful and slightly irritated response, wondering if there were yet more revelations coming her way.

'Um, well, you know…just in case,' I replied, red-faced and a little embarrassed.

To date, 'touch wood' the Viagra hasn't been required and once the use-by date expired, Katherine, ever practical, discovered they could extend the life of cut flowers if you dissolve the little blue tablets into a vase of water.

Without our parents having sex, we wouldn't be here. Yet, it is one of those thoughts you probably don't want intruding into your brain, so I was somewhat surprised to hear that Vicky's friends had a light-hearted conversation about how often they thought her parents had any kind of physical interaction.

Wedding anniversaries and maybe birthdays, they surmised.

It's probably better to let them believe what they want rather than to know the truth and the mental scarring that might potentially result.

To misquote Shirley Valentine.

'Sex! Young people think they invented it.'

Further Help and Guidance -

Having read this chapter, some people may realise they have a problem of their own and seriously consider seeking further help. If that is you, your partner, or someone you know, I hope the information here might help you to find a path out of this challenging maze. As always, if you are in need of definitive help and opinion, always consult a qualified health professional or suitable therapist.

Firstly, recognise that you have a problem and recognise your problem as a potential addiction. Acknowledge this as a positive step forward for realising and wanting to stop.

Accept that ADHD may be part of the reason for your addiction. But also feeling rejected, depressed, stressed, unloved, or experiencing an unmet emotional need might be the issue. Once this problem has been addressed, the habit may reduce and eventually disappear without further help.

You must actually want to stop and decide to get rid of every trigger you know of. If you don't or won't, then how serious are you about recovering? You may have to give up some aspects of your life if you think there may be a trigger lurking in there somewhere.

Talk to a therapist, find a hobby, meditate, try to make a better environment for yourself and get physically fit. If you are religious, you may find some assistance within your church. In addition, there are self-help groups and charities, such as Relate.

Remove the apps that make it easy to hide your viewing and can delete your internet history with one click. I believe the comedian Michael McIntyre referred to the private browsing feature as '…the secret wank button,' and that probably isn't far from the truth. However, the search engine may still have those not-so-secret details stored somewhere, even if you have deleted them from your own computer.

When you have a bad day at work or an argument at home, it isn't justification for a relapse or telling yourself that you deserve or have earned it. Those with ADHD have numerous plus points, one of which is an advanced level of determination. If you do relapse, this isn't failure and doesn't mean it's over. Learn from it and start again, don't view it as a reason to give up.

Give up junk food, chocolate and highly processed food, anything that may develop into cravings for a quick dopamine release. Protein, fresh fruit and vegetables are a better diet for your brain and body.

Porn is unlikely to be harmless, and keeping this in mind may help as a stepping stone to quitting.

Recognise the positive impact that halting your addiction will have on your life. You are taking steps to improve, and you are likely to feel happier, enjoy better concentration and be more pleasant company. There will also be less secrecy resulting in less stress for you and a better relationship with everyone, including yourself. The only secret you should ever have from your life partner is the present you buy for their birthday.

Recovery is seldom, if ever, likely to be a straight road, it is natural and very likely you will falter. When this happens, try not to be disheartened, don't give up and always be kind to yourself.

The most repeated word in this chapter is probably shame, but please try not to feel it. There are blogs and Ted Talks on porn and sex addiction from highly respected and successful people. This affects millions of people from virtually every background. It can happen to anyone.

People with ADHD can suffer from many kinds of addiction, including alcohol, drugs and gambling. Professional help is available from charities and specific organisations that I have listed at www.timmacwilliam.com.

CHAPTER TWENTY-ONE

Living With Tim: Katherine's Story

The impact of adult ADHD can be very difficult for couples,
and it is thought to cause significant problems
in more than half of relationships.

———————

'You must have been a nightmare as a child!'

I've lost count of the times I've said this to Tim. But, perhaps now, I finally understand why.

Tim could either be a playful puppy or an angry bear. He has made me laugh with tears of joy and bitter tears of sadness. As with any couple, we have had our share of ups and downs, but I couldn't bear to be without him, and I know we have something that is both unique and amazing.

From early in our relationship, we both knew that this was 'it.' Everything felt just right. My own life had been misfiring for a while, and it was a new experience to have someone so energetic, overwhelming and loving in my world. Due to us working closely together in the hotel where I also lived within the staff quarters, we were together virtually 24/7, so our relationship rapidly fast-forwarded, allowing us to get used to each other very quickly and, with hindsight, I now realise this is an ideal scenario for someone with ADHD.

Tim was nothing like any of my previous boyfriends. He was kind, loving, warm and very funny, but he would never sit still and be forever larking about. He could be difficult too, and it was maddening that he would lose absolutely everything, especially keys. So I bought him a giant key fob, a whistling key ring, one that vibrated, one that played music, and even one that floated when dropped in water. However, none of them proved to be 'Tim Proof.'

I tried to stay calm and reasoned whenever the keys were lost or I heard his cry of 'Where's my wallet?'

Tim's sister is very similar. When she came to visit and lost her purse, she would also become agitated, turning in circles and repeatedly searching in exactly the same place while her ever-patient partner was trying to be rational.

At family gatherings, I would sit quietly with my fellow in-laws while Tim, his brother, and his sister constantly moved from room to room like characters in a game of Pac-Man.

This must run in the family, I thought.

I wondered how someone seemingly as intelligent as Tim had left school without a qualification or a career plan. He ran a successful bar in the hotel, but I have no idea how, as Tim and his staff were always messing around with high jinks involving fake spiders, silly masks, ridiculous jokes, beer fights, locking people in the cellar, and a mad game of 'smash the bottle.'

When his staff gave away their uniforms to a charity shop as they didn't like the style, I was quite annoyed, but Tim just laughed. His staff were always loyal, even the frustrated housewives that had a schoolgirl crush on him, but his fun and carefree attitude lightened me up too and I'm so glad that it did. Management might have been a bit wary of his style, but the monthly stock-take results were always very good, and money was all they seemed to care about, so a blind eye was turned to the daily circus.

If I had known about ADHD in 1985, I would probably have realised that's what my boyfriend had. He would refuse to queue anywhere, and he dragged me to three different Post Offices because the queue was too long. Finally, I put my foot down at the third attempt and insisted we stay, even though it was the longest queue of all, while Tim marched up and down singing jingles from radio adverts.

We would travel to a beach, then, just twenty minutes later, he wanted to move on to another one even though we had paid for half a day's parking. He would then get upset with me for pointing out the waste of money.

When our daughters were young, he wanted to take us out every weekend. Eventually, the girls begged, 'Mum, can we just stay at home and hang out with our friends?'

Tim would sometimes quite literally be bouncing off the walls, such was his need to burn off energy. I found this particularly difficult to cope with.

Following almost every holiday, he decided we should sell our house and live there, whether it be in Greece, Spain, Portugal, France or Italy. It used to scare me, but it was his dream, and he realised it would have to wait a while longer. However, he was desperate to do something of this kind, and we offered to buy an old ruined house in France to rebuild, only for a constructor friend to talk him out of it.

Fortunately, soon after, a golden Labrador puppy came to the rescue and became his inseparable friend for the next fifteen years.

I've never seen him so broken as when Pebbles died.

Tim would talk so fast that people couldn't always understand him. It's another ADHD symptom. Yet when he was on the radio, he was relaxed, coherent and sounded great.

He believes one key to our relationship is that we are both really clever at finding solutions to problems that no amount of PhDs could untangle, but, by the same token, we can be really stupid. As a result, we have ended up in some ridiculous situations, such as walking two hundred metres across an empty beach to an idyllic sea-view restaurant forgetting the tide times and having to negotiate three miles of single-track roads in pitch darkness back to the car park with every sound and dark shape seemingly more sinister than the last.

We hired a caravan in a remote part of Cornwall. Unfortunately, the electricity cut out, followed moments later by the most dramatic thunderstorm. Tim described seeing a figure holding a pitchfork, highlighted by each flash of lightning, walking towards us. It sounded like a scene from a horror film, and I thought he was teasing me until there was a loud knock on the door that I greeted with a scream before I heard my boyfriend's now rather shaky voice ask,

'Who is it?'

'Tis' I, the farmer!' Was the reply, as the banging on the caravan door continued.

'What do you want?' Tim replied, his voice now rising.

'I forgot to show you the electricity meter.'

Tim was brilliant with our young daughters, but at times it was like having three children. He was always playing around with them, and when I tried to get them to behave, the three of them would be on the floor laughing. His own dad wouldn't allow him to help with decorating, so he insisted our two girls aged three and five, were allowed to paint the kitchen. There was soon a river of paint on the floor, and the girls covered in blue emulsion ran through the house, depositing walls and carpets with their footprints and handprints. Tim laughed, but I'm not sure I did.

There were sometimes disagreements on our parenting style, particularly when Tim decided that Norwich City's appearance in the play-off final at Cardiff was more important than the planned family event in Essex and perhaps more so Vicky's School SATS that were scheduled for the following morning. This caused a significant degree of household unrest. However, Tim always tried to find a solution to please everyone, even when two people wanted the opposite outcome. He found some relatively cheap flights from Stanstead to Cardiff, which meant I could go to the family event, and we agreed on the promise that Vicky would be back home and tucked up in bed by 11 pm. Unfortunately, extra time, penalties, and a delayed flight home meant it was 3 am before Vicky finally got to sleep, although it was only quite recently I found out about their long-held secret.

Thankfully Tim went into responsible parent mode and got Vicky to her SATS in good time the next morning, and then travelled down to Essex to pick me up. I think her results were very good, but none of us can quite remember. It seems they weren't all that important after all, but Vicky still talks about the excitement of that event in Cardiff to this day.

When Vicky was fifteen and heading towards her exams, I asked her if she'd had a good day, expecting her to tell me about events from school, only for her to recount the lovely day at the beach she had with her dad and Pebbles. Tim told me she had been particularly low that day and it did her a world of good. But, of course, I wasn't impressed, and no amount of reasoning on his part helped me to agree. However, looking back decades later, now dealing with the consequences of my M.E. and being unable to enjoy a day on the beach, I'm glad they had that time together as I'm now far more aware of the importance of mental health.

Over the years, Tim has gone through several weird buying obsessions, including telephones, faxes, running shoes and fitness equipment. Often spending money we didn't have. He bought and sold four cars in six weeks but usually made a profit on each re-sale, reducing my concern. More recently, he either opened or closed nine separate bank accounts in a month, which drove our accountant to distraction.

Months after the football World Cup had ended, I took down his wall chart and threw it away. He was so annoyed that he kicked an empty watering can, not realising I had just filled it up, leaving him with a broken toe. As a result, Tim couldn't drive, so I had to rush out and collect our daughters from their after-school club and promptly reversed the car into a fence.

'That was your fault!' I screamed at him as we surveyed the damage to the car and fence post.

Who knew he was so attached to a world cup wall chart for a tournament for which England didn't even qualify?

Tim would often talk about the torture of meal times when he was young and was insistent that he wouldn't lecture his own children on table manners, but predictably having few rules led to further problems.

Everyone likes eating out, but it was seldom plain sailing for our family. We would arrive to be seated at a nice restaurant that looked perfectly good to me, but something apparently wasn't right for Tim, so we would move from table to table and from restaurant to restaurant, often ending back where we'd first started. Thankfully, he doesn't do this anymore; since I have become unwell he has become ever more protective and understanding.

Tim would cook a roast dinner, but it would take days to clear up after him. Carrot peelings covered the walls, blackcurrant jelly would be on the ceiling, and once a birthday cake from our two daughters was made almost entirely of icing. They obviously had fun making it, but we may have needed to redecorate afterwards.

I would often wonder why Tim had taken so long to wash up, but upon further investigation discovered the dishes were all piled up and still dirty while he was standing as far away from the swing bin as possible, throwing used tea bags towards the open lid, with about half of the soggy mess having missed the intended target, with damp splodges on the wall leaving permanent brown stains as a reminder of his poor accuracy.

Similarly, I would ask him to hang the washing on the line to dry and find him outside twenty minutes later with half the clothes on the grass while he saw how many pegs he could throw into the peg bag. Not many! They were mostly scattered on the ground.

I would give him a shopping list which he promptly lost, and returned home with an entirely new set of ingredients for me to make dinner with while, on other occasions, I would ask him to buy three or four things, but he had disappeared out of the door before I got past the second item.

Although Tim had a great memory of the past, he didn't seem to remember important details I had told him moments earlier. I would almost cry with frustration, wondering how anyone could be so forgetful that he needed to pick our daughters up from a club after school at a set time.

'You don't listen!' I would shout in frustration.

'I do listen; I just didn't hear.' I think I may understand what this reply means now.

Eventually, I learned the best place to talk about important things and get his full attention was while on a long car journey when he couldn't escape.

Tim often acted impulsively and came up with ideas that I never expected to succeed. He got a sponsored car and developed his own business in such a way that he could spend as much time as possible with his greatest passion, his family.

He would book holidays and events we couldn't afford, telling me, 'We don't know if we will get the chance to do this again.' I thought this was a silly attitude, but it came true when I was forced to retire due to ill health, as we are far more limited in what we can do now. Tim had been one of the first to take out critical illness cover, having seen the bailiffs knock on his parents' door when his own father had a stroke. He would be annoyed when his projects were developed by others who had sufficient capital to succeed, often protesting, 'I'm sure I thought of that first!'

In the early 1990s, when buying and selling property was near impossible due to high-interest rates and negative equity, Tim somehow managed to sell our home and buy an empty house that wasn't even for sale, just through sheer persistence. One or two of my relatives told him his idea would fail, but this was all the motivation Tim needed. He also managed to persuade the estate agent to give him the keys two weeks before we had even exchanged contracts and then decorated from top to bottom so our new house immediately felt like home. We still live in that same house.

At times I felt like I was being pulled along by my arms and flying through the air, hoping that he would be proven right on his latest venture. However, he sometimes crossed the sanity line, and I would virtually have to pin him down to stop him from doing something ridiculous, such as when he was serious about re-mortgaging our house to gamble every last penny we had on the Brexit referendum. He was absolutely certain the vote would be to remain!

I have, at times, found it challenging to deal with Tim's spontaneity.

Many years back, I had a circle of friends who would meet up for coffee while our children were at playgroup. My friends would recount the frustration with their husbands, who didn't always give them enough time to paint their foundation and make-up on before going to the beach.

'Make-up!' I would laugh. 'I'm lucky to get my clothes on once Tim decides we are going out.'

He would often jump around with energy and joy, but Tim could also quickly get upset and moody. I often thought he might be suffering from depression, but I now realise it can live side by side with ADHD and will sometimes be mistaken for the condition, but he laughed at the suggestion anything was wrong with his mental health.

I don't think he properly grieved for his mum when she died, so a constant dark cloud festered over him for years, and when Pebbles died, he just fell apart.

It can be really tough helping someone with growing or unknown mental health issues. All you can do is be there for them, listen to them and support them. He also displayed some physical symptoms and underwent endless tests and brain scans. Fortunately, these came back negative.

I never knew what I might wake up to each morning. Either a short-lived attempt to be jolly or a person so morose he wouldn't even speak to me. Running and the radio were his twin passions, but he became injured from overuse and disenchanted with the radio, so the demons duly resurfaced.

I'm ashamed to admit that I was pleased to be away from him for a few hours while in my car and at work. Tim always made me a fresh pot of coffee on my return. Still, I resented him for apparently doing nothing else all day when in fact, he was suffering quite significantly with his mental health, and I hadn't even realised or supported him properly. I kept busy with my job, housework and as a Brownie leader as distractions to sub-consciously avoid him. He told me years later that he would sometimes sit in the corner of the kitchen floor and cry when he was alone in the house. I had no clue how desperate he was for help and how awful it must have been carrying undiagnosed ADHD and the issues that go with it.

I didn't know about Tim's suicidal thoughts until I read this book. It brought me to tears. The thought of losing Tim is devastating, and I still worry about it happening, especially when he is having a bad day.

The anger he displayed often came from his frustration and sensitivity. I had to be careful before I spoke, never knowing whether he would laugh or be annoyed. The slightest comment could ruin his day and then, in turn, ruin everyone else's.

He would then be so upset with himself for causing the problem the resulting self-loathing would last for days. I know for a fact he would never dream of physically hurting me or anyone else, although doors, cupboards and phones did occasionally feel the full force of his wrath. I wish he could have just said sorry.

Tim gets bored with everything so quickly, and adults with ADHD can be unfaithful or even have multiple partners. I've often joked that I'm amazed he didn't run off with another woman, but I don't think I could have forgiven him if he had. His mother told me it's one thing I would never have to worry about. She said, 'Tim is definitely a one-woman man.' Happily, she was right. My own mother advised me soon after I bought Tim home for the first time, 'Make sure you hang on to him. He's a goodun.' Although I have never doubted him, I once found what I assumed to be my unwritten Valentine card in his office drawer. He later presented me with an entirely different card. I was momentarily stunned and confused, so I checked back in the drawer, only to find the unwritten card still there.

'Oh, I decided that one wasn't nearly nice enough for you, so I bought another,' he explained, laughing at the notion of a secret valentine.

I know he trusts me completely, although he once found I had made thirty calls on my mobile phone to the same number and perhaps wondered if something was going on, I eventually had to admit I had been voting for Darius on the reality television show, *Pop Idol.*

I know he had a previous relationship with a woman he refers to in this book as the emotional wasp. Of course, Tim is super sensitive, so the mental scarring she caused him might not have been such a problem for those more resilient, but if we ever do meet, my inner 'angry ninja' that Tim referred to in a previous chapter is likely to resurface.

He really cares what his brother thinks, and James was probably being protective and worried that Tim might have found another complete bitch, so he decided to test my sense of humour. He gave me a cup of coffee, and as I took a sip, the eyes of a realistic porcelain frog bobbed up from the bottom of the mug. I may have let out a tiny shriek of surprise, but I think I passed the initiation test.

At times, I may have been a little too controlling or didn't trust Tim to do things properly because of the potential mess and jeopardy involved. He would forget or stop halfway through a task to begin something new and wonder why I was annoyed. For example, when he left the freezer door open, leaving food to defrost and then went outside to mow the grass. When he returned, he proceeded to traipse green stained footprints throughout the house.

He would become frustrated that I needed to do some housework, as he was desperate to go out and do fun things while our home resembled a bomb site. But he never seemed to realise.

Tim would insist on making the porridge in the morning but would then leave it unattended while he went to shave or change the cat litter. I don't know if it's the ADHD diagnosis, my own condition, or the therapy, but he gets far more done now. Since becoming ill, I've had to let go and understand that he has his own way of doing things. With hindsight, I wish I hadn't seen cleaning and housework as such a priority.

Nowadays, as my own health fails, it is almost a role reversal where Tim is the sensible one who keeps me in check from overdoing things. He does nearly all the housework and cooking but, thankfully, no longer deposits half of the ingredients up the wall. Somehow, he also finds time to run a business that, thanks to doing things in his own, 'thinking out of the box' way, survived the Covid-19 lockdowns and continues to prosper. He also reads to me every night, which I adore.

I often need a wheelchair when we go out these days, and I've had to get used to the high speeds Tim likes to employ when pushing me along, sometimes running down a hill, but so far, I have only been tipped out onto the pavement once.

I'm so proud that Tim never gave up and battled through the challenges to beat his demons and become his true loving and kind self again.

OK, I'll spare the false modesty here. I know he couldn't have done it without me, and there may be some who might wonder why I didn't give up on him like 99% of other women might have done. That's because our marriage has mostly been wonderful, and when it wasn't, I'm the 1% per cent that could ride the highs and lows. I also enjoy the warm feeling deep down inside that I have something, although I'm not entirely sure what Tim loves and no other woman possesses.

Today, I love Tim more than ever. However, we both know there might be a few more bumps in the road to come. He has changed so much in recent years, firstly opening up about his problems and getting some decent therapy, while his confirmed ADHD diagnosis has belatedly made sense to many of those in our family circle.

However, it's still not unusual for him to bring me a knife and fork, instead of a spoon, to eat my porridge with or to find him standing outside hula-hooping, having failed to produce the cup of tea he offered to make sometime earlier.

Further Help and Guidance

Becoming the partner of someone with ADHD is a life choice that only the person involved in the relationship can decide. It may be the best or worst decision they ever make.

Once aware their partner has ADHD, the other half of the relationship will, no doubt, endeavour to learn as much as they can about the disorder and may believe, somewhat misguidedly, they can rescue, manage, tame, overcome or even conquer the condition and become a real-life action hero or heroine for saving their loved one from the perils of an apparent lifetime curse to once again become normal.

However, accepting the condition and your partner for who they are is a far more positive way forward.

Many people with ADHD are special or different, usually in a positive way, and they might be amazing partners if you can adjust to them and ride the wave. However, not surprisingly, It can be too much for many and not be for the faint-hearted. A partner may not fully realise what they are getting themselves into and, quite often and understandably, can be worn down by the daily stress, strain and unpredictable behaviour.

There is research to suggest the divorce rate among couples affected by ADHD may be as much as twice that of the general population. Add to this, in many cases, including Tim's, where the condition is often undiagnosed, the chances that a partner will simply walk away are much greater as there is no apparent reason or an excuse for their behaviour.

An ADHD partner may have to deal with being ignored, repeating themselves, being shouted at, being emotionally hurt and hearing nonsense. They probably know they are in for a bumpy ride, but perhaps not quite the amount of turbulence that may be involved.

As a partner of someone with ADHD, it isn't an easy ride, and no one will blame you if it's all too much. I've been on the brink more than once over the years. However, when troubles come along, it is important to forgive, forget and move on.

Yet, if you can overcome the potential difficulties and stay by the side of someone with ADHD, you are likely to receive a more intense kind of love and loyalty. A partner who is often brave, passionate, spontaneous, funny, a good parent, often intelligent, generous, warm, and kind with a continual spark that many an 'ordinary' person might struggle to match.

So, if you truly love them, please don't give up too easily.

———————

There are further suggestions to help partners of those with ADHD in the final chapter and at www.timmacwilliam.com

CHAPTER TWENTY-TWO

Super Powers & Super People

Some believe that ADHD shouldn't be regarded as a problematic medical condition as there are too many plus points to consider.

———————

In the early part of the twentieth century, my Great Aunt Alice, then aged just sixteen, travelled from Scotland to America, searching for a new life and adventure.

She was eccentric, outgoing, relentlessly positive, bright, clever, funny, unpredictable, a happy sort of risk taker and always on the go. It was almost as if she was 'driven by a motor,' a phrase that anyone who has completed an ADHD diagnosis test will recognise. Alice was never diagnosed, of course, although it is widely believed that the man who employed her when she arrived in the USA did have the condition, and we should probably all be grateful.

Her boss was an inventor who had a plan to improve the quality of life for all. He'd encountered numerous setbacks but never gave up. It is thought to have taken him three thousand attempts to finally succeed with his invention. Determination is a known bonus of ADHD, and if he had given up on his idea, we might still be lighting candles every night, but he refused to admit defeat and finally, through his brilliance and sheer determination, succeeded. Her boss was Thomas Edison, the inventor of the electric light bulb. Just three years earlier, Alexander Graham Bell, invented the telephone. It is well documented that he also lived with the condition.

Where would we be if everything was left to 'ordinary people?'

Success has many fathers, it seems, and who doesn't have a strange bit of Swedish flat-pack furniture somewhere in their home, wondering who on earth would design anything so unusual?

The answer is the late Ingvar Kamprad, founder of Ikea. He had ADHD. Not a world-saving idea, admittedly, but a hugely successful worldwide business. Can you imagine the sales pitch if he had tried to sell his wares via a traditional furniture seller?

I wouldn't for a moment compare myself with those mentioned, but I do perhaps understand their thought process. For example, If I have an idea in the morning, I want it up and running as soon as possible, ideally by the next day. This may be through impatience or perhaps before I forget what my potentially 'brilliant' idea was in the first place. Historically, when I have pitched something new, I'm told by a potential investor to write a long-winded first-phase business proposal and then report back. So, I don't bother. Instead, I look for alternative ways to achieve my goals.

Richard Branson had many ideas to do things differently, from record shops to radio stations and banking to hot air balloons and space travel. He even found a way to buy Necker Island because he had the ambition to go for it while others didn't dare even to try.

I managed to read Branson's business advice book *Screw It Let's Do It* from start to finish. Partly because it was in a short and easy-read format and partly because someone on my wavelength wrote it. He talked of having an idea while taking his morning bath and having it up and running by the end of the day. Richard Branson has ADHD.

Many famous and highly successful people may owe their success because of ADHD, not despite it. If you conduct an online search, you might be surprised how many well-known people have this 'condition.' – The Diversity Honours List is released each year with a string of names who have succeeded in life.

I had a friend who never wanted to leave his job at a huge supermarket chain because it was secure. He told me that if he stayed another year, he would get an extra discount on all his purchases and an increase of £250 in his salary. Yet his real passion was radio, and he could edit and make audio content to the very highest standards. I never entirely understood why he wouldn't take a chance and follow his dream, although perhaps now, following my diagnosis, I do because my friend doesn't have ADHD and had no intention of ever taking any risks with his income.

I've always enjoyed what other people might think of as a risk. Many years ago, I bought a car on eBay, much to the bemusement of those who thought I would be the victim of fraud, but in fact, I saved nearly £3,000 on the forecourt price. I also arranged foreign holidays by dealing directly with the hotels abroad and booking our flights separately. As a result, the price of the holiday was around half of the typical cost. A travel agent acquaintance insisted this was a huge mistake and we would probably be left stranded abroad. But, decades later, many people now travel this way.

I guess we all like to think we are pioneers, even in some minute way. I have started many projects with so much energy but often failed to complete them, only to see others succeed years later with 'my idea.'

New cars have become so expensive there is a system known as PCP (Personal Contract Purchase). This involves a loan for half of the vehicle's cost based on the amount of mileage you drive then, at the end of the loan period, either hand back the car or finance the other half. But, you don't effectively own the car during the early years and have a list of rules to abide by. Several years before this system was in place, I already had my own possibly superior version of PCP with unlimited mileage and complete ownership of the vehicle. Did I really think of this idea before any of the world's car giants? Who knows? Maybe it runs in the family as, in the early 1960s, my dad and his inventor friend designed a 'Cushion Car' with the idea that you wouldn't get badly hurt if there was an accident. Every car manufacturer they spoke to dismissed their invention and some laughed in their face.

However, the idea was, of course, well ahead of its time as sixty years later, every new car had an airbag fitted as standard.

I was 19 when my father had a stroke. I fear that I may have caused it.

My dad suffered from high blood pressure and was often stressed. He had run a cottage industry print shop since before I was born. Late in his working life, he ditched his job of thirty years to try and make a go of it full-time, but unfortunately, this coincided with the recession of the early 1980s and his business soon ran into debt.

Maybe I learned from this and managed to keep my own business afloat when it was forced to launch amid the recession a decade later—a time when interest rates increased by 5% in a single day.

My dad printed the match day football programmes for non-league Wokingham Town FC. In the middle of one season, there was increased pressure on him to finish the magazines in time for a post-Christmas match with Maidenhead United. Unfortunately, things often went awry with my dad's printing machines, even the new one he couldn't afford but decided to buy on a costly hire purchase deal. Everything seemed to go wrong with that Christmas edition, but somehow, he got them completed by the deadline. I folded and stapled each one by hand so they reached their destination on time.

It's possible the stress of this work, faulty machinery, and everything that comes with Christmas might have caused his blood pressure to rise to a dangerous level, or it could have been that I got him so very drunk on a bottle of Scotch that New Year's Eve to jolly him along and help him to relax that caused him to have a life-changing stroke that night, or perhaps it was a combination of all three. He also ate poorly, smoked heavily and took no exercise.

Whatever the truth, he was never the same man again. The advice given for after-stroke care seemed virtually non-existent in those days.

I think we had bailiffs knocking on our door at least once, but, very fortunately, a nearby printing business stepped in to take on and pay for the machine, so we kept the roof over our heads.

Bitter irony followed as heavy snow fell between Christmas and New Year, which meant that the game was called off. So the match-day programmes were no longer required. Instead, they remained unsold, unread, and I think, unpaid for. Had my father hung on for just another year at his old job, he would have received a large redundancy payment as the firm that was once this post-war new town's biggest employer closed down for good.

Each person with ADHD will likely experience at least some unique feelings as the symptoms are so wide-ranging. So when I'm asked for advice on how newly diagnosed people should react, my advice is to own it, live it and love it as It's part of who you are.

I have found there are varying degrees of positives and negatives to my ADHD and I think of them as *'The Good, The Bad, and The Ugly.'*

The Good

From all of the potential positives that ADHD can give (and we don't get them all). I like to think mine is persistence. If there is a dead end or a blind refusal for something I believe in, I will try again and again, often driving those around me to distraction.

Whenever I get the familiar feeling of failure, I remind myself that I was made redundant with two kids under five and proceeded to run a successful business for over thirty years. I achieved other goals in life simply due to having a go and taking a chance that others wouldn't dare to. I often wonder if, without ADHD, I would have succeeded.

I sometimes liken the particularly challenging episodes in life, when I feel I cannot go on any longer but somehow find the strength to do so, to when Tyson Fury, a heavyweight boxing champion, fought Deontay Wilder in their first world title bout. Fury was seemingly knocked out cold in the twelfth round, and everyone assumed the fight was over until Fury somehow sprung to his feet, beat the count and then came close to knocking out his opponent before the final bell rang. As the Japanese proverb states *Fall down seven times, get up eight.*

There have been times when my emotions are running on empty, and I cannot take any more, but somehow and from somewhere, I find the strength to take another step and last another day, reminding myself that, however much life is beating me up, I always have Katherine in my corner.

A bonus of ADHD can be offering help and support to people even when they believe they don't need or want it. For example, when we first met, Katherine could drink most people under the table. There is a kind of pathetic rivalry among drinkers about how much alcohol it takes to get them 'sozzled,' and it was undoubtedly a competition she would win with me. Katherine later confided that she had drunk so much for so long that her kidneys hurt.

I have never been one for drinking much alcohol or particularly enjoyed sitting in pubs for the sake of it. I would rather engage in some form of activity such as a walk, a run, a swim, go to the theatre, or cinema, play tennis, or take up an introductory kickboxing lesson.

So, we hardly ever went to a pub unless it was to enjoy a meal, which helped her to stop drinking. In time, her kidney pain subsided, and years later, Katherine quietly confided in me that I had probably saved her life. I doubt that is really the case, but she has certainly saved mine more than once.

It wasn't a problem for her to stop, but it was a habit to drink. Working in hospitality can lead to late-night social occasions, and it's easy for alcohol consumption to get out of hand. I wonder what may have happened if Katherine had married a bloke who liked a drink in a pub rather than one who preferred messing around on the beach.

Katherine is the most gorgeous woman I've ever met, but when we first met, she was rather unfit and could barely walk up a hill without stopping to catch her breath. As someone who had been crazy about sports all his life, I found this difficult to understand. We travelled to

Bournemouth for a weekend, and I literally had to push her up one steep hill, otherwise, she would not have made it to the top.

Fortunately, my passion for sport and fitness won through, and years later, she was into all kinds of classes and a regular attendee at a gym with various T-shirts that displayed how many sessions had been completed.

On one occasion, as we watched the end of our children's trampolining class, their coach invited us to compete in a seated bouncing race on a trampoline. So, urged on by our two young daughters and their friends, we agreed. It looked easy, but the coach warned us it would take some rhythm, flexibility, coordination and strength. I couldn't find any rhythm and hardly get off the starting blocks before Katherine crossed the finish line, being wildly cheered by all the girls in the class as she was declared the winner. It was meant as a bit of fun, but I didn't expect to lose, let alone have my backside handed to me.

'You let me win, didn't you?' Katherine asked, slightly disbelieving at the ease of her victory.

'No, I was really trying' I replied, red-faced and out of breath.

I was so happy and proud of the woman who struggled to walk up a hill when we first met had just won our sporting contest.

'Just wait until I take up karate!' she teased later. I'm not sure if I was more relieved or slightly disappointed when she signed up for Pilates instead.

Other examples of the 'Good' include -

Often being a good judge of character and usually able to see right through anything fake or false, therefore perhaps knowing full well when someone, perhaps a businessman or builder, is a fraud, although I still often refuse to challenge them, thus avoiding any unpleasantness. A positive and a negative of my ADHD symptoms right there.

A report in Germany found that symptoms, such as being impulsive and hyper-focus, make those with ADHD great entrepreneurs. When you consider the historically famous people named earlier in this chapter there is little doubt this is true.

Thinking so far outside the box to the extent that I often can't think inside the box! I've listed this as a 'good' because inventions and ideas might occur as a result.

I often drive my family mad when they are halfway through watching a detective or murder series on television. I'll walk into the room and announce who I think the killer is, then walk out again. They are annoyed because I'm quite often right. Although, as Katherine would remind me, not always.

Those with ADHD are thought to be good in a crisis. This is perhaps due to the speed of thought in everyday life so when it comes to an emergency, they are already up to full speed and have an extra gear of potential available.

The benefit of ADHD most often spoken about is 'hyper-focus,' an extra level of concentration where the rest of the world is blanked out, and if required, a further degree of determination to be the last person standing if ever it was really needed.

Don't fight your ADHD. Instead, try to embrace it.
There are so many benefits.

The Bad

Living in the present and not the past is good advice for those with ADHD, but it is easier said than done, as one of the downsides of this condition can be a failure to be present in the moment or to 'seize the day.'

266

Rather than enjoying an event, I will often think ahead and miss out on what is happening there and then. This can happen even on the most important of days.

I could not believe how beautiful Katherine was on our wedding day. I was stunned and amazed, open-mouthed, eyes wide, staring. It literally took my breath away. I shed tears to see her so happy, carefree, confident and beautiful. However, this wasn't at the altar or at any point during our wedding day. In fact, it was more than two decades later as we looked through some photographs.

If I could travel back in time and tell myself just one thing from that day, other than, 'Why are you wearing such ridiculous glasses? Take them off now!' It would be to understand the reason your bride looks so full of joy is simply because she is marrying you.

As Katherine walked up the church aisle, I was directed to stay looking forward. I wish I had ignored that particular piece of advice. I would love to have banked the vision of her walking towards me, looking so happy in that beautiful dress. But, I guess if I had turned around, I might have charged halfway down the aisle towards her.

Katherine lived and loved every moment of our wedding day. But I don't think I took it all in. At least now I am able to understand why.

Of course, not everything from our wedding day is a blur, and I have some very happy memories, but there are always things to distract. Some are important and some perhaps less so.

There had been a rolling light-hearted disagreement between Katherine and her dress designer on one of the finer points of her attire. He was adamant that Katherine would only get the full sensation of her silk wedding dress if she forgo wearing underwear.

'But I'll be cold!' She typically argued.

With so much going on and the buzz of the day, I had completely forgotten Katherine's tease until later that night when I discovered she had won the argument and revealed a stunning piece of underwear.

Sadly, she never wore them again as these beautiful ivory silk knickers were somehow mixed up with a bag of washing that I had given to my mum before we departed for our honeymoon. So unfortunately, they ended up being washed with a lot of snotty hankies. And, as my mother was still in the habit of boiling hankies on a stove, Katherine was returned a brown, misshapen, and crunchy piece of material with an accompanying query, 'I'm not sure what these are?'

Was this a genuine mistake, I wondered, or had my mum perhaps thought they were just a little too racy for her new daughter-in-law to seduce her innocent young son with?

Either way, she duly apologised and replaced them with something far more practical from Marks & Spencer. Katherine's mum hadn't fared much better, having thrown away the wedding bouquet that seemingly contained an entire field of roses.

More recently, there are photos and videos of Katherine looking healthy and happy. At our daughter's graduation, she looked like a film star. If I had a time machine, I would stop right there and tell her just how amazing she looked, but the thought, the comment, and the day apparently passed me by.

There is no point in regret, but unfortunately, it plays a big part in a life with ADHD, especially when diagnosed late and there is a regular annoyance, or perhaps it is a form of grief at the missed opportunities and having missed out on aspects of life.

There have been times through my life when I've had a thought that may be profound, even controversial, but I decided to keep it to myself, only to find the idea written about in the media weeks later by someone else who was then put on a pedestal for their outstanding piece of thinking. Of course, I may not have been the first person who thought of this apparent bit of genius, but I would, nevertheless, regret keeping it to myself. This is perhaps another example of both the good and the bad side of ADHD.

Other examples of the 'Bad' include -

Having all four seasons of emotion during the same day and witnessing the effect it has on those around me.

Being in a hurry, making rash or silly decisions that I may instantly regret, then spending ages rectifying an issue that I had unnecessarily created.

Perhaps the most challenging part of my ADHD is the issues with sensitivity. I can still remember put-downs and sleights from those who crossed me, stupid things I've done, or the times I've embarrassed myself and the people with me.

Feeling overwhelmed when there is more than one thing to do as I can't decide what to do first, and the tasks are left incomplete or sometimes never started.

Forgetting people's names or getting them wrong. It took me five years to realise the man I cheerily greeted at the running club each week as Keith, was actually called Ian.

Regularly cracking an egg then throwing the yolk in the bin and the shell into a frying pan or potatoes in the bin and peelings in the cooking pot.

I will focus so much on a project because I know if I don't get it finished, I may lose interest or enthusiasm, and it won't get completed. So everything else in life is put on hold until I get it done, much to the annoyance of others.

Having handwriting so bad even I can't read it - Simultaneously believing everything and nothing is possible - Being desperate for an answer but often having no idea what the question is.

There is often frustration when my mind races so quickly that I can't convey things fast enough, so words spew out of my mouth incoherently, leading to further irritation of not being understood.

I may seem impatient with loved ones when they don't give information to me more speedily. This is often because I'm likely to forget if they take too long or use too many words.

Beginning a sentence, digressing and then forgetting what the original point was, Although, perhaps that is just me getting old!

Being asked to buy items in a shop, forgetting and bringing back the wrong things, then returning to the store and repeating the same error.

Walking in and out of endless restaurants and cafes as I can't bear to queue, or there was something within the building that annoyed me. Ultimately I'll go hungry or buy chocolate from a corner shop instead.

People with ADHD may have difficulties falling asleep or staying asleep. I will often wake during the night with a brain like an excited puppy, waiting to jump on me and demand attention. Simultaneously there will be a loud random song blaring in my mind akin to a strange personal disco while accompanying new thoughts flood into my mind leaving any chance of getting back to my dreams rather unlikely.

Outgoing and impulsive behaviour can sometimes be mistaken for something less appropriate, as I sometimes found out to my cost.

'Hello beautiful, how are you?' Come on, say hello. This was my uncontrolled and natural response when I noticed a tiny black and white kitten approaching to have its chin gently scratched, but the little feline decided it was safer to disappear up a small tree just behind a parked car.

Moments later, I was face to face with the driver of the car. A furious-looking woman who gave a rather judgemental stare before shaking her head, tutting loudly and driving away.

'I wasn't talking to you. I was talking to the cat!' I shouted towards the rear bumper as it disappeared over the horizon.

I'm always interested in the latest running kit technology and saw a young woman wearing the Adidas Boost shoes that had recently been released to great acclaim. It was a big story in the running world and they sold out very quickly. As the woman approached, I stared more intently at her shoes with the never before seen foam that apparently can help you run faster. As I looked up, I was met with her intense and angry stare.

'Do you want to stop staring at my arse!' she shouted loudly enough for those nearby to turn and look.

'Er, I was looking at your shoes,' I replied before embarrassing myself further by shouting after her, 'Where did you buy them?'

There was no reply as she had quickly disappeared over the horizon while passers-by pretended not to have noticed our excruciating exchange.

The Ugly

One of the most unwelcome symptoms of my ADHD is the mood swings. This added to taking risks and doing and saying stupid things that I may not realise are upsetting or unhelpful, has also put a strain on close relationships. There is also the feeling of failure, fraud, self-loathing, and a feeling of insecurity. Having such low self-esteem that I feel I'm being constantly judged and criticised.

Low self-esteem is a common problem for people with ADHD, and some believe it should be a listed symptom specifically linked to diagnosis. I would literally bounce around with frustration with myself, wanting to do something but without the confidence to try for fear of failure or getting things wrong and therefore looking stupid. I always knew that I was capable of far more than I achieved in life and therefore became frustrated with myself and envious of those who had accomplished more.

There are times when I am so over-sensitive that the people closest to me don't know what to say as they fear everything will sound like a criticism.

I dislike rules, especially those that I view as unnecessary. Therefore, when I'm challenged, I will often become more resolute, leading to a conflict that seldom ends well.

I will interrupt someone in mid-sentence. It looks and sounds ugly and I know it's rude. This is something I will often do without thought, although there are occasions when if I don't interrupt, my train of thought may be gone.

Two of the words I've heard or said most in my life are 'sorry' as I'm forever apologising for my behaviour even when I might have no need to. The second is 'idiot'. Not only because of the name-calling when I was young, but whenever I get something wrong, I'll often shout the word out to myself.

I would imagine that quite a tidy sum of money has been lost from the daily drip, drip effect of my ADHD. For example, buying the wrong items, forgetting the shopping list or the cost of travelling back into town to purchase the missing items, putting the delivery of ice cream in a cupboard instead of the freezer, or making the wrong tea. I'll inadvertently drive in a bus lane or type my licence plate incorrectly into one of the complicated (for someone with ADHD) parking machines and duly receive a hefty fine in the post a few days later.

Past behaviour doesn't necessarily dictate your future.

If I had been diagnosed at a younger age, I would likely have found life easier and accepted myself more for who I am. It is probably true that many people with ADHD have underachieved, possibly through misdiagnosis or the negativity thrown at them at a young age. I know I could have done far more with my life, and it is one of the most difficult things to accept. A person with ADHD is also in danger of self-destruction as feelings and emotions can boil over.

I was once told to imagine my last day on earth where the person I became met the person I could have become—that is quite a profound and slightly scary thought.

However, with ADHD, you should be proud of what you are. Being different or standing out from the crowd isn't wrong. You have something that others don't, so let yourself off the lead and allow yourself to become something brilliant, as we obviously can't rely on 'ordinary people' for the next life-changing business or invention. On the other side of the coin, I still get occasional genuine praise for leaving the shower gel the right way up and on the odd occasion when I remember the drinks order correctly. 'Well done, Timmy.'

It's funny how unexpectedly you can be taken back to times and places you'd rather forget.

Katherine and I were watching a hits and headlines show from the early 1980s, and I was expecting to enjoy reliving the music and the memories from that time. Katherine certainly did, as she could remember living and working across Europe in her carefree days before she had me to deal with. But I was almost in tears by the end of the show as I was taken back to the misery and hopelessness of my life at that time of missed opportunities, a lack of direction, and the failure to have an ADHD diagnosis that might have been life-changing for me. I was also reminded of the many disappointments and endless dead-end jobs at that time of my life.

However, I now realise none of that really matters because if I hadn't gone through the years of mishap and misadventure, I would never have met Katherine, the single best thing that has ever happened to me. I was so lucky to find someone who was prepared to ride the highs and lows of a seemingly never-ending emotional wave, fight for me, love me, and always be on my side.

For any person to find their true love, it is something to be treasured and valued far more than the biggest lottery win, and for someone with ADHD, it is beyond measure. I doubt I would still be alive if Katherine hadn't come into my life and simply refused to let go.

Nil desperandum.

CHAPTER TWENTY-THREE

It's Always Darkest Before the Dawn

'It'll all work out' I declared.
Although not many shared my optimism.

———————

The term 'Sliding Doors' has crept into everyday language, and many of us have a moment in time that we look back upon when our lives were irrevocably changed.

I wonder if my impulsive ADHD behaviour actually helped me to find a positive that would finally grow from the ashes of underachievement I had encountered throughout my formative years.

At the age of twenty-three, I was sick with dread at starting yet another live-in job, feeling completely lost and alone, waiting in the reception area to be shown to the staff quarters of a large soulless hotel situated next to a busy dual carriageway.

I would have walked out there and then, but I was intrigued by the presence of a television crew and the yellow and green ribbons that were strewn throughout the reception area. I then recognised a couple of footballers walking through the foyer and realised that Norwich City were staying at the hotel prior to the 1985 Milk Cup Final due to take place that weekend at Wembley Stadium.

As a huge football fan with a deep interest in broadcast media, I watched the players and then Ken Brown, the manager, being interviewed by a television reporter. This, I thought, would be my dream job, the one I always wanted but never considered I had even the tiniest chance to succeed in.

Having listened intently to the interview and fascinated by the way it was filmed and recorded, I was slightly disappointed by the reporter's lack of knowledge on the subject. I'm sure I could have asked more suitable questions than he did, and I had only been to Carrow Road once while on holiday in Norfolk as a twelve-year-old.

Instead, I was beginning yet another job that I loathed before I had even started. It was a job for the sake of a job. It wasn't a career move and was far removed from where I wanted to be, although I had no idea where that place might be.

The Norwich City manager, Ken Brown, noticed me staring, looked over and smiled. He is the kind of guy who knows and responds to everyone. He is always warm and friendly, with a permanent twinkle in his eye. I was trying to summon up enough courage to go over and talk to him, but at that very moment, the manager arrived to show me around the hotel and escort me to the live-in accommodation.

The living quarters were small, dark, and squalid, with no windows, but I kept trying to be positive. It was a new start at a decent hotel with an instant chance of a promotion. Deep down, I already knew I wouldn't be staying there long. It just felt wrong. I was looking for any excuse to pack my bags and go. I felt sick with the anxiety of it all while my undiagnosed ADHD brain refused to be still or comply. I had promised myself and my family that I would stick it out for at least a year, but any hope of staying evaporated that same evening.

I managed to fight off my apprehension and doze off when an intruder, possibly another member of staff, burst through my door, breaking the lock as they did so. He proceeded to search around the darkened room, presumably to find what he could steal. He obviously didn't know I was in there asleep, and once I sat up, he scampered away, apologising as he left.

'…sorry wrong room.'

'That's OK,' I replied in a bizarrely cheerful voice.

I should probably thank whoever that midnight intruder was because it gave me the excuse to get packed up and get out of there, thus starting a chain of events that would change my life.

I impulsively stuffed everything into plastic bin bags and then, without a word to anyone, tip-toed out of the hotel via a fire exit so no one saw me leave. I was back at my parents' house by morning, less than twenty-four hours after promising that I would stay in this job for at least a year. I watched as Ken Brown leapt up and down with joy as Norwich City won the newly named Milk Cup that same afternoon.

As my life went down yet another level of hopelessness, I moved back to live with my Mum and Dad to start yet another job at a large nearby hotel. I thought this would do for a few weeks, although I was already searching for holiday jobs on the coast.

'Please try and stay put if you can,' begged my mum.

It was a nightmare for my parents, never knowing what I would do next. As soon as I started a new job, I would immediately decide to leave. I was like a beached whale violently flapping around on the wet sand, not knowing how I'd got there or what to do next but desperately hoping the next move would magically take me into my natural world.

If I had an ADHD diagnosis back then, at least it would have made sense to those around me.

My brother offered some positivity, telling me that 'It's always darkest before the dawn,' and so it proved, although it took a series of bizarre and tragic events.

At home one afternoon, I was ranting to my parents once again, threatening to hand in my notice to a job I had been in for barely three weeks when our neighbour manically knocked at the front door to inform me, 'Your hotel is on fire!' The cause was later thought to be arson, a copycat from the previous weekend's Bradford City fire disaster, where fifty six people had tragically lost their lives.

When the hotel re-opened, my future wife was one of a raft of new employees. She had several job offers and only decided to move to Bracknell because her mum was evacuated nearby during the war. She saw it as a sign in the stars that maybe her life would also find some new direction here. Perhaps there was something in this, as when Katherine's mum first arrived at Moor House, a large stately home on the outskirts of town, for the very first time, she experienced an extreme form of *déjà vu,* certain that she had been there before and apparently already knew the exact layout of every room in detail.

At our wedding, my mother recounted, 'Tim told us almost every day that he hated his job and was going to leave, it drove us to distraction, then for no apparent reason he became happier, calmer and stopped talking about leaving but we didn't have a clue why. Then a short while later in, through the door walked Katherine.'

We soon planned to marry, but as yet didn't have our own property, so we virtually stuck a pin in a map and bought our first home together in Norfolk.

In the mid-1980s, houses were bought and sold like hotcakes, increasing in value by thousands of pounds every week, so we purchased our bungalow rather hastily en route to a holiday in Scotland. We began the day at the crack of dawn and succeeded in viewing, then immediately purchasing the property with the deal all wrapped up by noon. Somewhat embarrassingly, things caught up with us later that day as we both fell asleep while a solicitor tried to explain the finer details of our mortgage contract.

For months afterwards, we travelled back and forth from Berkshire to Norfolk, often leaving at 1 am following a twelve-hour work shift. Katherine kept me awake through the journey with coffee, and I would use the white lines in the middle of empty roads as a guide to keep me driving straight. After the three-hour journey, we would arrive at our freezing bungalow that was yet to be fitted with any central heating.

This was intended as a relatively harmless adventure, and if things didn't go the way we hoped, our alternative plan was to sell the house at a decent profit and take a coast-to-coast adventure across the United States—and then Katherine became pregnant.

A new home, an expensive mortgage, and a baby on the way rather more quickly than either of us had expected. But unfortunately no job.

'It'll all work out' I declared. Although not many shared my optimism.

Exactly two decades later, from walking out of that job in Beaconsfield where my life was at such a low point, I was now sitting in a radio studio presenting a chat show with a big red 'Microphone Live' sign shining down on me from the facing wall.

It's the twentieth anniversary of Norwich City's victory at Wembley. The years have been kind to my guest, and he doesn't look very much different from when he was jumping for joy at Wembley Stadium on that sunny afternoon in 1985.

'What a fantastic day, the best ever,' Ken Brown tells me with the same twinkle in his eye. He can still recall every detail of one of the greatest days for both himself and the football club.

'Were you at the match, Tim? You must have been,' he asked me.

'No, Ken, I couldn't make it.'

'Why not? What were you doing back then?'

'Well, Ken, it's a long story!'

CHAPTER TWENTY-FOUR

Further Help and Guidance

*If you are passionate enough about something,
then you are likely to succeed.*

Additional help and advice are contained within several of the previous chapters, and I have added some further thoughts below. First for those with ADHD, then their partners and finally for wider family members. As ever, these are purely my own thoughts and experiences or those I have researched.

Advice for those with ADHD

First and foremost, it is essential to get a proper diagnosis. It may take years to get or be very expensive, but it is vitally important for your own well-being and those around you. Talk to your doctor and get on the waiting list as soon as possible.

Try to think positively about the condition and keep in mind your good qualities. Remember, those without ADHD probably won't have some of the benefits you have.

If you are prescribed medication, give it time to work. However, this may not be the first one offered. Be aware that medication won't be for everyone and isn't the only help available.

You have ADHD. So it's OK to be wrong and to get things wrong. It's also OK to be you!

Forgive others while you still have the chance to do so. Not because they deserve forgiveness but because you deserve the peace it gives. Life may be short, as the two famous sayings on the next page suggest, it is seldom wise to hold a grudge.

'Holding on to anger is like grasping a hot coal with the intent of throwing it at someone else; you are the one who gets burned.' (Buddha).

'Before you embark on a journey of revenge, first dig two graves.' (Japanese proverb)

Listen to everyone but always make your own decisions and then own them. Never blame others for your actions.

Keep mentally and physically busy. The more 'flowers' you plant in your mind, the less chance there will be for 'weeds' to grow.

If you can do so, exercise frequently and release those natural feel-good chemicals in your brain. Find a sport or an activity that you enjoy so it doesn't become a chore. If you are healthy, take some comfort from being physically well, building on this, even when your mental health is a struggle. Eat well and try to cut excess sugar from your diet.

Everyone is good at something, so find out what yours is, and then go for it!

Don't beat yourself up when things go awry. You are always doing the best you can at that moment, so always be kind to yourself.

Always be yourself. If you can't be yourself, you are likely in the wrong place with the wrong people. It is important to say what you really think, not what you believe others want to hear.

Each night, before you go to sleep, think of at least one thing that made you happy or proud, however small, that you can look back on, knowing you did something well that day.

Therapy only works if you are honest with yourself and with the therapist, so it may take some time to find the right person for your needs. If you can't or won't open up to a therapist, it is probably a waste of your time and money.

Find someone who loves you for who you are, and don't compromise on this.

There is a difference between being nice and being weak. People with ADHD are often people pleasers, and this may backfire, potentially leading to mood swings. If you try to please everyone, you may end up pleasing no one. Remember, not everyone in life will like you. Unfortunately, I have learned this the hard way.

Understand that ADHD doesn't often travel alone and that you are likely to have at least one other co-existing condition that may require additional help or treatment.

Never give up on yourself or the people you love, and don't complain about the people around you as one day you will wish they were still there.

Life isn't about always getting what you want but enjoying, loving and appreciating what you already have.

Whenever you make a mistake recognise it, admit it, learn from it, then forget it. (Dean Smith)

Solutions may only exist if you actually want to find them.

Enjoy special moments and bank the memory, as one day they will be more precious than any amount of money.

Enjoy the good days when they come along, and remember to have fun without guilt or fear of what tomorrow might bring.

Learn to be happy in your own skin. I was often trying to show off or carry out tasks for others or acting like a clown just to get their approval or reassurance, but in reality, I was looking for my own approval, which is more important to have but perhaps more difficult to achieve.

Try not to compare yourselves to others. Always be kind, and never give up on your dreams.

If you are passionate about something, you will likely be successful. I have always dreamt of being a writer and a broadcaster. Despite the many obstacles involved, I have managed to reach my goals. So if I can achieve my dreams, then surely anyone can!

Advice for partners of those with ADHD.

Adults with ADHD often have problems with relationships. This is a fact. They can be overly sensitive, awkward, and complex. They almost certainly wish they didn't feel this way.

A person with ADHD may get easily frustrated, insist they are right and lack understanding. The wrong words will often spew out of their mouth, and it would be very easy to walk away from this kind of relationship. However, having a loving and understanding partner is a massive bonus that should never be understated or underestimated. Remember, as a partner, you are loved and valued, even though it may not always feel that way.

If your partner hasn't yet been diagnosed with ADHD, talk with them and complete some reputable or accredited tests. Choose carefully, as some online questionnaires and diagnoses may lack validity.

ADHD can sit with or hide behind any number of other problems or conditions, so try and keep an open mind about what the problem might be.

Don't spoil today's sunshine by worrying about tomorrow's weather or remembering yesterday's storm. Sometimes your partner's mood is just like the weather and can't be controlled. So, enjoy the good days when they come along and remind yourself why you love them.

If you suggest something and your partner rejects it, don't give up. Try again at a different time with another approach. It might just be a case of bad timing.

Make some mental notes of where things are kept so they may be more easily found, as this can save stress and tempers from being frayed.

Be encouraging and offer praise, but only if it is deserved and genuine. A person with ADHD will often see right through any attempt to be patronising and may also find accepting praise challenging.

Be constructive when you criticise. Choose your words carefully, or their sensitivity might lead to a lengthy dose of the sulks.

Trust and believe in them. People with ADHD tend to think outside the box, so if they have a crazy idea and it isn't too dangerous, go with it. The idea might not be so crazy after all.

Try to exclude comments such as 'You never listen.' Instead, get your partner's attention beforehand by using their name.

Choose your battles. In the grand scheme, many things in life really don't matter.

Sometimes it is better to laugh at a situation instead of criticising or crying. Make sure they know you will always be on their side, but only if you really are!

Try to be kind and patient even when you are at breaking point.

Advice for wider family and friends

Please have a large bucketload of love, patience, and kindness available. Whenever possible, embrace the person and try to enjoy their qualities.

People with ADHD are often highly sensitive but might also be a little needy. This can be difficult for some people to understand. So, please be nice, and when deserved, give compliments; although people with ADHD might also find accepting praise challenging, so don't be offended if they struggle to say thank you.

If 'we' (a person with ADHD) say something negative about ourselves, please don't instantly agree, as we are likely to be looking for some reassurance.

We might interrupt without thinking or ask a question that you have just answered.

We may zone out mid-conversation. Try not to feel upset, ignored, or devalued if this happens. We do try to listen, but our minds can often be somewhere else, so please don't be offended if it seems we have switched off. We are probably just 'multi-tasking.'

We sometimes think we know what you are going to say next even before you do and have worked out a reply plus multiple scenarios of the conversation. However, it might look as though we aren't listening.

We know we can be difficult and talk nonsense. We might say the wrong thing at the wrong time, which may hurt. However, we don't always realise the words have caused offence or harm. So, choose to forgive, forget and move on.

Unless a problem or disagreement is dealt with and appropriately discussed, taking into account the emotions, thoughts, and details of everyone involved, the issue will only fester.

Having ADHD is not an excuse for bad behaviour or displays of anger, but consider that it may be part of the reason.

We are usually trying to please those close to us, but it may not always seem that way as we mindlessly agree to do something and then forget to carry out the task.

Be kind, happy, and optimistic to those with ADHD. It will always be appreciated.

Thank you for reading Sit Still Timmy!

There are further updates on my ADHD journey with links and details of organisations offering help and support at www.timmacwilliam.com

Printed in Great Britain
by Amazon

22773771R00169